SOLDIERS AND STATESMEN
1914-1918

BY
FIELD-MARSHAL
SIR WILLIAM ROBERTSON, BART
G.C.B., G.C.M.G., K.C.V.O., D.S.O.

VOLUME ONE

With Four Plates

CASSELL AND COMPANY, LTD
LONDON, TORONTO, MELBOURNE AND SYDNEY

First Published 1926

Printed in Great Britain

DEDICATED

TO THE MEMORY OF

THE SOLDIERS OF ALL RANKS AND RACES

OF THE BRITISH EMPIRE

WHO GAVE THEIR LIVES IN THE WAR

1914–1918

CONTENTS

CONTENTS

CONTENTS

CHAPTER VI

CHAPTER VII

LIST OF PLATES

LIST OF PLATES

PREFACE

THE vast problems which British soldiers and statesmen were jointly called upon to solve during 1914–1918 would, in any circumstances, have tested to the utmost the ability and forbearance of both parties. They were the harder to solve because of the inadequate means with which the war was begun, and because no one had sufficiently thought out beforehand the organization of Government and of a High Command for war purposes. For months and even years after August, 1914, these disadvantages hampered the consideration of practically every question that came up for decision, and only by keeping that fact in mind can the operations be properly understood or the triumphs ultimately achieved be rightly appreciated.

Being employed in France until December, 1915, first as Quartermaster-General and then as Chief of the General Staff, my connexion with the supreme management of the war before that date was but local and occasional. It was, however, during these early days of hurry and stress that the defects in our war machinery were the most acutely felt, and in dealing with the various campaigns I have accordingly thought it desirable to recall the main events from the beginning, and not to restrict them to the particular period (December, 1915–February, 1918) when, as head of the Imperial General Staff, I myself occupied the post of chief military adviser and executive officer at Government head-quarters.

This means that the narrative is not wholly derived from personal knowledge, but has been supplemented from other sources, the two principal instances being the operations in Gallipoli and Mesopotamia. With the Gallipoli Expedition I had nothing to do except in regard to the evacuation, and information concerning it has been largely taken from the reports of the Dardanelles Commission. For the early stages of the Mesopotamia campaign the report of the Mesopotamia Commission and the official history have similarly been drawn upon.

With these exceptions, the narrative is mainly confined to matters which fell within my own experience, and the endeavour has been to give the General Staff views as expressed at the time, not those formed after the event. This is not an easy thing to do, as everybody knows, and in order to ensure it as far as possible, and so enable the reader to see for himself upon what advice the Government acted, and what the difficulties, ministerial and military, were, I have quoted freely from documents written either by myself or members of my staff when the different problems were being investigated. The good work done by the Directors of Military Operations and Intelligence (Major-Generals Sir Frederick Maurice and Sir George Macdonogh) and the officers who served with them, in the preparation of these important State papers, was not merely helpful to me but of great value to the country.

Not unlikely it will be said, as often before, that information acquired by public servants in the course of their duties ought to be treated as confidential, but seeing the amount and nature of such information which has already been published by Prime Ministers, Foreign Secretaries, Admirals, Generals and others, the claim seems to be no longer tenable. Further, the rules and customs which ordinarily govern the disclosure of official information can hardly be held to apply to the special conditions which attended the Great War.

The present book deals, moreover, with events none of which are less than eight years old, and so far as it may be held to disclose documents or discussions which were once classed as confidential, it cannot, I think, injure any public interest now existing. On the contrary, to place on record for the guidance of future generations of soldiers and statesmen the experiences gained in the first war in which the Imperial General Staff, as such, took part, should be to the benefit, not to the detriment, of the State, and the record can, so it seems to me, best be made by one who himself actually underwent those experiences and, militarily speaking, was responsible for them. It so happens that I held the post of C.I.G.S. for rather more than half the duration of the war, and that of the four other officers who held it for the remaining half three have since died. Hence, with one exception, Sir Archibald Murray, who was C.I.G.S. for about three months, I alone am available to publish the record.

Finally, I may remind the reader that the inner history of any war is seldom to be found complete in the official account of it. Parts of the story are, for one reason or another, not allowed to be published, and while the operations themselves are usually described at great, and sometimes wearisome, length, not much is said—especially in cases where failure occurs—about questions of high policy, upon the decision of which the operations ought to be founded. We are told what was done, but not always why it was done, or who was responsible for causing it to be done.

the period was reduced to seven years or less, the remainder of the engagement being passed in an "Army Reserve," the members of which, in the event of a national emergency, were liable to be called up and sent abroad wherever required. The bulk of the infantry was organized in two-battalion regiments, so that each regiment might have one battalion at home and one abroad, the latter being fed with trained men by the former, which, in its turn, drew upon the Army Reserve when ordered to mobilize. The militia and volunteers in each district were grouped with a regular battalion, one of the first steps thus being taken towards founding the Territorial Force system established some thirty-six years later. The custom whereby officers obtained advancement in rank by purchase was abolished, and the way made clear to promotion by merit.

These measures and others met, as can be imagined, with strenuous opposition No less an authority than Lord Roberts, when speaking at a Mansion House banquet some years after they were introduced, pronounced the shortening of army service to be a mistake, while the power to purchase promotion was also vehemently defended. Ample financial means and aristocratic birth were still regarded as the first qualifications of an officer, the others falling into second category.

Training and education were even more difficult to reform, and for long after 1870 continued to be based mainly on the ideas inherited from the Waterloo and Crimean campaigns. Pipe-clay, stereotyped forms of drill, blind obedience to orders, and similar time-honoured practices were the principal qualities by which the proficiency of a regiment was judged. Combined training of the four arms, so essential to war efficiency, was never attempted except on those rare occasions when facilities for it were specially provided at "sham fights" or "manœuvres." Cavalry training was the business of an Inspector-General of Cavalry located at the Horse Guards, not of the General under whom the regiments were actually serving, who was considered to know little or nothing about the mounted arm or its duties and not much more about the artillery and engineers. The artillery was kept inside a ring-fence at Woolwich and at a few other stations, while the engineers were similarly kept to themselves at Chatham, each arm having its own special General and staff in London.

For this backward state of affairs the Commander-in-Chief, the Duke of Cambridge, must be held primarily responsible. He had been appointed to the post in 1856, not on any grounds of military qualifications but, following the advice given by the Duke of Wellington in 1850, because it was considered necessary that the Army should be commanded by a member of the Royal Family, so as to ensure, in the event of a revolution, that the troops would be used in defence of the Throne, and not in obedience to the orders of Parliament! Since his appointment he had exercised unrestricted control over the forces without being under any obligation to consult the War Minister, who was nevertheless held responsible to Parliament for his actions—that is, so far as parliamentary responsibility for the public services can be said to rest with an individual Minister and not with the Cabinet, where in practice it ultimately does rest. Mr. Cardwell rightly changed this system by making the Secretary of State the supreme authority, and the War Office Act of 1870 and certain Orders in Council vested him with "the direct and immediate control of every branch whatsoever of Army administration."

Responsibility for war efficiency remained, however,

ministration of both the fighting services, and their relation to each other. Like Mr. Cardwell, the Commission was careful to repudiate the old-fashioned idea that the Sovereign should exercise direct control over the Army, and it laid down as a first premise that this control, like any other power of the Crown, should be exercised through a Minister. The Commission went on to recommend the abolition of the office of Commander-in-Chief ; the formation in its stead of a new department, under a " Chief of the Staff " ; and the establishment, under the presidency of the Secretary of State, of a War Office Council, of which the heads of the several military departments, Parliamentary and Permanent Under-Secretaries, and the Financial Secretary, would be members. The military heads (i.e. Chief of the Staff, Adjutant-General, Quartermaster-General, Director of Artillery, and Inspector-General of Fortifications) were to be equally, separately, and directly responsible to the Secretary of State, as well for the advice they offered to him as for the conduct of the business of their departments. The Chief of the Staff was to be freed from all executive functions and charged with the following duties :—

(*a*) To advise the Secretary of State on all matters of general military policy.

(*b*) To collect military information.

(*c*) To prepare a general scheme for the military defence of the Empire.

(*d*) To prepare " plans of actions in certain contingencies."

As regards the duties of actual command and inspection of the troops, a General Officer Commanding was to be appointed for Great Britain ; elsewhere the local Generals were to report to the War Council ; and in time of war a Commander-in-Chief to take charge of the operations would be selected by the Government as heretofore.

So far as it went there was much to be said for this system. It was, in fact, a close approximation to the one established in 1904, which still obtains. One member of the Commission, however, Sir Henry Campbell-Bannerman, while agreeing with the proposed abolition of the Commander-in-Chief, dissented from the creation of a Chief of the Staff. He considered such a department to be "unnecessary," and that although it existed in continental countries those countries differed fundamentally from Great Britain, in that they were

concerned in watching the military conditions of their neighbours, in detecting points of weakness and strength, and in planning possible operations in possible wars against them. But in this country there is in truth no room for "general military policy" in this larger and more ambitious sense of the phrase. We have no designs against our European neighbours. Indian "military policy" will be settled in India itself, and not in Pall Mall. In any of the smaller troubles with which we may be drawn by the interests of our dependencies, the plan of campaign must be governed by the particular circumstances, and would be left (I presume and hope) to be determined by the officer appointed to direct the operations. And as to the defence of these Islands, and of our depots and coaling stations, although there may have been some slackness and delay in the past, we have reason to believe now, if full provision has not yet been made, that complete schemes at least have been matured for protection against attacks which cannot vary greatly in character. I am therefore at a loss to know where, for this larger branch of their duties, the new department could find an adequate field in the circumstances of this country. There might indeed be a temptation to create such a field for itself, and I am thus afraid that while there would be no use for the proposed office, there might be some danger to our best interests. All that is in fact required for our purpose can be amply obtained by an adequately equipped Intelligence Branch, which, under the direction of the Adjutant-General, could collect all necessary information, and place it at the disposal not of one officer or department alone, but of all the military heads, whose duty it would be to advise the Minister.[1]

A further objection taken by Sir Henry to the proposal was that the appointment of a Chief of the Staff would, if carried out, vitiate the entire scheme of reform contemplated in the abolition of the Commander-in-Chief, since it was considered essential that the Secretary of State's advisers should be " on a perfectly level footing."

The conclusion to be drawn from the foregoing is that Sir Henry was so afraid that the Chief of the Staff, not content with planning wars, would precipitate them, that he preferred to have no plans at all until the necessity for them actually arose. For the continent no plans would be wanted, since, in his opinion, we were not likely to fight there. For the defence of the United Kingdom schemes had already been " matured." For the dependencies and elsewhere plans were to be " left " till they were required for use, and then they were to be prepared by the selected Commander-in-Chief. Until war came, it was deemed sufficient to collect information, and pass it on to the various military heads of the War Office. It was nobody's business to study and present to the Government the information so collected as a basis for our own military policy and plans. Sir Henry seemed, moreover, entirely to ignore the possibility that although Great Britain had " no designs " against her European neighbours, those same neighbours might have designs against her, in the future if not at the moment. Again, instead of the British Government having, as he suggested, less need of expert advice on military questions than continental Governments had, it surely required such advice more because of the world-wide conditions

[1] Further Report of the Hartington Commission, February 11, 1890, page xxix.

by which British interests might, in one quarter or another, any day be affected.

Twenty-six years later the heresy of the principles advocated by Sir Henry was exposed by the Commission appointed to investigate the conduct of the expedition to the Dardanelles, who attributed our failures largely to the fact that the General Staff was not allowed to do the work for which it was intended, and did not prepare beforehand a plan of operations for the guidance of the General in command.

Sir Henry's views were apparently shared by both political parties, for the Hartington Commission's recommendations were not adopted either by the Conservative Government of the day, by the Liberal Government which came into power in 1892, or by the Conservatives when they were returned to office in 1895. So long as these views prevailed it was not possible for the Empire to be provided with the requisite measure of military security, and nothing of much value was in fact done until some fourteen years later.

As Sir Henry Campbell-Bannerman had dissented from the chief proposal made in the Hartington Report it was not to be supposed that when he became War Minister in 1892 he would be in any hurry to disturb matters. There were other reasons which may have induced him to go slow. The Duke of Cambridge apparently took it for granted that no change would be made as long as he lived, while the Queen's private secretary wrote to the War Minister in 1893, that Her Majesty thought that the Commission's report "was dead." From the autumn of 1894, however, Sir Henry is said to have addressed himself seriously to the question, and to have designed the scheme introduced by the Conservatives in 1895.

In that year the Duke of Cambridge resigned, and the concentration of military responsibility on the Commander-in-Chief was abolished, the Adjutant-General, Quartermaster-General, and Inspector-General of Fortifications being removed from his authority and placed directly under the Secretary of State. Lord Wolseley, the new Commander-in-Chief, was expected, according to official phraseology, to exercise general "supervision" over all the military departments, but this was a different thing from having them under his orders. Even training and education were entrusted not to him but to the Adjutant-General, and indeed the only duties over which he had definite control were those appertaining to mobilization, intelligence, and the military secretariat. Hence, while the name remained, the Commander-in-Chief, as such, was practically done away with, and the supreme management of Army affairs devolved upon a civilian Minister, assisted by a number of military officers of equal status. It thus came about that whereas the Duke of Cambridge, admittedly not a great soldier, had for thirty-nine years been accorded full powers of management, his successor, who was eminently qualified to exercise those powers, had his authority cut down to the point of extinction.

The change was defended by Mr. Balfour on the plea that "if the Secretary of State is to take official advice from the Commander-in-Chief alone, it is impossible that he should be responsible. In this House he will be no more than the mouthpiece of the Commander-in-Chief." Mr. Balfour apparently attached no importance to the fact that a plurality of advisers would mean that the Secretary of State might have to decide between conflicting technical opinions on matters about which he, being a civilian, would have no expert knowledge.

The defects of the new system were soon afterwards exposed in the mismanagement of the South African war, which led to a heated discussion in the House of Lords between Lord Wolseley (ex-Commander-in-Chief) and Lord Lansdowne (ex-War Minister), each maintaining that the other was to blame. Without attempting to say who was right, there can be no doubt that Lord Wolseley must have been greatly hampered in the discharge of his duties by being deprived of the powers which, as Commander-in-Chief, he was entitled to possess.

The failures in South Africa may also be attributed to the absence of an appropriate military policy before the campaign was undertaken, and for this the blame unquestionably rested with the Government. When it decided to go to war our State policy became aggressive, whereas for years past our military policy had been quite the reverse. In a memorandum [1] by Mr. Stanhope, the War Minister, of June 1, 1888, it was laid down that the requirements of the Army were to have for their object (*a*) The effective support of the civil power in all parts of the United Kingdom; (*b*) To find the troops required for India; (*c*) To provide garrisons for the fortresses and coaling stations at home and abroad; and (*d*) To be able to mobilize for Home Defence two army corps of regulars, one of regulars and militia combined, and the auxiliary troops not allotted to those three corps. Subject to these considerations, and to their financial obligations, a further aim was to be able to send abroad, in case of necessity, "two complete army corps, with cavalry division and line of communication. But it will be distinctly understood that the probability of the employment of an army corps in the field in any European

[1] "Official History of the War in South Africa, 1899–1902," Vol. I, page 5.

war is sufficiently improbable to make it the primary duty of the military authorities to organize our forces efficiently for the defence of this country."

In accordance with this instruction regarding the "improbable probability" of even one army corps being employed in any European war, preparations were directed mainly to Home Defence, and only in a minor degree to operations abroad. Consequently, when the Army was required to engage in a peculiarly difficult campaign in South Africa, it was asked to do something for which it had been neither organized nor equipped. This lack of harmony between State policy and military policy was in its turn largely owing to the neglect to act on the recommendations of the Hartington Commission and to create a General Staff. If, said the report of the Esher Committee, 1904, these recommendations "had not been ignored the country would have been saved the loss of many thousands of lives, and of many millions of pounds, subsequently sacrificed in the war."[1]

As no General Staff was formed it is not surprising to find that, as late as 1901, there was not in the War Office archives, with one solitary exception, any comprehensive statement of the military resources of any foreign country in the world, or of the manner in which they might, in the event of war, be used for or against us. The "mobilization section" concerned itself chiefly with arrangements for defence against invasion, while the "intelligence section" collected foreign military information but was not responsible for making practical use of it. A few memoranda and minor schemes dealing with certain expeditions which might have to be undertaken were occasionally produced, but they did not contain, or pretend

[1] Part III of Report, dated March 9, 1904, page 1.

to contain, a complete survey of the resources of the assumed enemy, or anything like it.

To make matters worse, the activities of the several State departments were without any useful form of co-ordination so far as war preparations were concerned. "No combined plan of operations for the defence of the Empire in any given contingency has ever been worked out by the two departments" (War Office and Admiralty) was the evidence given before the Hartington Commission,[1] and for all practical purposes it would have been equally true of the state of affairs in 1901. The nearest approaches to a central authority of the kind required were the Defence Committee of the Cabinet and the Colonial Defence Committee. But the former seldom met except when an emergency had already arisen[2]; it kept no records, had no permanent nucleus, and therefore ensured no continuity of policy. For several reasons it could not, and did not, give timely or useful consideration to the many complex problems that awaited investigation. The Colonial Defence Committee performed a vast amount of valuable work, but its duties were chiefly confined to the Colonies, and, being composed of subordinate officials, it had no power to decide the questions with which it dealt. It could only make recommendations, and submit them for the approval of the departmental Ministers concerned.

[1] *Vide* Report dated July 10, 1889, page vi, paragraph 10.

[2] It met, hurriedly, in the "black week" of the South African war, when the war was some two months old, and amongst other things decided that Lord Roberts should replace Sir Redvers Buller in the chief command. I am not aware that it had met before, and if it did meet the results of its deliberations did not reach the South African section of the Intelligence Division of which I was then in charge, vainly trying to cope with duties sufficiently onerous to find employment for half a dozen General Staff officers.

The need for a drastic change of system was pointed out by the Prime Minister (the late Marquis of Salisbury) in the House of Lords shortly after the three defeats of Magersfontein, Stormberg, and Colenso at the end of 1899, when he said :—

> It is evident that there is something in your machinery that is wrong. . . . I do not think that the British Constitution as at present worked is a good fighting machine. . . . It is unequalled for producing happiness, prosperity, and liberty in time of peace ; but now in time of war, when Great Powers with enormous forces are looking at us with no gentle or kindly eye, it becomes us to think whether we must not in some degree modify our arrangements in order to enable ourselves to meet the dangers that at any moment may arise.[1]

As the 1895 system gave satisfaction to nobody, not even to the Government which introduced it, further alterations were made when, in 1901, Lord Wolseley was succeeded by Lord Roberts. They amounted, however, to little more than another attempt to adjust the irreconcilable. The Government was still bent upon withholding from the Commander-in-Chief those powers which rightly belonged to him, and at the same time it hesitated to abolish the office altogether and put something else in its place. The Adjutant-General was once more brought under the Commander-in-Chief's "control," and the other military departments were officially described as being under his "supervision," but exactly what was meant by these ambiguous terms it is hard to say. Whatever it was, the Army derived no benefit therefrom. The training of the troops, for example, continued to be dealt with at head-quarters by two junior officers of the Adjutant-General's branch, and was combined with such incongruous subjects as cooking, school of music, and sergeants' messes !

[1] "Hansard," January 30, 1900.

In some, and not unimportant, directions slight advances were made. The non-regular forces, not inaccurately described by a military writer at the time as " a collection of units having no systematic proportion to each other, unconnected with the special needs of the localities in which they were raised, and in no sense an army," were, with the regular troops, formed, on paper, into six army corps ; improved equipment and much better training grounds were provided ; and, as far as possible, the regular troops were more suitably located for training purposes. Military policy was extended to embrace, over and above Home Defence needs, the ability to send three army corps abroad. The personnel of the mobilization and intelligence sections (the nearest approach to a General Staff) was strengthened, the Defence Committee of the Cabinet became a more active organization, and broad strategical problems began to receive more scientific treatment. Of these the defence of the North-West Frontier of India occupied the principal place, and in a memorandum entitled "The Military Needs of the Empire " the Defence Committee was furnished by the Intelligence Division with a detailed statement of the organization and strength of the Army that might be required in the event of a great war. Later this document was included in the records of the Committee of Imperial Defence as I.A., and, as that number indicates, it was the first attempt made to deal comprehensively with the important subject to which it related. But, after conceding full allowance for these and other improvements, our war preparations were still defective. The reforms did not go deep enough down to reach the roots of the evils from which the Army was still suffering.

Lord Roberts, on becoming Commander-in-Chief, missed a great opportunity for putting matters on a more efficient footing. His high reputation as a commander and administrator had been enhanced by the skill and rapidity with which he had retrieved the situation in South Africa in 1900. The Secretary of State for War (the present Earl of Midleton) was anxious to have his advice and as far as possible to act upon it. The Cabinet welcomed him as one upon whose judgment they could rely, and there is reason to believe that they would even have hesitated to reject the principle of universal military service had he declared it to be necessary. He was a popular favourite, and the nation, angry at the defects brought to light in the early stages of the war, was ready to support him in almost any demands which he might put forward.

Why he did not make better use of these unique conditions it is difficult to say, but some possible reasons may be mentioned. He was over sixty-eight years of age, and the arduous campaign through which he had just been, coupled with the loss of his only son, did not tend to make him feel younger. Having served in India till over sixty years of age, his opportunities for keeping abreast of modern military thought had been limited, and he had had no official dealings with those European military questions which almost daily came before senior officers serving at home. His numerous campaigns against uncivilized and ill-armed tribes on and beyond the Indian frontiers were probably more misleading than helpful to him in his endeavour to appraise the characteristics of European warfare. He apparently saw little necessity for a General Staff department, and had but a partial knowledge of the methods by which staff duties in the field should be carried out. When commanding in South Africa, for instance, where the most careful staff work was needed because of the numerous detachments employed, he would not infrequently send orders to column commanders through the medium of his aides-de-camp—young officers without staff training and with but little military education of any kind—instead of through the recognized channels, and the responsible staffs might thus be left in ignorance of the orders that had been given.

If these suggestions do, in any way, explain why his term of office was not more fruitful, Lord Roberts, no less than the Government, must be held accountable for the small progress accomplished. I make this observation with some reluctance, for although employed in the War Office at the time when he was Commander-in-Chief, I was not in a position to know what passed between him and the Government, while I do know, from subsequent personal experience, that ministerial sanction for military measures is sometimes very difficult to obtain. This difficulty inevitably occurs, sooner or later, let the relations between the civil and military chiefs be as good as they may, and as a rule it springs from one of two causes. The Minister may be unable to appreciate the technical reasons underlying a given proposal, while the soldier finds it hard to explain them in such a way that they can be understood. Further, however ready a Minister may be to act on professional advice, he is always embarrassed by the necessity of having to consider, first and foremost, how such action may affect the political well-being of the Government of which he is a member. Lord Salisbury was right when he said that the British Constitution as worked before the Great War was not a good fighting machine.

At the end of 1903 another Secretary of State, Mr. Arnold-Forster, assumed office, and brought with him a fresh scheme of Army organization. I need not describe it beyond saying that it left matters little better than they were before. What the Army needed, and had needed for years past, was to be given a real, not a paper, organization, based on a definite and stable policy, and then to be left alone to do its work. An essential preliminary to this was the reconstruction of the War Office itself,[1] which would include either the restoration to the Commander-in-Chief of the powers which belonged to him, or the creation of some other professional authority in his place.

This was at last realized, and in 1904, following the recommendations of the Esher Committee, the office of Commander-in-Chief was abolished in theory as for the last nine years it had been in practice ; an Army Council, composed of four military and two civil members, with the Secretary of State as President, became the supreme military authority ; and a General Staff, under a Chief holding the position of First Military Member of the new Council, was to be formed. Another important innovation was the formation of the Committee of Imperial Defence. It absorbed the functions of the Defence Committee of the Cabinet and of the Colonial Defence Committee, and was intended to ensure continuity of policy, as well as effective co-ordination of all State departments concerned with defence questions.

Good though this new system was in the main, it was faulty in two respects. It assigned the inspection of troops at training to an Inspector-General of the Forces,

[1] Referring to this question, the Esher Committee reported that, " The War Office has been subjected (since the Crimean war) to successive tinkering processes, by which improvements in minor matters may occasionally have been accomplished, but which left great principles entirely out of sight."—Report dated January 18, 1904, page 8.

who was made independent of the Chief of the General Staff, and reported the results of his inspection not to the latter but to the Army Council. The anomaly was therefore created that while the Chief of the General Staff issued all instructions in regard to training, he was given no opportunity to see for himself how they worked in practice. The Inspector-General had this opportunity but was without the power to change the instructions if found to be unsuitable. Assuming that it was necessary to have an Inspector-General—an assumption not accepted by everyone—he ought to have been under the orders of the Chief of the General Staff, the chief military adviser of the Government.

The other mistake made was in nominating the Chief of the General Staff as First Military Member of the Army Council, since this saddled him with an administrative responsibility equal to that of his colleagues, and so prevented him from giving his undivided attention to his own special business of fighting.

In other respects the system stood the test of war well, and in its main principles it still holds good. For a proper organization of the forces themselves, however, we had to wait for a further three years, and in order to show the extent to which these forces met our needs it is necessary to glance at the general situation in Europe at the time.

At the end of the last century the two Great Powers from whose hostility we were deemed to have most to fear were France and Russia. France was feeling sore over the Fashoda affair ; her " Colonial Party " were, so we thought, unduly aggressive ; and we had disputes with her regarding Egypt, Siam, New Hebrides, and the fishing rights of Newfoundland, the latter wrangle dating back to the period of the old French ascendancy in North America. In general, it had become the fashion for the two countries to regard each other with unfriendly suspicion if not with actual enmity.

With Russia the chief bones of contention were Afghanistan, Persia, and Tibet, and from them Germany, the real enemy, was bent upon extracting all the advantage that she could. For years she had systematically egged on Russia and England against each other, her object being to stand neutral in a war which she believed to be inevitable and hoped would end in the ruin of both her great rivals, or would at least paralyse them for a long time to come. " If," said one of her leading journals in 1902, " German diplomacy knows its business it will avail itself of the Russian-English rivalry, which occupies the first place in international policy at the present time, to make England amenable, without in any way compromising itself as regards Russia."

That Germany, and not Russia, was the Power which most needed watching was, however, a conclusion which those holding responsible Government positions in Britain were slow to admit. For instance, in November, 1899, Mr. Joseph Chamberlain advocated an alliance with her as a remedy for our isolation in Europe, and the same alliance was later suggested by other authorities as a means of checkmating Russia, who, like Germany herself, was then seeking to acquire predominance in Mesopotamia and a footing on the Persian Gulf. In October, 1902, a suggestion of this nature came before me, as head of the foreign intelligence section, for military opinion.[1] The reply I returned included the following :—

It is not an exaggeration to say that in no other European country is hatred of England so general or so deep-rooted as in Germany. . . .

[1] I have no record of who initiated the suggestion.

This is due to several causes, one of which is that Germany in her dealings with the other Great Powers is always doubtful whether we can be relied upon to help her, and she is embarrassed accordingly. It is because of this embarrassment that she has at different times endeavoured to stimulate our interest in an alliance by a course of policy calculated to irritate us. Another, and the most potent, cause is the rivalry in trade and colonial enterprise, and in this respect Germany is the aggressor. Indeed, the hope of superseding us in the commercial and naval supremacy of the world is the governing idea of the German imagination. It may be argued that this is a perfectly laudable ambition, but it should be remembered that the fact of one nation being engaged, with every right, in undermining the foundations of another is not in itself an aid to good relations between them, and certainly not to a reliable alliance. Moreover, it must not be supposed that the anti-English feeling is a product of the Boer war, and that it sprang only from an uncontrollable Press and the lower orders. On the contrary, it has existed in every grade of German society for many years past, and it has come to stay.

Nor can we reckon on the good offices in our behalf of the Kaiser. He has duties to his own people, and might not always be ready to stem the national current of feeling against us. Those who believe that sentimental considerations of a purely personal kind will be allowed to stand in the way of the Kaiser's political ambitions, can hardly be aware of the diplomatic steps he is said to have undertaken against England when he dispatched the telegram to Kruger. It may be noticed, too, that he placed himself unreservedly on the side of the Turks in the Turco-Greek war, notwithstanding that his own sister is married to the heir of the Greek throne.

From whatever standpoint the question of terms is regarded, it seems indisputable that we would have to pay a very high price for the alliance, and this conclusion is corroborated by the recent statement of a prominent German professor: "Truly, with the feeling of animosity towards England which permeates Germany at present, public opinion can probably be satisfied in no way whatever; it would rather make no terms of any kind with ambitious Albion!" . . .

But because Germany is an unfavourable, if not an impossible, ally, it does not follow that Russia would be a desirable one. It is, perhaps, just as difficult to reconcile the interests of England with those of Russia as it is with those of Germany. At the same time, once Russia is convinced that we have no intention of taking sides with

Germany, or of encouraging those German projects which are hurtful to her, she will probably be far more amenable in her dealings with us than she has been in the past, and the same may be said with respect to France. Both countries, much as they may dislike us, would prefer our supremacy to that of Germany.

The argument that because we have practically become a continental Power in Central Asia we ought to follow continental methods and combine with other Powers, is not so conclusive as it is usually thought to be. We may be face to face with Russia (in Central Asia), but the amount of force which Russia can use against us is restricted by her means of communication and supply. There is no question, as on the continent (of Europe), of throwing, within the space of a few days, a million or more men across the frontier, directed at the very heart of the kingdom. The most Russia can employ, actively, against us in Central Asia may be roughly estimated at about 150,000 men, while in three years' time this number may be doubled.

It has also been argued at different times that unless we combine with one or other of the Great Powers, the latter may combine against us; but this argument ignores the fact that we are indispensable to Europe. Our function has long been to help to maintain the balance between continental Powers, which have always been divided by their interests and sympathies into opposing groups. . . . We have thwarted, or helped to thwart, each and every Power in turn which has aspired to continental preponderance, and concurrently, and as a consequence, we have enlarged our own sphere of Imperial ascendancy. This preservation of the balance of power would still seem to be our true rôle, and in playing it at the present time we should recognize that a new preponderance is now growing up, of which the centre of gravity is Berlin. If its growth is really as great as Germany proclaims it is high time that we abandoned all notions of effecting an alliance with her.

Six or seven years ago the idea of co-operation between the two countries could be defended, though even then it seemed paradoxical. To-day the situation is different. In 1895 or 1896 the policies of both France and Russia seemed to involve assaults on British rights in Asia and Africa, and it may then have been desirable that we should be associated with Germany. These conditions still exist, but to a less extent. There was, moreover, little evidence of a vital conflict between British and German interests; the German colonies and colonial designs did not seem worth a quarrel with a Great Power. To-day, however, we know that Germany is pursuing a policy which can only be successful at our expense, and that she is making great efforts to recover her former close connexion with Russia, and would not be likely to imperil that hope for any advantage that Great Britain could offer. Thus, the assumption on which, until a few years ago, an Anglo-German alliance could be regarded as practicable or desirable from our point of view has been shattered.

At first sight it might seem that isolation will involve the conclusion of treaties under pressure, instead of their being concluded after calm deliberation, and that we ought not to assume that alliances will be offered to us at the critical moment by Powers to whom, until we ourselves are in imminent danger, we refuse assistance. Also, that if we are to be everybody's friend, but to be on nobody's side, the interpretation placed by the rest of the world upon our attitude will be that we are everybody's enemy. All this may be admitted, but it only shows how necessary we are to the rest of the world, and at any rate it is not sufficient justification, considering the many objections enumerated, for entering into the particular alliance here in question. . . .

I venture to submit:—

That the alliance is not practicable.

That even if it were it would not be worth the price we should have to pay for it.

That instead of regarding Germany as a possibly ally we should recognize her as our most persistent, deliberate, and formidable rival.

The memorandum found its way through the Commander-in-Chief and Secretary of State to the Foreign Office. Whether it helped to check the pro-German tendencies of the time I cannot say, but it did nothing to correct the military position. Our oversea liabilities continued to be fixed not by the possibility of war with Germany, but by the requirements of India for the defence of her north-west frontier in the event of war with Russia. Having passed the greater part of his life in India, it was perhaps only natural that Lord Roberts should advise the Government, as he did, to give prior consideration to that country, and it was not until two or three years later that he perceived the full meaning of the German menace. Lord Kitchener, the Commander-in-Chief in India, was equally persistent in emphasizing India's claims, and in pointing out the dangers to which he considered her to be exposed. It may therefore be said that up to this period, 1904, the military policy followed by the Government had the approval of the two principal military advisers.

Thanks to the foresight of King Edward, to the efforts of Lord Lansdowne and M. Delcassé, and to the sound instinct of the two nations in general, the causes of friction between France and ourselves were removed in 1904, but the differences with Russia in Asia were not finally adjusted until 1907. Meanwhile war with the latter Power continued to occupy the chief place in our military plans, though not as before to the almost total exclusion of the situation in Europe.

One of the problems examined by the newly-formed General Staff in 1905 was that of a war between France and Germany, in which the latter, wishing to turn the French positions on the Meuse, was assumed to send part of her armies through Belgium. It was also assumed that the British Government had decided to go to the assistance of Belgium in fulfilment of the treaty of 1839, and a "war game" was played in the Operations Directorate so as to elucidate the probable course of events. It fell to me to command the (imaginary) German side, and the decisions of the Director, or Umpire, went to show that there would be little chance of stopping the German turning movement unless the British forces arrived on the scene quickly and in considerable strength. Presumably these results were made known to the Government by the Chief of the General Staff, under whose instructions the war game took place.

There was some difference of opinion at the time, both in England and elsewhere, as to whether, in the contingency given, Germany would or would not go to the extent of violating Belgian territory, for much could be said both for and against that course. Officers employed under my orders in the German section were convinced that she would, and the statements we laid before the Government suggested that, treaty or no treaty, she would certainly not allow her military actions to be influenced by any considerations of public morality.

Some such opinions as these were expressed in a General Staff memorandum prepared for the information of the Committee of Imperial Defence, shortly before Mr. Balfour's administration was replaced by a Liberal Government at the end of 1905. When the memorandum came up for discussion the proceedings began with a Minister stating that he had just spent a week-end at a house in the country where the guests included a Lieutenant of the Belgian Army, whose views on the question were quite contrary to those held by the British General Staff. It is not unusual for young men to lay down the law on matters about which they know little, and unfortunately the account given by the Belgian officer seemed to impress some of the Ministers present as being of greater importance than it could possibly be. After a rather rambling conversation, in which everybody joined, the subject was dropped and an end thus put to a discussion which ought to have been a useful step forward in the direction of a definite policy designed to meet a situation with which, nine years later, we were actually confronted.

The truth was that the probability of our being drawn into a Franco-German war was not yet a question to which Ministers were disposed to concede more than an academic hearing, and they maintained that even if we had to intervene our rôle would necessarily be almost entirely naval, and scarcely at all military, in character. In this view they were supported by the Admiralty and others who did not make sufficient allowance for the historical fact that although a supreme navy may win victories it cannot impose peace, unless there stands behind it an army capable of completing and confirming on land the successes gained at sea. To admit that every Trafalgar must be clinched by a Waterloo, and that the Army might have to meet and defeat the hosts of Germany on land, would have entailed the entire renunciation of the doctrines by which British military policy had hitherto been governed, and the substitution of some kind of general military service in place of the voluntary methods from which it was our boast we had never yet departed.

The Indian standard of requirements, on the other hand, fell comfortably within the limits of existing means, as a long series of investigations conducted by the Committee of Imperial Defence had recently shown—assuming that various calculations and assumptions made in connexion therewith could be relied upon. Adherence to the Indian measure involved no addition to Army Estimates, no new system of recruitment, with its attendant unpopularity, and would give rise to no awkward debates in Parliament. A policy possessing these attributes was too attractive in the eyes of a moribund administration to be lightly relinquished, and, as already said, the defence of India accordingly continued for a further period to be officially regarded as the greatest task overseas for which military preparations had to be made.

That this is no fanciful picture is shown by a speech made in the House of Commons by the Prime Minister, Mr. Balfour, on May 11, 1905. He was describing the work done by the Committee of Imperial Defence since its formation about a year before, and whereas he devoted one-half of his statement to Home Defence, France being the potential invader, and much of the remainder to Indian defence, Russia being the aggressor, not a word was said about possible trouble in Europe with Germany as the enemy. Mr. Balfour explained, as is usually done in such cases, that neither France nor Russia was taken as an enemy because of any supposed ill-will on their part, but only for the purpose of illustrating the problems which the Committee had to consider. So far as it went the explanation may be allowed to pass, but at the same time the omission of all reference to the German menace in a statement purporting to prove that no important question of Imperial Defence had been neglected was apt to be misleading, and did not indicate a serious desire to look facts squarely in the face.

The situation was the more disquieting to those behind the scenes because not enough was being done to make the best of such forces as we had, which, for the most part, were allowed to remain a heterogeneous jumble of small units incapable of effective use. With the exception of the Aldershot army corps, so called, the regular troops had no formation higher than the brigade which could have mobilized without changing its composition. Cavalry were short of horses, infantry of men, artillery of ammunition, and everybody of other requisites of war. The second line, the militia, continued to be bled for the regulars, and only a portion of it was liable for active service abroad. The yeomanry and volunteers, the third line, were in most cases without any organization higher than the regiment and battalion. For thirty years and more the various categories had constantly been pulled to pieces and put together again in a different way by the twelve War Ministers who had followed Mr. Cardwell, and innumerable changes had been made in areas of command, periods of training, terms of enlistment, rates of pay, and other similar details. This never-ending stream of tinkering reforms, few of which were of real benefit from the standpoint of higher organization, had created a feeling of despair in the minds of senior officers, and the whole Army longed to be spared the infliction of further nostrums as a cure for its supposed ailments. Speaking in the House of Lords in July, 1905, Lord Roberts said : " I have no hesitation in stating that our armed forces, as a body, are as absolutely unfitted and unprepared for war as they were in 1899–1900."

Such was the position three years after our experiences in South Africa, and nine years before the Great War. We seemed to have learnt nothing, and done nothing, although a succession of Royal Commissions and Committees had urged the cause of reform with the greatest vigour.

Early in 1906, soon after the Liberal party was returned to office, the Operations Directorate submitted a " Memorandum upon the Military Forces required for Oversea Warfare," as a revision of the memorandum of 1901 to which reference has previously been made. The revision was not very aptly named, for it did not deal so much with the forces required in war as with the employment and maintenance of those already procurable, and it made no recommendation for the addition to the Army of a single man, gun, or round of ammunition. It did, however, and for the first time, discuss a "war in alliance with France against Germany," which was referred to as "an eventuality to be seriously considered," and the opinion was expressed that it was *upon land operations in Europe* "that the successful issue of the war as a whole will mainly depend." The proposal was that a force of at least four cavalry brigades and three army corps should be dispatched as soon as transports could be collected, while as to reinforcements it was recommended that, instead of sending additional formations, "the soundest policy would perhaps be to devote our attention to keeping up the force already dispatched in a state of absolute efficiency in all respects."

These measures cannot be classed as very far-sighted, but for the most part neither soldiers nor statesmen had yet sufficiently rid themselves of anxiety about Russia to admit of adequate attention being directed to Germany. The numerous "small wars" in which we had been engaged during the last two or three decades had also served to contract the military outlook, and few people, if any, visualized the dimensions of the great European conflict now slowly appearing above the horizon. Such as they were, however, the proposals constituted a definite beginning in the organization of the Expeditionary Force dispatched to France in August, 1914.[1]

[1] It was no business of mine at this period to make recommendations regarding the strength and organization of the forces required, nor do I claim to have possessed any greater foresight than the writer of the memorandum here mentioned. But it so happened that, in an informal document, dated 1906 and now lying before me, I did argue that, for effective intervention in a Franco-German war, we ought to be prepared to send to France as a first contingent a force of 500,000 men.

For the moment no action was taken on the memorandum, its chief object being to place before the new War Minister, Mr. Haldane, a brief summary of what our oversea responsibilities consisted. Mr. Haldane, it may be observed, did not, as some of his predecessors had done, enter the War Office with his mind made up and a scheme in his pocket for putting his ideas into practice, but he tried first to ascertain what was wrong by inquiry from those who were qualified to enlighten him. He found the revised War Office constitution working well except that many vexatious delays had occurred in the formation of the new General Staff, owing to the jealousy and suspicion with which that body was regarded by the heads of some of the other branches of the department. These obstructions he removed, and although he did not combine the branches of the Adjutant-General, Quartermaster-General, and Master-General of Ordnance in one great administrative department, as is the custom in continental armies, he liberated the General Staff from as many irrelevant duties as possible and so enabled it to pursue its own special work.

He held, moreover, to the sound doctrine that the security of the British Isles demanded not only the possession of a powerful Navy, but the provision of appropriate land forces as well, and he realized that, in addition to meeting this first call upon our resources, we ought to be capable of undertaking certain operations abroad. For this purpose the regular troops serving in the United Kingdom, together with the army reserve, were made to form the "Expeditionary Force," while the militia was converted into a "Special Reserve" charged with the duty of training and providing drafts for the regular units at the front, these two categories thus becoming the first line. The yeomanry and volunteers, made to constitute the second line, were given an organization similar to the first line, and became the "Territorial Force" of fourteen infantry divisions and fourteen mounted brigades for Home Defence.

The introduction of these measures in 1907–8 was a good step in advance, but it still left the position far from satisfactory. The Expeditionary Force of 160,000 men was obviously not strong enough to intervene effectively in a European war; the Special Reserve could not be kept up to strength, and never was; and, owing to shortage of training, a considerable portion of the Territorial Force could not be made efficient. These defects remained without remedy up to the commencement of the Great War. The favourable moment—after the South African war—for introducing a military system more consistent with the situation had been allowed to slip by, and the people, intent only on matters connected with domestic reforms, concerned themselves scarcely at all with the trend of affairs in Europe. So long as naval supremacy was assured they regarded the Army as being of little or no account, while a large section of the supporters of the Government, adapting their attitude to this insular outlook, preached dangerous theories regarding the reduction of armaments, and insisted upon the cost of the Army being cut down. As to the Government itself I will let a war historian speak [1] :—

Their leader, Mr. Asquith, held the House of Commons in his hand, and developed a singular adroitness in party management; but his robust philosophy was apt to live in the hour, and his inclination was to wait till a difficulty became urgent before seeking a solution. It is a temperament most valuable in the head of a government in

[1] "A History of the Great War," by John Buchan, Vol. I, page 38.

normal times, but it has grave defects in seasons of crisis. This spirit set the tone in the Cabinet, and the unwillingness to look far ahead was strengthened by the temperament of one of the strongest personalities in the Government. Mr. Lloyd George made domestic reform his special subject, and brought to it a unique gift of rhetoric and an energy not always scrupulous. By schemes which were rarely more than emotional impromptus, he roused intense antagonism and a wild enthusiasm among those who saw a Machiavellian purpose of spoliation and those who discerned the dawn of a new world. The fact that he was the most conspicuous public figure in Britain at the time switched the attention of the nation still farther away from such unfruitful topics as defence and foreign affairs. For Mr. Lloyd George's imagination, vivid and notable as it was, was essentially short-range; his mind was wholly uninstructed in the problems of international policy, and though he was chosen in August, 1911, to convey a warning to Germany after the Agadir affair, he spoke only from a brief, for there were few matters about which he knew less or cared so little. Finally, the new power of the party caucus encouraged this narrowing of view. It is the business of skilful whips to know what the people want and to see that programmes are shaped accordingly. To an electorate scared or exhilarated by the prospect of large social changes the husks of foreign policy would not be acceptable. Warnings of the probability of war would be regarded as merely a trick to distract. Expenditure on defence was a waste of money which might otherwise be spent on objects from which there was a sound return. Such matters, whether right or wrong, had no electioneering value, and the comfortable delusion was fostered that, so long as Britain chose to desire peace, peace would follow. There were men in the Government who to their honour refused to prophesy smooth things, but the cotton-wool with which the political atmosphere was thick deadened their warnings.

The efforts made by Lord Roberts about this period to introduce obligatory military training unfortunately lost something of their weight because he had made no such recommendation to the Government when Commander-in-Chief and in a position to press officially for its acceptance. Moreover, as his scheme provided men for Home Defence only—which was already secured by the Territorial Force—and did nothing to increase the strength of the Expeditionary Force, it readily lent itself to criticism by anyone desirous of cutting down military expenditure.

But this unofficial action may be left on one side. The provision of appropriate military forces was the business of the Government, not of unemployed Field-Marshals, and the Government decided to rely upon the numbers furnished by the organization of 1907. This decision, as will be recalled presently, was deliberate and in no sense attributable to lack of knowledge as to Germany's aims. Her writers had been publicly discussing them for years past; everybody knew that she was increasing the facilities for concentrating troops on the frontiers of Belgium and Luxembourg; and every addition to her Army and Navy was brought to the notice of the Government by the Admiralty and War Office staffs.

There was, too, the fact that in 1905 the Kaiser had landed at Tangier and proclaimed the integrity of Morocco, and that the Algeciras arrangement which followed left Germany angry with Great Britain and Russia because they had stood behind France. Two years later she took revenge for this humiliation by backing Austria in the annexation of Bosnia and Herzegovina, and the Kaiser then made his notorious speech about Germany's "shining armour." In 1911 Germany again interfered in Morocco, dispatching the gunboat *Panther* to Agadir to emphasize her claims, and when Great Britain announced her intention of supporting France, Germany was once more filled with rage.

Going back to 1900, her Naval Bill of that year had contained the preamble that she "must have a fleet of such strength that even for the mightiest naval Power a war with her would involve such risks as to jeopardize its own supremacy." This was reinforced by other Bills in 1906, 1908, and 1912, the object of the latter being to place the German Navy in the North Sea permanently on a war footing. In 1912, again, Lord Haldane returned from his visit to Berlin with the conviction, apparently, that Germany was determined to proceed with her full naval programme, and was not likely to come to any amicable understanding with us except on the basis of unconditional neutrality in a European war. We had, too, "shown our readiness to meet her over the Baghdad railway, and (as far as we could honourably do so) in the matter of the Portuguese colonies; and an agreement on those subjects had practically been completed in the early months of 1914,"[1] but she declined to sign it. Humanly speaking war had become inevitable, and, as the American Ambassador in London wrote in the autumn of 1914, it seemed that "no power on earth could have prevented it. The German militarism, which is *the* crime of the last fifty years, has been working for this for twenty-five years. It is the logical result of their spirit and enterprise and doctrine. It *had* to come."[2]

Notwithstanding the significance of these events no material change in British military policy was made. The strength and equipment of the Army continued to be determined not by the sum of our military liabilities, but by what the voluntary methods of recruiting could produce within the financial limits of such annual estimates as the Cabinet deemed politically expedient to lay before Parliament. Beyond the forces

[1] "Twenty-five Years, 1892–1916," Vol. I, page 303.

[2] "The Life and Letters of Walter H. Page," Vol. I, page 300.

so provided war was not allowed in the picture at all. The following figures are worth recalling :—

Army Estimates for 1912–13 . . .	£27,860,000
,, ,, ,, 1913–14 . . .	£28,220,000
,, ,, ,, 1914–15 . . .	£28,845,000

The "establishment" (or authorized strength) and the actual strength at home and abroad on August 1, 1914, were approximately as under :—

	Establishment.	Strength.
Regular Army	256,798	247,432
Army Reserve	145,000	145,347
Special Reserve	80,120	63,933
Channel Islands, etc., Militia . . .	5,742	5,613
Territorial Force	316,094	268,777
Territorial Reserve		2,082
Bermuda and Isle of Man Volunteers .	445	330
Totals	804,199	733,514

Of the Regular Army about 120,000 men were abroad, while of the Territorial Force less than 20,000 had undertaken the liability to serve overseas. Hence, in round numbers, the total force immediately available for active service outside the United Kingdom amounted to about 350,000 men. It is of interest to note in comparison with the total of 733,514 that the strength of the British Army in November, 1918, was 3,563,466, while the Imperial Forces as a whole numbered 5,336,943.

Mr. Asquith claims [1] that by August, 1909, the Government had "investigated the whole of the ground covered by a possible war with Germany—the naval position; the possibilities of blockade; the invasion problem; the continental problem; the Egyptian problem." The utility of this investigation is not very strongly confirmed by the comparative figures just quoted.

[1] "The Genesis of the War," page 116.

The same authority further tells us [1] that any Government which had proposed that England, in addition to her other liabilities, should convert herself into a military Power on the continental model

> would have committed political suicide. It would have split the Cabinet, split the House of Commons, split both political parties, and split the whole nation; if indeed that can be described as a split which would have been regarded as the vagary of a minority, insignificant both in authority and in numbers. Neither for the assumption by Great Britain of the obligations of partnership in a continental alliance, nor (still less) for the militarization of her people, could any countenance have been afforded by national opinion.

Similar views were held by Lord Haldane :—

> To raise armies under the stress of war, when the people submit cheerfully to compulsion, and when highly intelligent civilian men of business readily quit their occupations to be trained as rapidly as possible for the work of every kind of officer, is one thing. To do it in peace time is quite another.[2]

To quote Lord Grey, another member of the Cabinet :—

> A change of our Army system to conscription would have involved a transition stage that would have offered a moment peculiarly favourable to Germany. A scheme was actually considered in the War Office by high military authority in the year before the war. It was put aside as futile because no political party was prepared to consider it, because the country would not have conscription.[3]

The opinions of Ministers were, it appears, shared by the General Staff, for Lord Haldane says [4] :—

> In the year 1912 the then Chief of the General Staff told me that he and the General Staff would like to investigate, as a purely military

---

[1] "The Genesis of the War," page 139

[2] "Before the War," page 171.

[3] "Twenty-five Years, 1892–1916," Vol. II, page 55. The "high military authority" is apparently the one named below by Lord Haldane.

[4] "Before the War," page 174.

problem, the question whether we could or could not raise a great army. I thought this a reasonable inquiry and sanctioned and found money for it, only stipulating that they should consult with the administrative staff when assembling the materials for the investigation. The outcome was embodied in a report made to me by Lord Nicholson, himself a soldier who had a strong desire for compulsory service and a large Army. He reported, as the result of a prolonged and careful investigation, that, alike as regarded officers and as regarded buildings and equipment, the conclusion of the General Staff was that it would be in a high degree unwise to try, during a period of unrest on the continent, to commence a new military system. It could not be built up excepting after much unavoidable delay. We might at once experience a falling off in voluntary recruiting, and so become seriously weaker before we had a chance of becoming stronger. And the temptation to a foreign General Staff to make an early end of what it might insist on interpreting as preparation for aggression on our part would be too strong to be risked. What we should get might prove to be a mob in place of an army. I quite agreed, and not the less because it was highly improbable that the country would have looked at anything of the sort.

What truth there may be in these various views the reader must judge for himself. The dilemma in which we had become involved was, like other situations of the same kind recorded in history, a very awkward one, and no doubt it was difficult to decide what to do for the best. But, after all, if there was a possibility that we might have to fight for bare life, it was essential that a new system of recruiting should be started, or at any rate be considered and worked out, before and not after the crisis arose, if only in a latent form. A middle course of this kind was advocated in 1910 by General Sir Ian Hamilton in a memorandum which he prepared for Lord Haldane, and there can be no doubt that if legislative authority for enforcing national service, in case of need, had been acquired before 1914, and registration and other preliminary measures had been completed, when war broke out our man-power resources could have been utilized much more rapidly and scientifically than they were. Men could have been called up for service according to the requirements of their civil professions, and in numbers suitable to the equipment and training facilities available, everybody being put at once into their proper places. As things were left it was unavoidable that there should be during the first part of the war immense wastage of good material owing to men who should have been trained as officers being put into the ranks, and men who should have remained in the factories leaving them, and afterwards having to be withdrawn from the trenches and returned to their civil work. To refrain from taking these and other precautionary measures for fear of incurring the displeasure of Germany was a futile solution of the dilemma if, as indicated by her actions, she could be appeased by nothing less than complete submission to her will.

Again, however much the people might object to compulsory service, it was surely the duty of the Government to inform them of the dangers which threatened so that at any rate they might have an opportunity of considering how to meet it. Not only were they not adequately warned of it, but they were sometimes asked to believe that no such danger existed, as, for example, in January, 1914, when Mr. Lloyd George publicly derided the possibility of war, and urged that the season was "the most favourable moment for twenty years" for cutting down expenditure on armaments.[1] This being the opinion of a responsible Minister it was not to be expected that the people would see the necessity for compulsory service or any other special military precaution.

As late as July 23, 1914, when speaking in the

[1] *Daily Chronicle* interview.

House of Commons on the Finance Bill, Mr. Lloyd George made the further statement that

> next year there will be substantial economy without interfering in the slightest degree with the efficiency of the Navy. The expenditure of the last few years has been very largely for the purpose of meeting what is recognized to be a temporary emergency. . . . I think it is a very serious thing . . . to assume that this expenditure on armaments is going on and that there is not likely to be a stop to it. I think there are symptoms, not merely here but in other lands, not merely that the industrial classes, but that the financial interests of the world are getting alarmed. . . . The encouraging symptom which I observe is that the movement against it (expenditure on armaments) is a cosmopolitan one and an international one. Whether it will bear fruit this year or next year, that I am not sure of, but I am certain that it will come. I can see signs, distinct signs, of reaction throughout the world.[1]

On the same day, and at about the same hour, that Mr. Lloyd George was seeing these signs Austria-Hungary presented to Serbia the ultimatum which started the greatest war ever known.

The attitude of the soldiers is even more difficult to understand than that of the Government. Ministers frequently stated in Parliament that our preparations aimed at no more than the dispatch oversea of the six divisions of the Expeditionary Force, and the Chief of the Imperial General Staff must have known that much larger forces would be needed before we could hope to emerge successful from a great war in Europe. Knowing this, he ought to have brought the question of man-power before the Army Council, who, after making the requisite investigation, should have informed the Government that, so far as they could judge, the men procurable were inadequate to meet the demands that might arise. In this way the Government would have known exactly

[1] "Hansard," July 23, 1914.

where it stood and where the policy it was then following in Europe would inevitably lead.

But the General Staff, as far as their views were voiced by their Chief, seemed to think that no initiative on their part was required. In proof of this it may be observed that in 1912 the National Service League advocated the increase of the Home Defence Forces, and a reply in the shape of an unsigned article appeared in the *Army Review* which was commonly believed to have been the work of a senior General Staff officer who had been instructed by his Chief to write it. It contained the following statement :—

> Until the Government tell us that the Expeditionary Force is too small to enable them to carry out a sound national policy, we must presume that it is sufficient for requirements, and we must rely on the Government to foresee the need for augmentation in time for the necessary additions to be made and perfected before the machinery is put to the test of war.[1]

This was a most extraordinary presumption to entertain, and was unjustified by any experience in this country, or by any proper division of responsibility as between the statesman and the soldier. The truth probably is that the vision of the General Staff did not extend much, if at all, beyond that of the Government, and at any rate the view they put forward was that the addition of the Expeditionary Force to the French armies would give just that numerical superiority over the armies of Germany that was required to turn the scale against her.[2]

[1] " Our Requirements for Home Defence," *Army Review*, July, 1912.

[2] " A careful study had made us think that the addition of even a small force of such quality to those of France and Russia would provide the combined armies with a good chance of defeating any German attempt at the invasion and dismemberment of France." —" Before the War," page 160.

That the appreciation of the General Staff was badly at fault is shown by the fact that the majority of its members employed at the War Office, of whom I was one, accompanied the Expeditionary Force to France. Had the appreciation been more accurate these officers would presumably have remained at their posts at home, so as to furnish the Government with the assistance it required and to supervise the organization and training of such additional forces as might have to be raised.

The insufficiency of guns and ammunition was even more serious than the shortage of personnel, and there was less excuse for it. The substitution of compulsory for voluntary service involved many considerations of an economic and political character, and the soldiers could not press it to the same extent as in the more technical case of war material. This was chiefly a matter of asking for more money, and of spending more usefully what was allotted. Everybody knew that Germany had a large amount of heavy artillery and a formidable array of machine guns, but the British Army had none of the former suitable for the field and very few of the latter. In 1909 the School of Musketry recommended that infantry battalions should have six machine guns each, but the recommendation was rejected on financial grounds, and when the Expeditionary Force was sent to France battalions had but two guns each, or less than 200 in all. Of the 500 pieces of artillery 24 only were of medium type, the remainder being the ordinary "light" field guns or field howitzers. On Armistice Day we had in France alone well over 50,000 machine guns and 7,578 guns and howitzers, of which over 2,200 were of medium or heavy calibre. We began the war with a reserve of considerably less than 1,000,000 rounds of artillery ammunition, whereas before it ended the reserve in France alone amounted to over 15,000,000, in addition to large reserves in other theatres and at home. The position was much the same with regard to the requirements of trench warfare, although the Russo-Japanese war of 1904–1905 had shown how great they might be.

Before the war, and in the early part of it, not one of the belligerents imagined that the demands for war material would attain the colossal figures they did reach, and there was everywhere much difference of opinion as to the most suitable kinds of artillery and ammunition. Still a very crude forecast would have shown that the British Army was much under-gunned, and that the reserve stocks of ammunition were, having regard to the rapid rate of fire, much too small.

It has been said that soldiers are never satisfied, and probably they may be prone, like other people, to ask for more than is really needed. But if they submit their demands in a temperate and well-considered manner, and show that they are unanimous in pressing for their acceptance, Ministers will quickly enough realize the importance of them. If the demands are refused, and are of first-rate importance, the soldiers should ask that a suitable statement be made public, otherwise it may happen—and often has happened—that they will have the mortification of seeing themselves quoted by Ministers, either directly or by implication, as being in agreement with measures to which, in fact, they are strongly opposed.

Unfortunately, the requisite unanimity is not always forthcoming. Up to a point it may be, but Army Councillors, like other men, sometimes weaken in resolve when big decisions have to be made, and Ministers may thus be left with two or three flabby alternatives from which to select one for themselves. Small blame to them if, out of patience with their advisers, they choose the alternative which is politically the most convenient though it may not be the one which, from a military standpoint, is the most desirable. One of the highest Ministers of the Crown said to me when I came home from France to take up the post of C.I.G.S. that his chief complaint against the General Staff was that he could not "get a definite opinion from it. We cannot make out what we ought to do for the best in order to win the war." (The General Staff had not yet been properly reconstituted after its dispersion in August, 1914.)

To sum up, if the Army Council did not definitely and officially represent that the men and material procurable under the existing system were insufficient to meet possible liabilities, the Government may justly complain that it was not well served. If, on the other hand, the Council kept the Government informed of the position, and if, in their judgment, the interests of the nation continued to be imperilled, they ought to have considered whether they were justified in remaining in office. Not everyone will agree with this view, but it seems to me that unless responsible soldiers are prepared, in times of national danger, to risk some personal sacrifice for the sake of their country, they will never either win or deserve their country's esteem. It is therefore submitted that, from whatever angle their action is viewed, those soldiers who held the office of Army Councillor in the years preceding 1914 were, no less than Ministers, accountable for the inadequacy of the means with which the war was begun.

CHAPTER II

THE WESTERN FRONT, 1914–1915

British Pre-war Policy regarding Infringement of Belgian Neutrality—The Outbreak of War—Disadvantages caused by the Absence of an Adequate Military Policy—Inadequate Arrangements for Co-operation within the Empire—Council of War, August 5—Government Instructions to Sir John French—Shortage of Munitions—Uncertainty as to Dispatch of Reinforcements from England—Necessity for Offensive Policy—French Staff Memorandum on Champagne-Loos Operations—Sir Douglas Haig succeeds Sir John French—Sir William Robertson becomes C.I.G.S.

"THE policy to be adopted in the circumstances you describe must necessarily be settled by the Government of the day, when the time comes. It cannot be decided now. All that can now be said is that the fulfilment of our treaty obligations will follow and will not precede the national inclination."

To the best of my recollection these were the words used in 1902 by the Prime Minister, the late Marquis of Salisbury, in reply to a War Office memorandum, written by myself, asking what British policy was likely to be should Belgium be invaded by either belligerent in the event of war between France and Germany. Such a war was already within the realm of possibility, and as many changes had taken place since the treaty guaranteeing Belgian neutrality was signed sixty-three years before, it was desirable to know whether, if it were infringed, we would, or would not, actively intervene in support of it.

Without some official guidance of the kind the study of possible future operations—a duty with which I was connected—could not be usefully prosecuted. Hence the memorandum, which was forwarded by the Commander-in-Chief, Lord Roberts, through the Secretary of State for War to the Foreign Office.

The reply just quoted was not very helpful, but it may have been the only feasible one at the time, and perhaps Lord Salisbury displayed more wisdom in answering the question than I did in asking it. Later, say from 1910 onwards, when Germany's aggressive designs had become more pronounced, and our relations with France and Russia had been put on a more friendly footing, the difficulty of supplying the information should have been less, while the need for supplying it was certainly greater. But it was not supplied, and indetermination accordingly continued until August, 1914, when the "time" referred to by Lord Salisbury arrived, and a decision one way or another had to be taken. We then had to face the fact that, whereas our foreign policy had gradually assumed a continental character, our military preparations had remained insular and almost parochial. In other words we were, for the reasons given in the preceding chapter, without the means required for enforcing the policy in which we had become involved.

On July 29, when France, Russia, and Germany were on the verge of war, the German Chancellor made the notorious proposal to our Ambassador in Berlin that Great Britain should remain neutral, and on the following day the French Ambassador in London asked us to join France. The German proposal was contemptuously rejected, and the French were told that we were not yet able to promise intervention. On July 31 the French request was repeated by the President of the Republic in a message which he sent to the King, and a similar reply was returned.

On August 2 the negotiations with France were appreciably advanced, the British Cabinet undertaking, subject to the approval of Parliament, to give all the naval assistance possible should the German Fleet come into the English Channel or through the North Sea to attack the French coast. On the same day Germany sent an ultimatum to Belgium demanding a free passage for her armies, and undertook that if it were conceded to evacuate Belgian territory at the end of the war. If it were refused, she would take it by force and treat Belgium as an enemy. King Albert then appealed to us to intervene. On August 3 Belgium rejected the German ultimatum, and the British Parliament approved of the promised naval assistance being given to France and of the mobilization of the land forces.

On August 4 we advised Belgium to resist the passage of the German armies, if attempted, and promised to join with France and Russia in supporting her. At the same time a telegram was dispatched to Berlin asking for an assurance before midnight that Belgian neutrality would be respected. To this no formal reply was made; Belgium was invaded the same morning; and thus, after a week spent in the vain endeavour to preserve peace, we found ourselves engaged in the war which had been hanging over our heads for more than ten years past, and was destined to entail the sacrifice of nearly a million British lives.

The British Government has been criticized for not coming to a decision more quickly, and, no doubt, it would have been an advantage if the divisions first sent out had had more time to take their places in the line of battle before being called upon to meet the German attack at Mons. But responsibility for the declaration of war rests with the Government alone, and soldiers are not justified in trying to force matters. "It is not their business," as Lord Haldane rightly says, "to have the last word in deciding between peace and war."[1] The time factor was exceedingly important from the military standpoint, but the Government was none the less bound to proceed with the utmost deliberation before taking the final step, which, once taken, could not be retraced. The essential thing was, as always, that the decision to go to war should receive the whole-hearted support of the nation, and if we may judge from the divided opinions which prevailed in the Cabinet there was at first no certainty that this support would be forthcoming. Instead of condemning the Government for proceeding with unnecessary precaution, history will not unlikely commend it for the prudence and sound judgment which it displayed.

The most regrettable feature was not the time spent in reaching a final decision when war became imminent, but the omission to lay down beforehand an appropriate military policy upon which comprehensive preparations and plans could be based. There were many difficulties in the way of doing this, as Lord Grey has since explained.[2] "I was quite clear," he says, in writing of the situation in 1906, "that no Cabinet could undertake any obligation to go to war (in support of France as against Germany) . . . We must therefore be free to go to the help of France as well as free to stand aside." Referring to 1911 he says: "No man and no Govern-

[1] "Before the War," page 74.
[2] "Twenty-five Years, 1892–1916," Vol. I.

ment could pledge this country in advance to go to war."

Unofficially, plans for military co-operation with France had, with the knowledge of Lord Lansdowne, Foreign Secretary at the time, been discussed between the Director of Military Operations and the French military attaché in London as far back as 1905. Lord Grey says that the discussions were carried on through an intermediary, the military correspondent of *The Times*, but, to my personal knowledge, they were also conducted, at least to some extent, direct. From 1906 onwards the conversations grew more intimate and frequent, and were always conducted direct between the General Staffs of the two armies. The fact of their taking place was not, however, made known to the Cabinet as a whole until 1912, when it was put into writing in a memorandum sent by the Foreign Secretary to M. Cambon on November 22 of that year. The arrangement laid down was that "if either Government had grave reason to expect an unprovoked attack by a third Power, or something that threatened the general peace, it should immediately discuss with the other whether both Governments should act together to prevent aggression and to preserve peace, and, if so, what measures they would be prepared to take in common. If these measures involved action, the plans of the General Staffs would at once be taken into consideration, and the Governments would then decide what effect should be given to them."[1]

Not only was the Cabinet unaware of the conversations, but even the Foreign Secretary, who gave permission for them, knew nothing about their results. Writing to the Prime Minister on the subject in 1911 he said[2]: "What they [the General Staffs] settled I never knew—the position being that the Government was quite free,

[1] "Twenty-five Years, 1892–1916," page 97. [2] *Ibid.*, page 94.

but the military people knew what to do, if the word was given." It was, however, of little use for the "military people" to "know what to do" unless adequate means were available for doing it, and this they could not be if the Cabinet knew nothing about what was taking place. On the principle that half a loaf is better than no bread the conversations were useful, but a more unsatisfactory method for ensuring co-operative action can hardly be imagined than that of leaving the two General Staffs to patch together a plan which the British Government, as such, declined to endorse with its formal approval. As the British official history of the war says, although there was an "obligation of honour," there was no actual undertaking to send the Expeditionary Force, or any part of it, "to any particular point or, in fact, anywhere at all."[1]

Moreover, since there was no such undertaking the French authorities were forced to frame their plan of campaign not knowing whether they would or would not receive British assistance, while we, on our side, were not able to insist upon our right to examine the French plan in return for our co-operation. When the crisis arose there was no time to examine it, and consequently our military policy was for long wholly subordinate to the French policy, of which we knew very little.

There was also a want of precision about the arrangements for co-operation within the Empire itself. Beginning in 1887, seven different conferences had been held for the purpose of considering questions of common interest, but the progress made in regard to Imperial Defence was extremely slow. Its importance was emphasized at the third conference in 1897, when Mr. Joseph

[1] "France and Belgium, 1914," page 14.

Chamberlain invited the Colonial Premiers to say what contribution they thought the colonies would be willing to make to establish the principle of mutual support, but the results were very disappointing. The entire naval responsibility was left, as before, to Great Britain, and the colonies merely undertook to provide their own local land defence. Three years later the South African war furnished a gratifying picture of the potential power of the Empire, which came as a surprise to many, but equally it afforded a proof of the need for more efficient methods in the application of that power, and at the fourth conference, held in 1902, Mr. Seddon, who represented New Zealand, tabled a resolution that an Imperial Reserve Force should be formed in " each of His Majesty's Dominions over the seas for service in case of emergency outside the Dominion or Colony in which such reserve is formed." The principle had already been embodied in the New Zealand Defence Act of 1880, and it constituted the first attempt by a colony to evolve such an organization as would enable it to place in the field trained troops available for Imperial service outside the colony. As might be expected the resolution did not meet with unanimous approval. The Prime Ministers of some of the states were willing to accept it, but others thought that the " infringement " of the rights of self-government which it entailed were such that its adoption might impede rather than further the object in view.

The fifth conference was held in 1907. It was noteworthy as being the first one known as an " Imperial " as opposed to a " Colonial " conference. The question as to whether the Dominions should undertake to provide contingents of given strength and composition for service outside their own territories, as proposed by Mr. Seddon in 1902, was again raised, but a General Staff memorandum on the "Strategical conditions of the Empire from a military point of view," considered that it was "impossible (at any rate for the present) to learn in advance the exact numbers of troops that might be placed in the field side by side with the Home Army." It was added, truly if tamely, "that the lack of definite provision for common action between the various military forces of the Empire deprives those forces of much of the power which they might otherwise exert at a time of national danger."

The conference of 1909 was brought about by the acceleration of the German shipbuilding programme. Various naval measures of importance were taken, while a General Staff paper containing "Proposals for so organizing the military forces of the Empire as to ensure their effective co-operation in the event of war," went more thoroughly into the whole subject than had been the case at any of the previous conferences. While acknowledging the progress made in matters of local defence, the paper complained that "in the Oversea Dominions no organization has yet been devised for rendering assistance to other parts of the Empire in an emergency," and declared that "the time seems to have arrived when this important question should be considered." The weakness of improvised forces was commented upon, and although it was not suggested that the Dominions should be asked to undertake definite obligations, it was urged "that in order to utilize the resources from overseas to the best advantage, the arrangements for organizing, training, and mobilizing the troops of the Oversea Dominions, while primarily directed to local defence, should include the possibility of the employment of such troops in a wider sphere."

After the conclusion of the main conference at the

Foreign Office a military conference took place at the War Office, at which it was agreed that " without impairing the complete control of the Government of each Dominion over the military forces raised within it these forces should be standardized, the formation of units, the arrangements for transport, the patterns of weapons, etc., being as far as possible assimilated to those recently worked out for the British Army." The duty of considering the detailed application of these decisions was entrusted to a sub-conference consisting of military experts and presided over by General Sir William Nicholson, acting for the first time in the capacity of Chief of the *Imperial* General Staff. These results represented a considerable advance.

Another conference was held in 1911, but not much was achieved beyond a mutual understanding that the various states would, in the future as in the past, give such assistance as they could. This position continued, with little change, until 1914. Nothing specific was settled as to the nature or amount of assistance that would be forthcoming, and even in the case of India, where 70,000 British troops were permanently stationed, the position remained unsatisfactory. As already mentioned, the question of reinforcing India in time of need had for long received considerable attention, but in respect of the help which she herself would contribute in the event of an Imperial emergency little was done. The Government of India was consulted as to the extent to which they could co-operate in a great war in Europe, and the suggestion was made that an appropriate contingent would be a cavalry brigade and two divisions. No sufficient steps were taken, however, to make even these small contingents readily available when wanted.

As the Dominions are in reality self-governing states

the provision of more definite arrangements for co-operation was perhaps not practicable. The matter is referred to here not so much by way of criticism as for the purpose of recalling some further disadvantages under which the Empire began the war. Seeing how splendidly the different states, great and small, hastened to the assistance of the Homeland in the hour of its need, and accepted the principle of single military control, it might seem that there is little ground for complaint, and that in time of peril sentiment and kinship will always prove a more effective bond of union than any links that can be forged by centralized authority in time of peace. On the other hand, when next we are forced into war circumstances may be less favourable to us than on the last occasion, and therefore it is to be hoped that the statesmen of the Empire will not cease trying to weld the Imperial Forces as closely together as the established rights of self-government will permit.

No authoritative plan of campaign being in existence, a Council of War was held at No. 10 Downing Street on August 5 and 6 to consider what number of troops should be sent to the continent and where they should be concentrated. Nearly all the members of the Cabinet were present, and in addition were no fewer than eight military officers—Field-Marshals Lord Roberts and Kitchener (the latter about to become Secretary of State for War), Sir Charles Douglas (Chief of the Imperial General Staff), Sir Henry Wilson (Director of Military Operations), Sir John French (Commander-in-Chief designate), his two Corps Commanders, Generals Haig and Grierson, and General Sir Ian Hamilton (as having been Inspector-General of the oversea forces).[1]

[1] *See also* Chapter IV, pages 151–2.

The Council left the question of concentration to be settled later, after consultation with French G.H.Q., and it recorded the following resolutions in regard to the distribution of troops :—

(*a*) To embark one cavalry division and ultimately five, but for the present only four, of the six divisions of the Expeditionary Force.

(*b*) To bring home the Imperial Troops from South Africa.

(*c*) To transport two Indian divisions to Egypt, and to urge the Government of India to send a division to capture Dar-es-Salaam in German East Africa.

The French representatives arrived in London on August 10 to discuss the question of concentration. The British and French staffs had already provisionally and unofficially arranged that the Expeditionary Force should concentrate on the French left, in the vicinity of Maubeuge, and the question now to be settled was whether the situation demanded any modification of this plan. Sir John French has placed it on record [1] that

> There was an exhaustive exchange of views between soldiers and Ministers, and many conflicting opinions were expressed. The soldiers themselves were not agreed. Lord Kitchener thought that our position on the left of the French line at Maubeuge would be too exposed, and rather favoured a concentration farther back in the neighbourhood of Amiens. . . . Personally I was opposed to these ideas, and most anxious to adhere to our original plans. Any alteration in carrying out our concentration, particularly if this meant delay, would have upset the French plan of campaign and created much distrust in the minds of our Allies. . . . The vital element of the problem was speed in mobilization and concentration. Change of plans meant inevitable and possibly fatal delay.

Sir John French was supported by the Director of

[1] "1914," page 6.

Military Operations and other British representatives; the French Mission, as instructed by General Joffre, pressed for the adoption of the same plan; and eventually it was accepted. Lord Kitchener appears to have yielded because he felt that he could not oppose the opinion of the combined French and British staffs, who for years past had devoted themselves to a study of the problem, and he made his consent subject to the approval of the Prime Minister. This was given for much the same reason—the disinclination to override the two staffs. Lord Kitchener's views, it will be remembered, proved to be correct. Before the Expeditionary Force had fired a shot, its line of communication became so menaced by the probability of an enveloping movement on its left flank that, as Quartermaster-General of the Force, I had to consider the possibility of having to abandon the sea bases at Havre and Boulogne and establish others farther to the south. On August 22, the day before the battle of Mons, I summoned the Inspector-General of Communications, Major-General Sir Frederick Robb, to G.H.Q. at Le Cateau so as to discuss future developments with him. The main principles upon which we would act in the event of new bases being required were then settled, and on return to his head-quarters at Amiens he made preliminary arrangements with the French authorities for effecting the change. About five days later the German advance had made such progress that Sir John French ordered the change of bases to be carried out, the new sea base being established at St. Nazaire, and an advanced base at Le Mans. Amiens, the previous advanced base, had then already been evacuated by us and the Germans occupied it on August 31. This change of base, at a very critical period, was a striking example of the value of sea-power, and of itself was an adequate return for the money we had expended in ensuring naval supremacy.

The fifth division, or fourth by name, reached Le Cateau on the day that the 2nd Corps began to arrive there in the retreat from Mons, and the sixth was retained for the defence of England until September. If the whole six had been dispatched in the first instance the retreat might have been a less arduous task for ourselves, and the pursuit could have been made correspondingly more costly for the enemy. Who was responsible for keeping the two divisions back I do not know, nor do I question the wisdom of the decision, but it was a significant commentary on the boast frequently voiced before 1914 that a supreme Navy would enable us in time of war to sleep peacefully in bed with the comforting assurance that not even a dinghy-load of men could land on our coasts.

Another result of having no comprehensive war policy was that the Government was unable to furnish Sir John French with the kind of instructions which he was entitled to have. It was essential that he should be clearly told the nature of his mission and the means that would be supplied for carrying it out. The instructions supplied to him by Lord Kitchener, on behalf of the Government, were sufficiently explicit on the first point, but contained nothing about the second. They were as follows :—

Owing to the infringement of the neutrality of Belgium by Germany, and in furtherance of the Entente which exists between this country and France, His Majesty's Government has decided, at the request of the French Government, to send an Expeditionary Force to France and to entrust the command of the troops to yourself.

The special motive of the Force under your command is to support, and co-operate with, the French army against our common enemies. The peculiar task laid upon you is to assist (1) in preventing, or repelling, the invasion of French territory, and (2) in restoring the neutrality of Belgium.

These are the reasons which have induced His Majesty's Government to declare war, and these reasons constitute the primary objective you have before you.

The place of your assembly, according to present arrangements, is Amiens, and during the assembly of your troops you will have every opportunity for discussing with the Commander-in-Chief of the French army, the military position in general and the special part which your Force is able and adapted to play. It must be recognized from the outset that the numerical strength of the British Force, and its contingent reinforcements, is strictly limited, and with this consideration kept steadily in view it will be obvious that the greatest care must be exercised towards a minimum of losses and wastage.

Therefore, while every effort must be made to coincide most sympathetically with the plans and wishes of our Ally, the gravest consideration will devolve upon you as to participation in forward movements where large bodies of French troops are not engaged and where your Force may be unduly exposed to attack. Should a contingency of this sort be contemplated, I look to you to inform me fully and give me time to communicate to you any decision to which His Majesty's Government may come in the matter. In this connexion I wish you distinctly to understand that your command is an entirely independent one, and that you will in no case come in any sense under the orders of any Allied General.

* * * * *

Sir John French knew that he was to take out four divisions, and that one or two others might follow later, but it will be observed that he was told nothing about any further reinforcements except that they would be "strictly limited" whatever that might mean. Something may have passed verbally, but nothing of much practical use, for no one could say what troops the Dominions might furnish, or what proportion of the Territorial Force might volunteer, if asked, to serve abroad, or whether or when it would be allowed to leave the country. Nor could anyone calculate how long it would take to enrol, train, and equip with rifles, guns, saddlery, ammunition, vehicles, etc., such new categories of troops as might be raised.

The whole position was one of extreme difficulty, and was aggravated by the fact that even the needs of such troops as were already available could not be supplied. Before the war was a month old the supply of ammunition began to cause anxiety. The daily receipts of 18-pounder ammunition in September amounted to only 7 rounds per gun per day, while the average daily expenditure—which was abnormally small at the time—amounted to twice that number. The daily receipts of 4·5-inch howitzer ammunition numbered 8 or 9 rounds per howitzer per day, the expenditure being over 40 rounds a day. In October, at the height of the first battle of Ypres, and when the receipts were still about the same, the 18-pounder expenditure averaged 80 rounds per gun per day, and in some cases as many as 300 rounds per gun were fired in a day. So depleted did the reserve stocks eventually become, and so precarious were the prospects of future supplies, that I had to obtain the Commander-in-Chief's authority to restrict the allowance to 20 rounds, and later to 10 rounds, per gun per day. In the case of the 4·5 howitzers the daily allowance was at one time fixed at the ludicrous amount of 2 rounds each. Owing to the appalling shortage, no effective artillery reply could be made to the enemy's guns, and the sorely tried infantry were thereby deprived of essential support to which they were entitled, and without which the best troops in the world are apt to give themselves up to despair. Entrenchments were no sooner constructed than they were battered down and had to be re-made; communications between the front and rear lines, and the conveyance of necessities across the shell-swept area, were carried out under the most trying conditions; and, in general, life in the trenches during the first winter spent in Flanders was wellnigh intolerable. When preparations for war are decried as being unnecessary, or as more likely to provoke war than to prevent it, or for any other reason, we shall do well to recollect that in the Great War thousands of lives were sacrificed and terrible hardships suffered because no suitable preparations for it had been made.

By the enforcement of strict economy during the period of comparative inactivity which followed the first battle of Ypres, a larger reserve of ammunition was accumulated by the beginning of March, 1915, than had hitherto been possible, and, partly with a view to restoring the morale of the Army after the long and depressing winter just ended, offensive operations were undertaken which led to the battle of Neuve Chapelle. Another prolonged pause then ensued for the accumulation of fresh reserves for use in the Franco-British offensive due to commence in the La Bassée-Arras area in the second week of May.

The daily allotment of ammunition to the Second Army, on the Ypres front, was meanwhile fixed at the miserable pittance of 2 rounds per 18-pounder, 3 per 4·5 howitzer, and 6 per 6-inch howitzer. On April 22 this Army had to meet the enemy's first gas attack, and in the fighting that followed the amount of ammunition it expended averaged about 100 rounds per gun per day. Moreover, many of the 4·7-inch guns, of an old and useless type, burst, their ranging was hopelessly unreliable, and a large proportion of the shells were "blind."

Matters were made worse by the occasional diversion to other theatres of war of consignments of material originally earmarked for France. During the second battle of Ypres, for instance, when the stocks were specially low, 20,000 rounds of 18-pounder ammunition were ordered to be sent from France to Gallipoli on a definite promise that they would be immediately replaced, but more than a week elapsed before this was done.[1] Towards the end of May the stocks had been almost entirely exhausted with the exception of a small amount of shrapnel, and the consequence was that British participation in the combined offensive had to be terminated.

The limited scope and spasmodic character thus imparted to the operations were repeatedly brought to the notice of the Government, and it was pointed out that unless the supply of ammunition was sufficiently increased to enable the Army to engage in a sustained offensive, the object in view—the expulsion of the enemy from French and Belgian territory—could not be attained. The War Office endeavoured to expedite a better supply, but it was not a matter that could be quickly put right, and uncertainty regarding the guns and ammunition which he might hope to receive by a given date accordingly continued to dog the footsteps of the Commander-in-Chief with maddening persistence for the greater part of the year. No one could say whether or when contracts for war material would or would not be fulfilled by the dates agreed upon, for besides the general upheaval of industrial conditions, the manufacture of the material could not in many cases be commenced until the machinery and factories required for making it had themselves been constructed. In January, 1915, the War Office furnished a statement of the amounts of 18-pounder

[1] To the best of my belief this was the fact. But I ought to say that in Sir George Arthur's "Life of Kitchener," Vol. III, page 239, it is stated that the ammunition was replaced within twenty-four hours.

ammunition which contractors had undertaken to supply by the end of May, but the amounts received fell very short of the estimates as the following figures show :—

	Number of Rounds.	
	Contract.	Received.
January	140,000	88,156
February	150,000	92,546
March	310,000	166,832
April	560,000	199,992
May	610,000	249,562

Similar disappointments were experienced in regard to the receipt of drafts and additional divisions, both of which were liable to be diverted at the last moment to other theatres. Large new armies were in process of being raised, but when they would be sent to France, if at all, was a matter about which no reliable information could be obtained, and throughout the first half of 1915 the Commander-in-Chief had little or no knowledge of what the military policy of the Government was supposed to be. Since August, 1914, the original policy—the defeat of the German armies and their expulsion from Belgium—had to a great extent been eclipsed by the campaigns started at the Dardanelles, in Mesopotamia, and in various parts of Africa, and the uncertainty thus created as to the men and munitions that might eventually become available for France made it impossible to utilize to the best advantage even such limited means as were provided.

Writing to the War Office on the subject on May 17, Sir John French said :—

It is not for me to do more than suggest where His Majesty's Forces can best be employed in order to bring the war to a successful conclusion, as the decision must of course rest with His Majesty's Government. But it is essential to the same end that both myself and the

French should be informed at once what the decision is, because it may prove impossible to continue to act offensively here unless adequate troops are sent in such numbers as I have hitherto been led to expect.[1] The War Office letter under reply leaves me at present quite uncertain as to when the New Armies will be sent out, as that is dependent upon when the Second Line Territorial Divisions can be satisfactorily "organized into a force capable of meeting the landing of such a German force as the Admiralty state they cannot under present distribution of the Fleet prevent landing on these shores." How long this is likely to be I have no idea.

In order that I may be able to concert plans for the future with the French, I have the honour to request that I may be informed whether it is still the intention to defer the dispatch of further new divisions and if so for what period, or whether I may expect them to arrive as previously arranged.

No sufficient information on these points having been received, it was again asked for in a letter dated June 23, which contained the following passages :—

The French propose shortly to employ larger forces and to widen their front of attack, and General Joffre is naturally desirous to have my co-operation. It would assist me and General Joffre in formulating our plans if I could be informed at once whether and when further divisions are likely to be sent out, and whether the supply of ammunition is likely to continue to improve. This information would be of great value, because it would enable General Joffre and myself to decide whether it would be desirable, having regard to the situation as a whole, to postpone the contemplated operations.[2] In this connexion I may point out that every day's delay means a corresponding strengthening of the hostile defences, and thereby adds to the difficulty of breaking through them.

A further reason for striking as heavy and early a blow as possible is the present critical situation in the Eastern theatre of war, which is such as to render it possible that the Russians may before long be

---

[1] The first battle of Artois was in progress at the time.

[2] The first battle of Artois had now ended, and operations which afterwards became known as the battles of Loos and Champagne were under consideration.

forced back to the line Riga-Grodno-Litovsk and the Galician frontier. Should this happen the line to be held by the enemy would be so much shorter than that held in February that he could, if he elects to act defensively, transfer sufficient Austrian troops to hold Italy and bring a considerable force against the Allies in the West during the month of August. While it may be hoped that this reinforcement would not suffice to inflict a decisive defeat upon the French and ourselves it would undoubtedly postpone for an indefinite period the prospect of driving the Germans from France and Belgium, and would leave the question of a favourable decision largely contingent upon Russia's recovery, which in view of the state of her supply of armaments must be slow.

The French are now about to make their maximum effort and will very shortly reach the high-water mark of their numerical development. It will not be possible for them to maintain this strength during a second winter campaign. The information at my disposal shows that the Germans have now at least 800,000 effective rifles on the Western front. The French effective rifles are about 875,000, the Belgians have 55,000 and we 255,000. The Allied superiority indicated by these figures is barely sufficient to fulfil the conditions necessary for successful attack which I have outlined in paragraph 5. That degree of superiority can only be obtained in the Western theatre with certainty, if I am reinforced with men, guns, and ammunition before the Germans can transfer troops from East to West.

It is not for me to say what reinforcements can or should be sent to this theatre, but I feel it my duty to point out what it is possible to do with reinforcements if they are sent, in sufficient strength, and what will be the consequence if they do not arrive.

As far as I have been able to judge, the French regard this war as our war even more than theirs, and if we leave them at what they, rightly in my opinion, regard as the most critical stage of the war without the fullest possible support, the effect upon their future attitude may be serious.

The paralysing effect of our unreadiness was, as it always is, most vividly to be seen in the unfitness of the personnel, whose collective value as fighting formations was much less in 1915 than it afterwards became as the result of more military experience and training. Of the divisions sent to France during that year the personnel of the Territorial divisions partly, and of the New Army divisions almost wholly, were at first in the position of recruits—they were soldiers in the making, learning how to perform the new and strange duties which, with admirable patriotism, they had voluntarily undertaken, but about which they knew practically nothing. The New Army divisions first formed, being comparatively well leavened with trained officers and non-commissioned officers, were soon capable of doing as good work as any other divisions on the Western Front. Those formed at a later date, although fully equal to their seniors in bravery and dash, had not the same leavening of trained leaders, and consequently exhibited many failings which required more time and instruction to correct than had yet been available.

Some Ministers with whom I conversed at the front found the defects of new troops hard to understand, and could not believe that they were as serious as I represented them to be. They insisted, when criticizing the operations, upon estimating the relative fighting strengths of the opposing forces by the misleading process of counting heads, and ignored the established fact that numerical superiority can never make up for defects in discipline and practical knowledge. In the latter part of the war of 1870–1871 the French levies were repeatedly beaten by forces less than one-quarter of their strength, although they fought with the utmost gallantry, and on the few occasions when an initial success was achieved they were not capable of reaping the fruits of it. The early years of the American Civil War taught the same lesson, and nowadays, when war has become more scientific, and the physical and moral effect of armament more terrifying and destructive, the demands made upon leaders and men alike are far greater than before. Fortunately for us, the most essential qualification needed, discipline, was acquired by the troops much quicker than had been anticipated in pre-war days, and to this was mainly due the rapidity with which a good standard of proficiency was subsequently reached.

It has been objected that, in view of the great strength of the German defences, the Entente should have deferred offensive action until 1916, when their armies would be better provided with guns and munitions, and the new British divisions could be put into battle better trained and as a whole, and not, as they were, indifferently trained and in driblets. These considerations were undoubtedly very important, and a waiting policy was, in fact, advocated by Sir John French early in July when discussing with General Joffre the French proposal for a double attack in Artois-Champagne. Other factors, however, had to be taken into account. Germany's original plan of crushing France before turning to dispose of Russia had been frustrated by her defeat on the Marne ; her second plan to seize the Channel Ports and advance on Paris from the north had been thwarted at Ypres, and she had then transferred her main effort to the Russian front. But she might, at any time, so far as we knew, bring her troops back and resume the offensive temporarily suspended in the West, in which case the situation there might again become serious.[1]

Moreover, Germany was still in possession of a large part of French territory, and no self-respecting nation could be expected to tolerate this outrage for an indefinite time without an effort being made to end it. Arm-

[1] See Chapter III, pages 147–8, where this contingency is further discussed.

chair critics and military students engaged in conducting campaigns on paper can afford to ignore public opinion, General Joffre could not, any more than von Moltke, Chief of the German General Staff, could at the end of August, 1914, when, as a result of alarm in Berlin, he dispatched two army corps from his right in France to meet the Russian invasion on the Eastern Front. The absence of these troops from the Marne probably went far to lose the Germans that battle. About two months later other German corps had to be sent from the Ypres front to the East just at the time when a little more pressure might have brought victory. General Joffre was in a similar position in 1915, and knew that his countrymen expected him to expel the German invaders with the least possible delay.

The situation on other fronts had also to be remembered. Russia, suffering from a series of heavy defeats, was calling for help, and the Entente armies in the West could not look idly on and leave her in the lurch, especially after the valuable assistance which she had rendered to them the year before. It was imperative, apart from any consideration of expelling the Germans from France, that they should come to her aid by means of a strong and speedy attack. Italy, too, a new partner in the war, needed to be assured of the resolution of her allies. For many reasons General Joffre had practically no alternative to an offensive policy, while Sir John French had no choice but to support him, although his army was, in fact, imperfectly trained and equipped.[1]

[1] The British Government was strongly in favour of adopting a passive defence on the Western Front at this time, *vide* page 127. It was discussed by the British and French staffs at Chantilly on June 24, when General Joffre said he " would not countenance it for a moment."

Sir John's instructions certainly laid down that he was to exercise the " greatest care " in respect of losses and wastage, and " distinctly to understand " that his command was " an entirely independent one." But he was also told " to support and co-operate with the French armies," and that " every effort must be made to coincide most sympathetically with the plans and wishes of our Ally." Perhaps it was not easy to express more clearly the meaning which these instructions were intended to convey, but they were, as all such conditional instructions are, difficult to apply in practice, and to me it has always seemed that Sir John interpreted them in the proper way. His command was very small as compared with the armies under General Joffre, and, loyally placing " co-operation " before " independence," he tried to fall in with the plans of his French colleague even though he might not entirely agree with them.

The second battle of Ypres (April-May) was an example, though General Foch rather than General Joffre was concerned. It will be remembered that a certain amount of ground was lost as the result of the enemy's first gas attack, the effect of which was to place the British troops occupying the Ypres salient in a precarious position. Several attempts to regain the lost ground having proved unsuccessful, Sir John French decided to withdraw from the salient. To this General Foch, then in command of the French army holding the line to the north of the British front, objected, and insisted that the armies ought to act " with the greatest energy and the most complete co-operation " in trying to restore the situation. Twice Sir John French reluctantly agreed to defer with-

The conclusion of the conference was that " A passive defence is out of the question, because it is bad strategy, unfair to Russia, Serbia, and Italy, and therefore wholly inadmissible."

drawal until further efforts had been made, and at last General Joffre intervened with the order that the loss of ground should be accepted and all resources be reserved for the coming offensive in Artois.

In the autumn offensive of 1915, Sir John French co-operated not only from a sense of loyalty to General Joffre but upon definite instructions from the Government. By mid-August Russia's position was becoming so critical that she might collapse any day, and as no relief would be afforded from either the Italian or Gallipoli Fronts, where the recent operations had been very disappointing, it could only be sought in the West. Lord Kitchener, as representing the Government, accordingly went to British G.H.Q. to tell Sir John to do his "utmost to help France in their offensive," even though that entailed "very heavy losses," while a later instruction, telegraphed from London, directed him "to take the offensive and act vigorously."

When America joined in the war some two years later she intended not to commit her troops to battle until they were fully ready and of sufficient strength to be self-supporting. In consequence of the enemy's action, she was compelled to abandon this intention and hasten to the assistance of the British and French armies as best she could. In her case, as in ours in 1915, was repeated the lesson—which is as old as the hills—that when a nation goes to war unprepared it will invariably be compelled by force of circumstances to put its troops into battle piecemeal and before they have learned how to fight.

A memorandum drawn up at French G.H.Q. in November, 1915, said of the September operations :—

This powerful offensive achieved brilliant tactical results. The French and English troops penetrated deeply into the German lines ;

on the Champagne front and in Artois they captured about 30,000 prisoners and more than 500 guns. We have therefore achieved a real victory, the importance of which has been certainly appreciated by our enemies. They have realized that their lines are not inviolable, and that the troops which they maintained on our front were barely sufficient to prevent our breaking through. Without desiring to insist on too close a connexion between events as they occurred, we may still point out that the checking of the forward movement of the Austro-German forces in Russia coincided both with the preparation and execution of our offensive. The Guard, Xth, and XVIIth Corps, and the 38th Division of the XIth Corps were transferred from the Russian front to the French front during the period of preparation, and made their appearance either at the moment of the first attacks or soon after. This movement was followed during October by the transfer of the 4th General Division, the 1st Guard Reserve Division, and the 10th Division of the IInd Corps, which brings up to ten the number of the divisions recently transferred from the Eastern to the Western Front.

It is true that the tactical successes gained could not be developed into a strategic success. The principal causes of this were partly the bad weather which, by paralysing our artillery, limited our rate of advance during the first days of the attack, and partly by a temporary shortage of ammunition and of fresh troops, which prevented us from either resuming or prolonging the operations.

These views have since been substantially confirmed by General Falkenhayn, who has admitted that " a serious crisis arose (in Champagne), leading the staff of the IIIrd Army to consider the advisability of a further withdrawal of the whole army front. Such a step would of necessity have led to very serious consequences." General Ludendorff tells us also, in referring to the " powerful offensive near Loos and Champagne," that " the troops which had been transferred from the East arrived just in time to support the defenders of the Western Front, who were holding out so gallantly, and avert a serious defeat."

Summed up, it may be said that although the operations

were unproductive of decisive success, and were attended by tactical miscalculations which would have to be corrected before the enemy's lines could be breached, they nevertheless rendered valuable aid to an ally in distress, and furnished useful experience in the handling of new troops and in the methods to be employed in the attack on continuous lines of field fortifications. They were, in fact, necessary stages in the preparation for the great battles that were subsequently fought. That the results might have been more immediately effective had greater resources and better-trained troops been available cannot of course be denied, but for the provision of these it was not possible to wait. Nor was the lack of means and training the only reason why greater progress was not made. As in all campaigns at this period the operations suffered from another and equally damaging cause—the absence of efficient Government machinery in London for the general direction of the war, and of close co-operation between the several Entente Powers, who had so far done but little to focus their political and military activities towards a common end. These questions will be dealt with in subsequent chapters.

On December 15 Sir John French was succeeded by Sir Douglas Haig. For some time past the Government had not been satisfied with the way in which affairs on the Western Front were being managed; the Army had greatly increased in size; Sir John French's health was not always as good as could be desired; and as he no longer possessed the complete confidence of the Government it was, as it always is in such cases, best that he should be replaced. Into the question of his relations with the Prime Minister and Secretary of

Photo: Vandyk.

THE EARL OF YPRES.

State for War I shall not enter. From the knowledge I acquired as his Chief of the General Staff I consider that both Mr. Asquith and Lord Kitchener invariably left him a free hand to make, in conjunction with General Joffre, such plans as he deemed fit, and gave him all the support within their power. This statement may perhaps require some qualification in regard to the retreat to the Marne in 1914, but as I was not Chief of the General Staff at that time I know nothing first-hand about the friction which then occurred. Leaving this incident aside, it may be said that Sir John was subjected to none of those discouraging ministerial questions and criticisms on purely military matters which later in the war were inflicted upon his successor.

In other respects his task was much harder than Sir Douglas Haig's. He had to withstand the first onslaught, when all the conditions were new and strange ; the enemy was then at his strongest and the British Army at its weakest ; and, having so small an Army, our actions had necessarily to be subordinated to those of France. Fortunately, Sir John was exceedingly popular with the troops, and I doubt if any other General in the Army could have sustained in them to the same extent the courage and resolution which they displayed during the trying circumstances of the first six months of the war.

Mr. Asquith and a Conservative member of the Government asked for my opinion as to the selection of a General to take Sir John's place, and both were good enough to refer to myself as a possible successor. Sir John, also, recommended that I should fill the vacancy. I felt, however, that Sir Douglas Haig's qualifications were superior to mine, he having held, next to Sir John, the most important command at the front since the commencement of the war.

Further, it was the wish of Lord Kitchener, as of other senior officers in the Army, that I should take up the work of Chief of the Imperial General Staff, and this was the arrangement which the Prime Minister eventually decided to make. It had no attractions for me personally. I did not wish to supersede the then occupant of the post, who had but recently been appointed to fill it ; I knew that it was beset with special difficulties ; while the general military situation had become so entangled, owing to the haphazard manner in which campaigns had been started in Gallipoli, Mesopotamia, Salonika, and elsewhere, that those charged with the duty of restoring it could at the best expect no thanks and much criticism for many months to come. It was necessary, however, to put these considerations on one side and go where it was thought that one could be the most useful.

CHAPTER III

THE DARDANELLES EXPEDITION

Importance of Decisive Front—Pre-war studies of Gallipoli Peninsula—First Naval Bombardment of Forts—Rival Policies and Plans at end of 1914—War Council's Consideration of Dardanelles Project as a Purely Naval Operation—Confused Ideas as to Meaning of the Decision reached—Ministerial Opinions as to Value of Naval Attack—Lord Fisher's Attitude—Admiralty Staff ask for Troops—Second Naval Bombardment of Forts—Vacillation of War Council as to Future Action—Military Expedition sanctioned—Instructions to Commander-in-Chief—Third Naval Bombardment of Forts—Landing of the Expeditionary Force—Further Divisions Dispatched—Landing at Suvla Bay—Suspension of Offensive Action—General Monro appointed to Command—Views of G.H.Q. in France—General Monro recommends Evacuation—Lord Kitchener sent out to Report—Government approves of Evacuation—Some Final Reflections on the Expedition.

AN essential condition of success in war being the concentration of effort on the "decisive front," or place where the main issue will probably be fought out, it follows that soldiers and statesmen charged with the direction of military operations should be agreed amongst themselves as to where that front is. Should any difference of opinion exist—as it usually will, sooner or later—it must be thrashed out and a definite conclusion reached, and this must be honestly and completely accepted by all concerned. If these precautions are not taken, the operations will be of the nature of half-measures and compromise, and may indeed end in disaster.

It is true that the Great War proved, as all previous

wars had done, that numerical superiority alone will not necessarily bring success, and that the attempt to break through well-defended positions with the object of immediately forcing a decision, is not a wise policy to pursue when opposed by an enemy whose morale is still intact, and whose general military efficiency is still good. On the other hand, it was also proved, again in confirmation of past experience, that one cannot be too strong on the decisive front, and that the attempt to score victories in two different theatres simultaneously may lead to failure in both. The Dardanelles Expedition was a case in point.

Again, while soldiers must never forget that the selection of the decisive theatre is influenced by political as well as by military considerations, statesmen should not forget that, once selected, the theatre cannot be changed without causing such dislocation in administrative arrangements as may, according to the size of the army and the distances involved, take several weeks or even months to readjust. In the meantime the army will be more or less out of action, and the enemy will enjoy a corresponding advantage in comparative strength on the fighting fronts. Hence, a change of plan which entails the transfer of the main effort from one theatre to another may, however attractive in appearance, be attended with great risks, and usually it can only be justified by exceptional circumstances.

The doctrine of concentration, like most other doctrines, is easier to preach than to practise, and particularly so in the case of a world-wide Empire such as our own. Troops for protection may be requisitioned by outlying territories, as they were by India and East Africa in the Great War; and new plans of operations may be advocated by amateurs at home or by the man-on-the-spot abroad, who is often thought to be the best judge, whereas he is frequently the worst. Ministers, too, may become impatient with the small progress made in existing theatres, be alarmed at the long casualty lists and their possible effect on public opinion, and begin to search for a "way round" to victory in preference to the direct method of fighting and defeating the enemy's principal armies.

The soldier has no choice but to resist all tendencies of this kind, unless they are well founded, remembering that dispersion of force is only admissible when, in one form or another, it subserves the main plan of campaign. For instance, it may be politically advisable, though strategically objectionable, to try to assist an ally in difficulties, as in October, 1917, when French and British troops were sent to Italy; or it may be necessary to detail detachments for the defence of the lines of communication, as was the object of our operations in the Sinai Peninsula for securing the Suez Canal; or, again, it may be desirable to threaten interests which are of importance to the enemy, so as to oblige him to detach for their protection a force larger than the one employed in making the threat, thus rendering him weaker in comparison on the decisive front.

In the Great War the decisive front was fixed for us by the deployment of the enemy's masses in France and Belgium, which compelled us to go to the direct assistance of those countries, and at first there was little or no inducement to disseminate our forces in other and secondary enterprises. The entry of Turkey into the war at the end of October, 1914, created a more complicated situation, and one offering many temptations for dispersion against which it was important to be on our guard. A careful review of the new conditions was therefore necessary in order to decide in what respect our war plans should be modified, and unfortunately there was at the time no adequate machinery available, in the shape of an efficient General Staff, for conducting the investigation. The field of strategy thus lay open to those Ministers who, as members of the Government, claimed the right to put forward for Cabinet consideration such schemes of operations as they deemed fit; who saw in our sea-power a ready means for undertaking such amphibious adventures as they might conceive and could persuade their colleagues to accept or not to oppose; and who were indifferent to, or ignorant of, the disadvantages which always attend changes of plan and the neglect to concentrate on one thing at a time.

Mr. Churchill has explained the activities of Ministers in this respect by saying that the General Staff at the War Office never presented the War Minister (Lord Kitchener)

> with well-considered general reasonings about the whole course of the war. They stood ready to execute his decisions to the best of their ability. It was left to the members of the War Council to write papers upon the broad strategic view of the war. It was left to the Chancellor of the Exchequer, Mr. Lloyd George, to discern and proclaim to the Cabinet in unmistakable terms the impending military collapse of Russia. It was left to me to offer at any rate one method of influencing the political situation in the Near East in default of comprehensive military schemes.[1]

To what extent Ministers really were impelled to write papers on naval and military strategy, which they would not have written had not that duty been "left" them to do by a defaulting General Staff, is a matter which the reader must decide for himself. It was commonly said at the time that Ministers did not give the General

[1] "The World Crisis, 1915," page 173.

Staff proper opportunities for doing their work, and, judging from the report of the Dardanelles Commission, much the same could be said about the Naval Staff. The planning of the Dardanelles naval operations seems to have been conducted far more by Mr. Churchill than by Lord Fisher, and at meetings of the War Council Mr. Churchill invariably acted as spokesman on all naval matters. There may have been special reasons for this procedure, but fundamentally they could not have been good reasons. The War Council would have obtained a much better knowledge of the questions with which they had to deal had they taken the technical advice they wanted direct from the professional, instead of from the ministerial, head of the Admiralty, as was, in fact, done after Mr. Churchill left that department.

Mr. Churchill's reference to the impending military collapse of Russia is also a little difficult to follow, for no collapse was "impending" as early as January, 1915. The real collapse did not occur until 1917, and consequently it could have had no connexion with the strategical plans which Mr. Lloyd George wished to see adopted two years before.

Plans for the seizure of the Gallipoli Peninsula probably received more attention before 1914 than those of any other projected operation of the kind, and they dated back at least as far as 1878, when Constantinople seemed about to fall into the possession of Russia. I, myself, as head of the foreign section of the General Staff, took part in the investigation on several occasions during 1902–1906, and in December, 1906, the problem was dealt with by the strategical section in a memorandum prepared for the Committee of Imperial Defence. Both the General Staff and Admiralty Staff expressed the view that unaided action of the Fleet was to be strongly deprecated, while the General Staff went further and declined to recommend that the project should be attempted even as a joint operation. They stated :—

> When the question of dispatching a military expeditionary force to the Gallipoli Peninsula comes to be passed in review, the first point to be considered is the general one of whether a landing is possible at all, in face of active opposition, under modern conditions.
>
> In regard to this, history affords no guide.
>
> The whole conditions of war have been revolutionized since such an operation was last attempted.
>
> Military opinion, however, will certainly lean strongly to the view that no landing could nowadays be effected in the presence of an enemy, unless the co-operating naval squadron was in a position to guarantee with its guns, that the men, horses, and vehicles of the landing force should reach the shore unmolested, and that they should find, after disembarkation, a sufficiently extended area, free from hostile fire, to enable them to form up for battle on suitable ground.
>
> In the opinion of the General Staff, a doubt exists as to whether the co-operating Fleet would be able to give this absolute guarantee.
>
> The successful conclusion of a military operation against the Gallipoli Peninsula must hinge, as already stated, upon the ability of the Fleet, not only to dominate the Turkish defences with gunfire, and to crush their field troops during that period of helplessness which exists while an army is in actual process of disembarkation, but also to cover the advance of the troops once ashore, until they can gain a firm foothold and establish themselves upon the high ground in rear of the coast defences of the Dardanelles. However brilliant as a combination of war, and however fruitful in its consequences, such an operation would be, were it crowned with success, the General Staff, in view of the risks involved, are not prepared to recommend its being attempted.[1]

Nothing could well be more definite than this advice. The Admiralty Staff thought that the General Staff had underrated " the value of the assistance which might be rendered by a co-operating Fleet by means of a heavy covering fire," and the difference of opinion between the

[1] Final Report of the Dardanelles Commission, page 7.

two staffs was subsequently recorded in the proceedings of the Committee of Imperial Defence as follows :—

> While the former (the General Staff) appears to regard the enterprise in question as too hazardous, the latter (the Admiralty Staff), while recognizing the great risk involved, is of opinion that it is within the bounds of possibility that an operation of this nature might be forced upon us . . . and that in such an event there is no reason to despair of success, though at the expense, in all likelihood, of heavy sacrifices.[1]

The General Staff view proved to be the more correct. Further, to the best of my recollection it was also laid down in the memorandum above quoted, and if not it was certainly well understood, that, as in the case of all landings on an enemy's coast, the element of surprise would be of supreme importance.

Having left the War Office early in 1907, before the examination of the project had been completed, I have no personal knowledge of the conclusions which the Defence Committee reached, but according to Mr. Churchill's account it was decided that a military landing on the Peninsula would involve such great risks that it ought not to be attempted if it could be avoided. As the narrative will show, little attention was paid either to this decision or to the very sound advice contained in the General Staff memorandum when, in 1914–15, the project came up for final settlement.

Shortly after war broke out Mr. Churchill, thinking that Turkey would sooner or later join the Central Powers, arranged with Lord Kitchener that their two departments should prepare a joint scheme for seizing the Peninsula, so that it might be ready for use if wanted. How far it materialized I do not know, but in a memoran-

[1] First Report of the Dardanelles Commission, page 48.

dum written by the Director of Military Operations on September 3 the statement was again made that an attack " from the sea-side (outside the Straits) is likely to prove an extremely difficult operation of war," and one which ought not to be attempted with a less force than 60,000 men. Attention was also called to the decision of the Defence Committee in 1907.

On November 3, three days after Turkey declared war, the outer forts of the Dardanelles were bombarded by British ships for about ten minutes, the object being to find out by a practical test the effective range of the guns of the forts. The orders to bombard emanated solely from the Admiralty, and the War Council was not consulted. Leaving aside the impropriety of opening up operations in a new quarter without Government sanction or knowledge, the bombardment undoubtedly was, as the naval authorities stated before the Dardanelles Commission, " unfortunate " and a " mistake," since it was calculated to place the enemy on the alert and so jeopardize the possibility of effecting a surprise should a serious attack have to be undertaken at a later date.

The question of making such an attack appears to have been considered by the War Council for the first time on November 25. Mr. Churchill then said " that the best way to defend Egypt was to make an attack on some part of the coast of Asiatic Turkey, and, as an extension of this idea he suggested an attack on the Gallipoli Peninsula, which, if successful, would give us control of the Straits and enable us to dictate terms at Constantinople. He added that it would be a very difficult operation and would require a large force. Lord Kitchener agreed that it might be necessary to make a diversion by an attack on the Turkish communications, but considered that the moment had not yet arrived for doing so."[1] Apparently he preferred a landing near Alexandretta, but neither troops nor material were available for this or any other new enterprise. For weeks past the British Army in France had been locked in a deadly struggle with the enemy in opposing his efforts to reach the Channel Ports; the shortage of shipping for mercantile purposes, due partly to heavy military demands, was also being felt; and for these and other reasons it was deemed desirable that the project should be laid aside.

The repeated attempts made by the enemy to break through our positions at Ypres having been repulsed with great loss, it seemed fairly clear by the end of November that further attempts would have no better chance of success, while on the other hand the Entente armies were not yet strong enough to justify the hope that they could break through the enemy's lines. Hence, for the time being, the whole Western Front stagnated into dreary trench warfare, and proposals began to pour in from all quarters as to what our future strategy should be. One of the first to appear on the scene was a memorandum circulated to the members of the War Council by its secretary, dated December 28. This paper called attention to the "remarkable deadlock" which had occurred on the Western Front. It invited consideration of the possibility of seeking some other outlet for the employment of the new armies then in course of formation. It suggested that Germany could perhaps "be struck most effectively, and with the most lasting results on the peace of the world, through her allies, and particularly Turkey." Finally, it asked whether it was not possible "now to weave a web around Turkey,

[1] First Report of the Dardanelles Commission, page 14.

which will end her career as a European Power?"[1] The weaving of this web was to prove a very costly business.

Three days later, on January 1, appeared the famous memorandum of the Chancellor of the Exchequer, Mr. Lloyd George, proposing that the entire Expeditionary Force, with the exception of a general reserve to be kept temporarily near Boulogne, should be withdrawn from France and sent to the Balkans, whence, in combination with the armies of Serbia, Greece and Rumania, our main military effort would be directed against Austria, instead of vainly continuing the attempts to break through the German defences on the Western Front. Simultaneously with this transfer, a force of 100,000 British troops were to be landed "in Syria" so as to cut off the 80,000 Turkish troops reported to be moving thence on Egypt.

These proposals will be discussed in a later chapter, and nothing more need be said about them here except that they found, as might be expected, no favour in French military circles. General Joffre insisted that all available strength should be concentrated in France, and was supported by M. Millerand, Minister of War, who very sensibly remarked, so it was said, that "*Un plan mediocre bien arrêté vaut mieux que de changer souvent de plan. Il ne faut pas encombrer nos généraux de suggestions.*"[2]

Sir John French, too, rejected the theory that the enemy's lines could not be breached, given a better supply of men, guns, and munitions. He further represented that, irrespective of breaking through, the safety of France, and of the Channel Ports in particular, was

[1] First Report of the Dardanelles Commission, page 48.

[2] "The Tragedy of Lord Kitchener," by Lord Esher.

vital to us, and that such troops as we could put into the field would afford no more than the margin of security which the situation demanded. His proposal was, however, to undertake a joint operation with the Navy for the purpose of clearing the enemy out of Ostend and Zeebrugge, in preference to what might be called a purely frontal attack. Lord Kitchener at first supported this plan, and the British Ambassador in Paris was informed that the " Government consider it most urgent and important that this step should be taken, and you should ask the French Government to agree to it and to arrange with General Joffre for carrying it out." But General Joffre was opposed to it, on the grounds that to undertake an offensive on the extreme left flank would needlessly weaken the Entente centre and so uncover the direct lines of advance on Paris. The French Government accordingly gave the proposal a cool reception.

Another scheme which frequently cropped up at this time was the one advocated by Lord Fisher for making a combined naval and military attack on the coast of Schleswig-Holstein. This had often been mentioned before the war and as often opposed by the General Staff. From a military standpoint it was not a practicable proposition, and I could never understand why Lord Fisher should think that it was.

Over and above this bewildering shower of proposals and projects, emanating respectively from the First Lord of the Admiralty, the Secretary of the War Council, the Chancellor of the Exchequer, the French Commander-in-Chief, the British Commander-in-Chief, and the First Sea Lord, the Government of India, under the auspices of the Secretary of State for India, had commenced operations at the head of the Persian Gulf, and their extension up to Baghdad, some 500 miles from the Gulf, was already being mooted.

These rival policies and plans, uncontrolled by any master-hand, and never discussed by the War Council in terms of available means, continued to jostle each other in the Council's deliberations until matters were brought to a head on January 2. On that day a telegram was received from the British Ambassador at Petrograd stating that the Russians were being hard pressed in the Caucasus, and that in order to relieve the pressure the Russian Government requested that a demonstration might be made against the Turks in some other quarter.

On January 3 the Ambassador was authorized to say that a demonstration would be made but that it was very doubtful if it would lead to the desired result —the withdrawal of enemy troops from the Caucasian front. According to normal procedure, the reply was drafted by the War Office and transmitted to Russia through the medium of the Foreign Office. The matter was not in any way referred to the War Council—the body charged with the supreme direction of the war—and even the Prime Minister did not see the reply until after it had been dispatched. It appears to have been entirely the outcome of a conversation which Lord Kitchener had with Mr. Churchill after the receipt of the Petrograd message, and in a letter written to Mr. Churchill on the same day Lord Kitchener said :—

I do not see that we can do anything that will seriously help the Russians in the Caucasus. The Turks are evidently withdrawing most of their troops from Adrianople and using them to reinforce their army against Russia, probably sending them by the Black Sea. . . . We have no troops to land anywhere. A demonstration at Smyrna would do no good and would probably cause the slaughter of Christians. Alexandretta has already been tried, and would have no great effect a second time. The coast of Syria would have no effect. The only place that a demonstration might have some effect in stopping reinforcements going east would be the Dardanelles. Particularly if, as the Grand Duke says, reports could be spread at the same time that Constantinople was threatened. We shall not be ready for anything big for some months.[1]

On the same day as the reply was sent to Russia promising the "demonstration," Mr. Churchill telegraphed to Admiral Carden, Naval Commander-in-Chief in the Mediterranean, asking for his view as to the practicability of forcing the Dardanelles by the use of ships alone. Other telegrams on the subject were exchanged later and the Admiralty Staff were directed by Mr. Churchill to prepare a memorandum which was afterwards described as a "Note on forcing the Passages of the Dardanelles and Bosphorus by the Allied Fleets in order to destroy the Turko-German squadron and threaten Constantinople without military co-operation."

Meanwhile, having in mind the many competing policies recently put forward, Lord Kitchener had written to Sir John French on January 2 asking what views were held by him as to the desirability of operating elsewhere than on the Western Front, where there seemed to be no prospect of breaking through the enemy's lines. In his reply Sir John dealt with the various alternative theatres of war and went on to say that any attack on Turkey (in Gallipoli, Asia Minor, or Syria) would be devoid of decisive result.

In the most favourable circumstances it could only cause the relaxation of pressure against Russia in the Caucasus and enable her to transfer two or three corps to the West—a result quite incommensurate with the effort involved. To attack Turkey would be to play the German game and to bring about the very end which Germany had in mind when she induced Turkey to join in the war, namely, to

---

[1] "The World Crisis, 1915," page 94.

draw off troops from the decisive spot, which is Germany itself. . . . There are no theatres, other than those in which operations are now in progress, in which decisive results could be attained.[1]

These views were considered by the War Council on January 8, when another long discussion took place as to whether, where, and when new theatres should be opened up. In the course of it Lord Kitchener expressed the opinion that the Dardanelles appeared to be the most suitable military objective, as an attack there could be made in co-operation with the Fleet, and he estimated that 150,000 men would be sufficient, but reserved his final opinion until a closer study of the problem had been made. The Council decided that, owing to the scarcity of trained men and the shortage of ammunition, the Belgian coast project of Sir John French must be abandoned, but that, "for the present, the main theatre of operations for British forces should be alongside the French Army, and that this should continue as long as France was liable to successful invasion and required armed support."[2]

The decision was communicated to Sir John French on January 9, and it was further stated that as the situation on the Western Front might conceivably develop into one of stalemate, the War Council considered it desirable that

certain of the possible projects for pressing the war in other theatres should be carefully studied during the next few weeks, so that, as soon as the new forces are fit for action, plans may be ready to meet any eventuality that may be then deemed expedient, either from a political point of view or to enable our forces to act with the best advantage in concert with the troops of other nations throwing in their lot with the Allies.

---

[1] "1914," pages 314–16.
[2] Final Report of the Dardanelles Commission, page 6.

This was the position on January 13, when the War Council again had the question of the Dardanelles under consideration. Mr. Churchill then referred to his communications with Admiral Carden, and informed the Council that the sense of the reply was "that it was impossible to rush the Dardanelles, but that, in his opinion, it might be possible to demolish the forts one by one." To this end the Admiral had submitted a plan, which Mr. Churchill explained to the Council and added that the "Admiralty were studying the question, and believed that a plan could be made for systematically reducing all the forts within a few weeks. Once the forts were reduced the minefields could be cleared, and the Fleet would proceed up to Constantinople and destroy the *Goeben*. They would have nothing to fear from field guns or rifles, which would be merely an inconvenience."[1] It was further recorded in the proceedings of the meeting that "Lord Kitchener thought the plan was worth trying. We could leave off the bombardment if it did not prove effective." He stated, however, that there were not, and would not for some months be, any troops available for the operations.

Lord Fisher "said nothing," and this apparently led to some misunderstanding on the part of Ministers who attended the meeting. Mr. Churchill maintained before the Dardanelles Commissioners that he was entitled to think that in what he said at the meeting he carried with him the "full agreement" of those who were present. The Commissioners themselves thought that it

is perhaps overstating the case to say that Lord Fisher was in full agreement, but it is undeniable that, by not dissenting, Lord Fisher might reasonably have been held to agree, and that, so far as we have been able to ascertain, he did not, before the meeting, express anything

[1] First Report of the Dardanelles Commission, pages 19–20.

approaching strong disapproval save on the ground to which we have already alluded, namely, that he feared that the Dardanelles operations would interfere with the execution of other schemes which he favoured.[1]

What Lord Fisher's views actually were it is not easy to guess, as the whole affair was so irregularly handled, but there need have been no doubt about it had he, and not the First Lord, acted as the naval spokesman. The principal question before the Council was one of practicability, not of policy, and it ought to have been dealt with, not by a civilian Minister, but by a man who possessed the necessary technical knowledge and practical experience enabling him to answer it.

The advantages to be derived from forcing the Straits were perfectly obvious. Such a success would, as the advocates of the project said, serve to secure Egypt, to induce Italy and the Balkan States to come in on our side, and, if followed by the forcing of the Bosphorus, would enable Russia to draw munitions from America and Western Europe, and to export her accumulated supplies of wheat. There is seldom any lack of attractive-looking schemes in war. The difficulty is to give effect to them, and one of the difficulties in the Dardanelles scheme was that nothing really useful could be achieved without the assistance, sooner or later, of troops, and, according to the War Minister, no troops were available. Moreover, it was necessary that the scheme should be considered in relation to our military policy as a whole, and the latter, as already indicated, had not yet been intelligently studied or settled.[2]

[1] First Report of the Dardanelles Commission, page 21.

[2] Referring to the final decision reached on January 28, Mr. Churchill says: "It was on that foundation alone (i.e. that for the present no troops could be spared) that all our decisions in favour of a purely naval attack had been taken. But henceforward a series of new facts and pressures came into play which gradually but un-

Into the dispute as to who was primarily responsible for originating the proposal to make a purely naval attack it would be presumptuous on my part to enter. Lord Fisher, in giving evidence before the Dardanelles Commission, spoke of the attack as "Lord Kitchener's proposal," basing his statement on Lord Kitchener's letter to Mr. Churchill of January 2, to which reference has just been made. The Commissioners reported that—

> We are unable to concur in Lord Fisher's view. Lord Kitchener suggested and pressed for a demonstration, but that did not necessarily involve a deliberate attempt to force a passage. The proper conclusion seems to be that when a demonstration appeared to be necessary the First Lord thought it was possible to convert and extend that demonstration into an attempt to force a passage.

Having accepted Lord Kitchener's statement that no troops could be made available for an indefinite time to come, the questions which the War Council should have considered and decided were :—

(*a*) Should the project of forcing the Dardanelles be accepted as part of our general war policy ?

(*b*) If so, should it be undertaken forthwith by the Fleet alone, or wait until troops became available ?

(*c*) If and when undertaken, what modification should be made in the policy tentatively laid down five days before, namely, that the Western Front was to be regarded as the main theatre ?

The project does not appear to have been sufficiently examined from these three standpoints, but mainly on its

ceasingly changed the character and enormously extended the scope of the enterprise."—" The World Crisis, 1915," page 170.

" New facts and pressures " invariably do come into play in all operations of war, and the possibility of their intervention needs careful consideration before any plan can be regarded as sound. This consideration was not conspicuously apparent in the case of the Dardanelles Expedition.

own merits, and the decision which the Council arrived at was couched in the following ambiguous terms :—

> That the Admiralty should consider promptly the possibility of effective action in the Adriatic at Cattaro or elsewhere—with a view (*inter alia*) of bringing pressure on Italy. (This operation was much to the fore at the time, but was later dropped as being useless.)
>
> That the Admiralty should also prepare for a naval expedition in February to bombard and take the Gallipoli Peninsula, with Constantinople as its objective.[1]

In regard to this second decision the Dardanelles Commissioners remarked :—

> It is impossible to read all the evidence or to study the voluminous papers which have been submitted to us, without being struck with the atmosphere of vagueness and want of precision which seems to have characterized the proceedings of the War Council. We have already mentioned that some of those present at the meetings of the Council left without having any very clear idea of what had or had not been decided. The decision of the Council taken on January 13 is another case in point.[2]

The Commissioners then went on to show how the decision was interpreted by the different persons concerned.

Mr. Asquith understood it to be " merely provisional, to prepare, but nothing more." It did not pledge the Council to definite action. It " was a very promising operation, and the Admiralty ought to get ready for it." But " no more than that."

Mr. Churchill thought it went further than the approval of mere preparation. It " was the approval of a principle, with general knowledge of how it was to be given effect to."

Lord Crewe and others of the Council thought that the operation " was approved subject to the occurrence

[1] " The World Crisis, 1915," page 110.

[2] First Report of the Dardanelles Commission, page 21.

of any unforeseen event which might have made it from one point of view unnecessary."

The staffs of the War Office and Admiralty understood the decision to mean a "definite serious project definitely to force the passage of the Dardanelles," and in no sense "to be anything of the limited character of a demonstration."

In regard to this point it should be noticed that the Council had drifted entirely away from their original purpose—a demonstration—and were now about to authorize an operation of a much more ambitious character. A "demonstration" is a feint-attack, or subsidiary measure, designed to draw the enemy temporarily into a course of action advantageous to oneself. In this particular case the intention—a futile one, no doubt—was to draw Turkish troops away from the Russian front in the Caucasus, and to prevent Turkish reinforcements being sent there from Europe. But the seizure of the Gallipoli Peninsula with Constantinople, the enemy's capital, as the ultimate goal, was an operation of the first rank, and, as the Commissioners said, it was

> almost inconceivable that anyone, whether military, naval, or civilian, could have imagined for one moment that Constantinople could be captured without military help on a somewhat large scale. It is clear that, by the decision of January 13, although the War Council only pledged itself for the moment to naval action, they were in reality committed to military action on a large scale in the event of the attempt to force the Dardanelles by the Fleet alone proving successful.

The decision went, indeed, even further than this. Not only would a large military force be required to consolidate and complete the work of the Fleet if successful, but it might be required to come to the assistance of the Fleet if unsuccessful, for there was no certainty that the operation could be abandoned once the naval attack began.

Ministers and experts both thought at the time that it could, but both should have known that this was an unreliable assumption upon which to build. Unsuccessful minor operations may possibly be broken off without causing much harm, but the case is different with great enterprises. The action of the enemy, the morale of one's own troops, public opinion at home, prestige abroad, and many other things may combine to render their continuance compulsory once they are begun. When drawing up plans of operations, there is no greater fallacy than to suppose that one can have as much or as little fighting as suits one's own purpose. As Lord Kitchener said during the Dardanelles discussions: "We have to make war as we must and not as we would like to."

The strength of the military force that might be needed before the Dardanelles fell into our possession had already been tentatively estimated by Lord Kitchener at 150,000 men, but the possibility of being compelled to provide those men should the Fleet fail received no attention. "I am unable to find," said one of the Dardanelles Commissioners, "that the War Council ever really faced or ever really decided whether it was within their power to undertake military operations on a large scale in another theatre of war, or that the great and obvious political advantages to be gained by operations in the East were ever considered in the light of military possibility. This was due to the complete absence during their discussions of detailed staff estimates in terms of munitions and men, and to the too confident belief in the success of the purely naval attack on the Dardanelles, in the chance of an ineffective Turkish resistance, and in the decisive effect of the appearance of the Fleet off Constantinople."[1]

[1] First Report of the Dardanelles Commission, page 55.

Shortly after the meeting of January 13, information was received pointing to Austro-German preparations for the invasion of Serbia, and Mr. Lloyd George thereupon made fresh efforts to persuade the War Council to sanction his Balkan project. Notes were addressed to Greece and Rumania pressing them to co-operate with Serbia, and on January 20 Greece agreed to do so on certain conditions, one of which was that the Greek army should first be reinforced by Entente troops. Aided by this news, Mr. Lloyd George obtained Lord Kitchener's provisional consent to the dispatch of the 29th Division from England, previously earmarked for France. It remained to enlist the co-operation of the French Government, and while negotiations were still going on the War Council decided, on January 28, to proceed with the naval attack on the Dardanelles. How this decision came about will now be explained.

The tentative instructions given by the War Council on January 13 caused the First Sea Lord (Lord Fisher) to become uneasy in his mind, and "there were at this time constant differences of opinion"[1] between him and the First Lord (Mr. Churchill). These differences eventually culminated in the submission by Lord Fisher to the Prime Minister, on January 25, of a memorandum dealing with the question of naval policy in general. It had no very direct bearing on the Dardanelles project, but it deprecated the use of the Fleet for coast bombardments or attacks on fortified positions. The memorandum was answered by another prepared by Mr. Winston Churchill on January 27, in which it was contended that the proposal to bombard the Gallipoli Peninsula did not conflict

[1] First Report of the Dardanelles Commission, page 26.

with the general principles of naval policy which Lord Fisher advocated.

Subsequently Lord Fisher intimated that he did not wish to attend any more meetings of the War Council, and as the Prime Minister was desirous that he should not absent himself from the one which had been fixed for January 28, he arranged that, prior to it, Lord Fisher and Mr. Churchill should meet in his room and discuss the matter with him. Mr. Churchill again pressed for a naval attack, while Lord Fisher spoke in favour of certain alternative plans but did not directly criticize the Dardanelles project on its own merits. The Prime Minister, after hearing both sides, expressed his approval of Mr. Churchill's plan, and immediately afterwards the War Council met and, as just stated, decided that the naval attack should be carried out. There was no longer any question of "preparing," and there was still no intention of using troops, save for minor duties.

Having regard to the importance of the project, the proceedings of this meeting and the arguments upon which the final decision was founded, seem to have been most extraordinary. They were as follows :—

Mr. Churchill informed the Council that he had communicated the project to the Grand Duke Nicholas and the French Admiralty. The former had replied that it might be of assistance to him, while the latter had promised to co-operate. Admiral Carden had expressed his belief in the success of the attack. He required from three weeks to a month to accomplish it. The necessary ships were already on their way to the Dardanelles.

The Prime Minister said that "in view of the steps which had already been taken the question could not well be left in abeyance." (This was not a good argument for going on with the project, for unless it were considered to be sound and to have a fair chance of success, the longer it was left in abeyance the better.)

Lord Kitchener thought " the naval attack to be vitally important. If successful, its effect would be equivalent to that of a successful campaign fought with the New Armies. One merit of the scheme was that, if satisfactory progress was not made, the attack could be broken off."

Mr. Balfour also dwelt on the advantages which would be derived from the attack, if successful, and concluded by saying that " it was difficult to imagine a more helpful operation." (There was no need to emphasize the advantages, and by constantly dwelling upon them there was a danger of obscuring the only points really at issue, namely, was the operation likely to succeed, and what might be the consequences if it failed ? This, according to the findings of the Dardanelles Commission, was exactly what happened. " The stress laid upon the unquestionable advantages which would accrue from success was so great that the disadvantages which would arise in the not improbable case of failure were insufficiently considered." The omission is a common and very natural one on the part of those who, from want of practical experience, do not realize the difficulties and uncertainties which attend operations of war, even of the simplest kind.)

Sir Edward Grey said the attack would " finally settle the attitude of Bulgaria and the whole of the Balkans." (This, again, was by itself a misleading argument. Instead of finally settling " the whole of the Balkans " it might reopen the whole Eastern question as to who should possess Constantinople after the overthrow of the Turk—a question about which the Balkan States and

Russia had been quarrelling and fighting for more than 450 years past. This proved to be the case. Russia would not at any price accept the co-operation of Greece, which we were endeavouring to secure, and Bulgaria and Greece would, had they joined the Entente, have been no less jealous of each other.)

Lord Fisher said practically nothing. He apparently attended the meeting under the impression that the Dardanelles question was not to be raised, and that further time would be given in which to think it over. When he found that he was mistaken in this opinion, and that a final decision was to be taken, he rose from his seat with the intention of leaving the room and intimating his wish to resign. Lord Kitchener rose at the same time, and urged him not to resign, and eventually he agreed and resumed his seat.

Finally, it has to be said that the important memorandum sent by Lord Fisher to the Prime Minister on January 25 was not in the hands of the War Council when the meeting took place, neither were the members informed of the conversation between the Prime Minister, Lord Fisher and Mr. Churchill, immediately before the meeting. The result, coupled with Lord Fisher's silence, was that the members of the Council were not well-informed of his views.

When asked by the Dardanelles Commission to explain the reasons of his silence, Lord Fisher said he did not want to have an altercation with his departmental chief at the Council. Mr. Churchill, he said, " was my chief, and it was silence or resignation." He " did not think it would tend towards good relations between the First Lord and myself, nor to the smooth working of the Board of Admiralty, to raise objections in the War Council's discussions. My opinion being known to Mr. Churchill in what I regarded as the proper constitutional way, I preferred thereafter to remain silent."

The majority of the Commissioners did not agree that it was Lord Fisher's duty if he differed from his ministerial chief to maintain silence at the Council or to resign. They thought that the adoption of any such principle generally would impair the efficiency of the public service, and that the "naval advisers should have expressed their views to the Council whether asked or not, if they considered that the project which the Council was about to adopt was impracticable from a naval point of view." Two of the Commissioners dissented from this opinion, but it was shared by all the Ministers who gave evidence.

The position in which Lord Fisher was placed was not, however, quite so simple as it might appear. In a later chapter [1] I shall describe how I found myself similarly situated at a meeting of the Supreme War Council at Versailles in 1918. I then took a course entirely opposite to the one followed by Lord Fisher, and the result was as unsatisfactory in my case as in his.

The Commissioners did not confine their criticisms to the shortcomings of the sailor. They went on to observe that

> considering what Mr. Churchill knew of the opinions of Lord Fisher and Sir Arthur Wilson, and considering also the fact that the other experts at the Admiralty who had been consulted, although they assented to an attack on the outer forts of the Dardanelles and to progressive operations thereafter up the Straits as far as might be found practicable, had not done so with any great cordiality or enthusiasm, he ought . . . not merely to have invited Lord Fisher and Sir Arthur Wilson to express their views freely to the Council, but further to have insisted on their doing so. . . . Without in any

[1] *Vide* Vol. II, page 287.

way wishing to impugn his good faith, it seems clear that he was carried away by his sanguine temperament, and his firm belief in the success of the undertaking which he advocated. Although none of his expert advisers absolutely expressed dissent, all the evidence laid before us leads us to the conclusion that Mr. Churchill had obtained their support to a less extent than he himself imagined.

Further, we are very clearly of opinion that the other members of the Council, and more especially the Chairman, should have encouraged the experts present to give their opinion, and, indeed, should have insisted upon their doing so. . . . It was common knowledge that naval opinion generally condemned the attack on forts by ships unaided by any military force. The Prime Minister was himself aware of this fact. Such being the case, it would appear that special care should have been taken to elicit a full expression of the opinions entertained by the experts, and that they should have been urged to state them in their own way.[1]

Everyone will agree with these conclusions, but, after all, the errors committed, whether by Ministers or experts, were largely traceable to the unsystematic methods by which the supreme direction of the war was being carried on, in Downing Street as in the two War Departments, and so long as those methods remained unremedied confusion and failure were inevitable. For instance, and as already mentioned,[2] at the very time that the War Council was deciding, on January 28, to start new and ambitious operations in the Dardanelles, for which a large number of troops must sooner or later be wanted, its representative, the Chancellor of the Exchequer, was arranging with the French to combine with us in still another new campaign, in the Balkans. On February 6 the Chancellor returned from Paris with M. Delcassé, who promised that his Government would send a division to Salonika if we would do the same. Lord Kitchener agreed that this was a cheap price to pay

[1] First Report of the Dardanelles Commission, pages 28 and 29.
[2] *Vide* page 93.

for the assistance of Greece, and proposed to send a Territorial division as well as the 29th Division already provisionally appointed to go. On February 15, while the discussions were still proceeding, Greece categorically refused to join the Entente and the idea of operations in the Balkans had once more to be abandoned.

The disregard of the General Staff memorandum of December, 1906, which pointed out the difficulties of seizing the Gallipoli Peninsula, and advised that the attempt should not be made, was another instance of the mismanagement which prevailed. Apparently the War Council held that the memorandum was not applicable to the conditions of 1915, and for the following reasons:—

Turkey had shown herself in the Balkan wars to be much less formidable as a military power than had been supposed. Naval ordnance had considerably improved, and the use of aircraft had increased the efficacy of naval bombardment. The development of submarines rendered the Turkish communications to the Gallipoli Peninsula through the Sea of Marmora more vulnerable. The rapid fall of the Liège and Namur forts was considered to justify the conclusion that " permanent works could easily be dealt with by modern long-range guns." In general, it was thought that the old-established principle of naval warfare which forbade the attack of ships on forts without military aid was no longer valid. Events were to prove that this conclusion was very ill-founded. There was, in fact, no analogy between the military bombardment of the Belgian defences with howitzers and a naval bombardment of the Dardanelles defences with guns, and before resolving to run counter to all previous teaching and to pit ships against permanent works, the War Council would have been wise to obtain the opinion of those who were the most competent to help them—Engineer and Artillery officers having special knowledge of fortress warfare. The General Staff memorandum, with the remarks thereon by the Naval Staff, was apparently not brought to the notice of the War Council as a whole until February 19. On that day, when too late to be of use, Mr. Asquith read out certain extracts from it, and it was afterwards circulated to all members of the Council.

After the meeting of January 28 "the objective of the Government remained the same, but the views held as to the means of realizing it underwent a profound change."[1] Day by day the unwelcome truth grew clearer that nothing useful could be accomplished without the aid of troops, and the idea of a purely naval operation was gradually dropped. But neither the Cabinet nor the War Council took the requisite steps to modify the policy which was now seen to be impracticable. It was not until some seven or eight weeks later, after two attacks by ships alone had been made, that the employment of troops was finally sanctioned.

On February 15 the Admiralty Staff wrote a long memorandum on the subject, in which it was stated that:—

> The provision of the necessary military forces to enable the fruits of this heavy naval undertaking to be gathered must never be lost sight of; the transport carrying them should be in readiness to enter the Straits as soon as it is seen the forts at the Narrows will be silenced. To complete their destruction, strong military landing parties with strong covering forces will be necessary. It is considered, however, that the full advantage of the undertaking would only be obtained by the occupation of the Peninsula by a military force acting in conjunction with the naval operations, as the pressure of a strong army on the Peninsula would not only greatly harass the operations, but would render the passage of the Straits impracticable by any but powerfully

[1] First Report of the Dardanelles Commission, page 29.

armed vessels, even though all the permanent defences had been silenced. The naval bombardment is not recommended as a sound military operation, unless a strong military force is ready to assist in the operation, or, at least, follow it up immediately all the forts are silenced.[1]

Next day an informal meeting of the War Council was held, at which Mr. Asquith, Lord Kitchener, Mr. Churchill, and other principal Ministers were present, and it was agreed, the decision being later incorporated into those of the Council, that the 29th Division should be sent to Lemnos at the earliest possible date ; another force was to be made ready for dispatch from Egypt, where a considerable number of troops from Australia, New Zealand and elsewhere were assembling ; and various other preparations for a joint naval and military enterprise were ordered to be made. Thus, although it was not yet decided to use troops on a large scale, they were to be massed and made ready for use, if required, when the Fleet had forced a passage.

On February 19 the naval bombardment ordered on January 28 took place, the results being only fairly satisfactory and in no sense decisive. Future plans were discussed by the War Council on the same day, and again on February 24 and 26, Lord Kitchener's anxiety about the situation on the Russian and Western fronts causing him to announce that, for the present, he must withhold his consent to the 29th Division being sent to the East. This led to an " acute difference of opinion " between him and Mr. Churchill, the latter demanding the immediate dispatch of the division; while Lord Kitchener, maintaining that the troops to be brought from Egypt must suffice, declined to yield. Eventually the Council decided in accordance with Lord Kitchener's advice.

[1] First Report of the Dardanelles Commission, page 30.

By this time it was evident beyond all possibility of dispute that troops were needed as well as ships, and that, contrary to previous ideas, the operation could not be abandoned now that it had been started. At a meeting on February 24 Lord Kitchener said that he "felt that if the Fleet would not get through the Straits unaided, the Army ought to see the business through. The effect of a defeat in the Orient would be very serious. There could be no going back. The publicity of the announcement had committed us." Lord Grey, too, said that "failure would be morally equivalent to a great defeat on land." These were very different views from those expressed by the same Ministers and others at the meeting of January 28, a month before.

The position was further complicated by still another endeavour on the part of Mr. Lloyd George to secure acceptance of his Balkan scheme. At the meeting of the 24th he "strongly urged that the Army should not be expected to pull the chestnuts out of the fire for the Navy, and that if the Navy failed we should try somewhere else, in the Balkans, and not necessarily at the Dardanelles."[1] This proposal, like the two which preceded it, fell to the ground. The question was, of course, not one of "chestnuts," but of doing the right thing, and Mr. Lloyd George's proposal is a proof that the Council was not yet agreed as to what the right thing was.

On March 10 Lord Kitchener, being then more reassured as regards the position in other theatres, informed the War Council that he was prepared to release the 29th Division for the Dardanelles, and in this way the decision of February 16, the execution of which had been suspended on the 20th, again became operative. He also announced that the approximate strength of

[1] First Report of Dardanelles Commission, page 56.

the forces "available against Constantinople" would be 128,700 men. This number included, however, besides a French division (18,000 men), a Russian army corps (47,600 men) whose dispatch would be contingent upon our gaining access to Constantinople through the Dardanelles and Sea of Marmora.

It has been argued that the failure of the Dardanelles campaign was largely due to the 29th Division being held back during the dates just mentioned, but the argument will hardly bear examination, and instead of speculating upon the effect produced by holding the division back, it will be more useful to observe that there must have been something wrong with the main project from the first, otherwise the employment of a single division could not have become so important a matter as Lord Kitchener found it to be. The wrong thing was, of course, that the troops required could not be provided without a complete reversal of the policy hitherto followed on the Western Front. To force the Dardanelles, dominate Constantinople, and open up the Bosphorus, was a task that might well call for the services of many divisions if the large forces likely to be encountered, eventually, were to be met, on their own ground, with a reasonable chance of success. Moreover, Lord Kitchener was being urged at the time both by General Joffre and Sir John French to reinforce the Western Front; he was disturbed about the Russian Front; he had to make Egypt safe and think of Home Defence. His hesitation to incur the further liability of a new campaign can therefore be well understood. His error, if he made one, was not so much in temporarily holding back the 29th Division, as in departing from his first, simple, and accurate instinct that sufficient troops for the new venture could not be found.

The crucial question was never whether or when the 29th or any other division should or should not be sent to the Dardanelles. That was a detail of a much larger problem, namely, whether the seizure of the Straits and subsequent domination of Constantinople constituted a sound, necessary, and practicable plan, and whether we really meant to carry it out? A definite decision one way or the other, and one which nobody could misunderstand, ought to have been reached before a shot was fired, and it was especially called for in the third week of February, when the original idea of being able to break off the naval attack at will was seen to be futile. The decision was not forthcoming, and consequently, as one of the witnesses before the Commission said, "we drifted into the big military attack." The fact was that the Cabinet aimed at the capture of Constantinople without a proper appreciation of what that task involved, erroneously hoping that it could be accomplished by the Navy alone, while neither the sailors nor soldiers were sufficiently insistent in pointing out the error until it was too late.

Referring to the proceedings of the War Council during this period, the Commissioners observed :—

> From the moment when large bodies of troops were massed in the immediate neighbourhood of the Dardanelles, even though they were not landed, the situation underwent a material change. Whatever may have been the intention of the Government, the public opinion of the world must have been led to believe that an intention existed of making a serious attack both by land and sea. The loss-of-prestige argument, therefore, naturally acquired greater force than had been formerly the case. From the time the decision of February 16 was taken, there were really only two alternatives which were thoroughly defensible. One was to accept the view that by reason of our existing commitments elsewhere an adequate force could not be made available for expeditionary action in the Eastern Mediterranean ; to face the

possible loss of prestige which would have been involved in an acknowledgment of partial failure; and to have fallen back on the original plan of abandoning the naval attack on the Dardanelles, when once it became apparent that military operations on a large scale would be necessary. The other was to have boldly faced the risks which would have been involved elsewhere, and at once to have made a determined effort to force the passage of the Dardanelles by a rapid and well-organized combined attack in great strength. Unfortunately, the Government adopted neither of these courses. Time, as Mr. Asquith very truly said to us, was all-important. Yet for at least three weeks the Government vacillated and came to no definite decision in one sense or the other. The natural result ensued. The favourable moment for action was allowed to lapse. Time was given to the Turks, with the help of German officers, to strengthen their position, so that eventually the opposition to be encountered became of a far more formidable character than was originally to have been anticipated. Moreover, even when the decision was taken, it was by no means thorough.[1]

It was not easy for the War Council to extricate itself from the position in which it had become entangled. It was committed to operations which had been consistently opposed by the General Staff as far back as 1906, and which, as a purely naval undertaking, responsible naval officers were almost equally reluctant to support. The Council now realized the truth of the professional advice which had been given, and was in the dilemma of knowing that troops were needed and that none were available unless diverted from other theatres, contrary to the advice of the War Minister and to the wishes of our French allies. Moreover, it was being persistently pressed by one of its most active members, the Chancellor of the Exchequer, to start a campaign in the Balkans, either in addition to, or in substitution for, the one already begun in the Dardanelles. There was no possibility of escape from these and other similar difficulties with which the Council was rapidly becoming

[1] First Report of the Dardanelles Commission, pages 33 and 34.

surrounded, except by instituting such a system of war-management as would cause Ministers to confine their activities to their own departments, and would allow the professionals to take that controlling share in the conducts of the war which, in the interests of the nation, they ought to take.

On March 12 General Sir Ian Hamilton was appointed to command the troops then in process of assembly, and on the following day he left London for Mudros. The written instructions given to him by Lord Kitchener, and presumably representing the wishes of the Government, were dated March 13, and read:—

1. The Fleet have undertaken to force the passage of the Dardanelles. The employment of military forces on any large scale for land operations at this juncture is only contemplated in the event of the Fleet failing to get through after every effort has been exhausted.

2. Before any serious undertaking is carried out in the Gallipoli Peninsula all the British military forces detailed for the expedition should be assembled, so that their full weight can be thrown in.

3. Having entered on the project of forcing the Straits there can be no idea of abandoning the scheme. It will require time, patience, and methodical plans of co-operation between the naval and military commanders. The essential point is to avoid a check, which will jeopardize our chances of strategical and political success.

4. This does not preclude the probability of minor operations being engaged upon to clear areas occupied by the Turks with guns annoying the Fleet, or for the demolition of forts already silenced by the Fleet. But such minor operations should be as much as possible restricted to the forces necessary to achieve the object in view, and should as far as practicable not entail permanent occupation of positions on the Gallipoli Peninsula.

5. Owing to the lack of any definite information we must presume that the Gallipoli Peninsula is held in strength and that the Kilid Bahr plateau has been fortified and armed for a determined resistance. In fact, we must presuppose that the Turks have taken every measure for the defence of the plateau, which is the key to the Western front at the Narrows, until such time as reconnaissance has proved otherwise.

6. Under present conditions it seems undesirable to land any permanent garrison or hold any lines on the Gallipoli Peninsula. Probably an entrenched force will be required to retain the Turkish forces in the Peninsula and prevent reinforcements arriving at Bulair, and this force would naturally be supported on both flanks by gun-fire from the Fleet. Troops employed on the minor operations mentioned above (paragraph 4) should be withdrawn as soon as their mission is fulfilled.

7. In order not to reduce forces advancing on Constantinople, the security of the Dardanelles passage, once it has been forced, is a matter for the Fleet, except as in paragraph 6 with regard to Bulair.

The occupation of the Asiatic side by military forces is to be strongly deprecated.

8. When the advance through the Sea of Marmora is undertaken, and the Turkish Fleet has been destroyed, the opening of the Bosphorus for the passage of Russian forces will be proceeded with. During this period, the employment of the British and French troops, which will probably have been brought up to the neighbourhood of Constantinople, should be conducted with caution. As soon as the Russian corps has joined up with our troops, combined plans of operations against the Turkish Army (if it still remains in European Turkey) will be undertaken with a view to obtaining its defeat or surrender. Until this is achieved, landing in the town of Constantinople, which may entail street fighting, should be avoided.

9. As it is impossible now to foretell what action the Turkish military authorities may decide upon as regards holding their European territories, the plan of operations for the landing of the troops and their employment must be left for subsequent decision. It is, however, important that as soon as possible after the arrival of the Fleet at Constantinople, all communication from the west to the east across the Bosphorus, including telegraph cables, should be stopped. Assuming that the main portion of the Turkish Army is prepared to defend European Turkish territory, it may be necessary to land parties to hold entrenched positions on the east side of the Bosphorus, and thus assist the Fleet in preventing all communication across the Bosphorus.

10. Should the Turkish Army have retired to the east side of the Bosphorus, the occupation of Constantinople and the western territories of Turkey may be proceeded with.

11. As in certain contingencies it may be important to be able to withdraw our troops from this theatre at an early date, the Allied troops

working in conjunction with us should be placed in those positions which need to be garrisoned, and our troops might with advantage be employed principally in holding the railway line until a decision is come to as to future operations.[1]

These instructions strike one as being more like military commands than ministerial directions—the result, perhaps, of being drafted by a Minister who was also a soldier. They prescribed, moreover, too far ahead and in too great detail to be practical, while the manner of their preparation was also somewhat singular. Referring to them in his diary, when *en route* to the Dardanelles, Sir Ian Hamilton says that when he went to the War Office to say good-bye before leaving, Lord Kitchener was " standing by his desk splashing about with his pen at three different drafts of instructions. One of them had been drafted by Fitz—I suppose under somebody's guidance ; the other was by young Buckley ; the third K. was working on himself." (Fitz was Lord Kitchener's private secretary, and Buckley a General Staff officer.)

Braithwaite (Sir Ian's chief of staff), Fitz and I were in the room ; no one else except Callwell (Director of Military Operations) who popped in and out. The instructions went over most of the ground of yesterday's debate and were too vague. . . . He (Lord Kitchener) toiled over the wording of the instructions. They were headed " Constantinople Expeditionary Force." I begged him to alter this to avert Fate's evil eye. He consented and both this corrected draft and the copy as finally approved are now in Braithwaite's dispatch-box more modestly headed " Mediterranean Expeditionary Force." None of the drafts help us with facts about the enemy ; the politics ; the country and our allies, the Russians. In sober fact these " instructions " leave me to my own devices in the East, almost as much as K.'s laconic order " Git " left me to myself when I quitted Pretoria for the West thirteen years ago.[2]

---

[1] Final Report of Dardanelles Commission, page 10.
[2] " Gallipoli Diary," Vol. I, page 14.

It is hardly necessary to emphasize that instructions given to an officer on taking up the appointment of military or naval Commander-in-Chief are of the highest importance, since they specifically define, or ought to define, the Government policy which he is required to carry out. They should, therefore, be very clearly drafted and each word be carefully weighed, the object being to tell the Commander-in-Chief in general, but in perfectly plain, language what his mission is. Obviously this will not be possible unless Ministers have themselves first made up their minds what it is they want him to do. If they are not agreed about this the instructions will inevitably lead to confusion and disappointment. It is because of their great importance that they are issued on behalf of the Government by a Minister—the Secretary of State for War or the First Lord of the Admiralty—and not over the signature of the chief of the Army or Navy Staff as in the case of operation orders designed to give effect to them.

The Commander-in-Chief, on his part, should be careful to satisfy himself that he correctly understands the instructions. If he is doubtful, he should say so, and ask for the necessary amendments to be made, and in writing. Verbal or other supplementary explanations are wholly objectionable, and instructions which require them are bad. They should be amended, so as to be complete in themselves.

The extent to which a Commander-in-Chief is entitled to be heard on the question of means depends upon the nature of his task. His rôle may be merely one of passive defence, or of holding up enemy forces in one theatre so as to provide a better opportunity for defeating those in another. In circumstances like these the strength of his force would be determined by the High Command, and although he would be consulted, he would, ultimately, have to do the best he could with what he was given. Clearly, the strategical allocation of armies cannot be settled by each Commander-in-Chief for himself.

The case is different when the intention is to undertake an entirely new and offensive campaign for the purpose of producing decisive results. For example, in 1916–17 the rôle of Sir Archibald Murray was, primarily, the defence of Egypt and the Suez Canal, and the strength of his force was fixed on that basis by the High Command in London. In the autumn of 1917 the Prime Minister wished to change the objective into the conquest of Palestine and the complete overthrow of the Turkish armies. General Allenby, successor to General Murray, was therefore asked to submit an estimate of his requirements, and as it proved to be in excess of available means the project had to be temporarily laid aside.

The Dardanelles campaign, as shown by Lord Kitchener's instructions, similarly aimed at decisive results. "Having entered on the project of forcing the Straits there can be no idea of abandoning the scheme. . . . The essential point is to avoid a check which will jeopardize our chances of strategical and political success." It is quite clear from these words that the project was meant to be a major not a subsidiary operation, and that if it fell materially short of complete success it would amount to a failure. When that is the position considerable latitude of action must be left to the Commander-in-Chief, and his opinion regarding the strength and composition of the force to be employed for carrying out the assigned mission should receive careful attention. Moreover, if he thinks that the force proposed is insufficient, he should, having estimated what it ought to be, ask that his views may be laid before the Government.

If the requisite means are not then allotted, and if the Government, in spite of his representations, persist in proceeding with the project with what he believes to be an inadequate force, he should suggest that another officer be appointed in his stead. The Government, on their part, should not hesitate to appoint one, for they could not have a more undesirable servant than one who foresees failure and not success.

Action of this kind is not, however, always easy to take, for in the stress of war questions as between soldiers and statesmen which relate to the distribution of troops do not as a rule present themselves in the simple and straightforward manner one is apt to imagine in time of peace. Usually they are interwoven with a dozen other questions which may be of great concern to Ministers though not to soldiers, and the latter cannot expect that their demands will always be given priority. There will, moreover, be a certain amount of hurry and bustle; decisions may have to be taken very quickly, and with little opportunity for consideration of all the factors involved; difficulties will abound on all sides, and everybody will be expected to do their utmost to assist in surmounting them and not to create new ones.

It may further be observed that, in addition to written instructions, the Commander of an Expeditionary Force is usually supplied with a plan of operations previously worked out by the General Staff, not necessarily for adoption as it stands, but rather for guidance and assistance. No such plan was supplied to Sir Ian Hamilton, and none had been prepared, although a month or more had elapsed since it first became apparent that extensive operations might have to be undertaken. When asked by the Prime Minister at a War Council meeting a week later whether the War Office had prepared a plan or scheme of disembarkation, Lord Kitchener said that though the question had been examined, sufficient information was not forthcoming to enable a detailed scheme to be drawn up.

It was the business of the Chief of the Imperial General Staff to see that the plan was supplied, and that the Commander-in-Chief was given all other information likely to be of assistance to him. When asked by the Dardanelles Commissioners as to whether it was not his duty, when the amphibious attack was decided on, to instruct his officers to prepare a plan, he admitted that under ordinary circumstances it was. When further "asked to account for not doing so, he said in effect that he was overshadowed by Lord Kitchener." A better answer would have been to say outright that no purely military plan could be prepared, for until it was known whether the Fleet would succeed in forcing a passage or not there was nothing definite on which a military plan could be based. Obviously the task of the troops would be different if the passage were first forced by the ships than if it were not. What was really required was a plan for a combined naval and military attack, drawn up by the joint naval and military staffs.

Seeing the importance which the instructions attached to the success of the scheme, and to the fact that a combined attack was more likely to succeed than one made by the Fleet alone, it is hard to understand by what process of reasoning it was thought right to hold the troops back until the ships had failed for the second time. The enemy had been put on the alert on November 3; he must have been still more alarmed by the bombardment of February 19; and already Sir Ian Hamilton had to assume—*vide* his instructions—that the Peninsula was held in strength and had been prepared for a determined resistance. Another bombardment was due to take place shortly, and, unless it succeeded in clearing the Peninsula, the enemy's preparations would be further intensified. Most indiscreet references to our intentions had appeared in the Press, and, in general, the longer the military attack was delayed the more formidable would the defences be found if it was eventually decided to make the attack.

Although, for the reasons given, an excuse can be made for not providing Sir Ian Hamilton with the usual plan of operations, there was none for not supplying him with the General Staff memorandum of December, 1906, and the opinions expressed thereon by the Naval Staff and Committee of Imperial Defence. He ought, moreover, to have been informed of the report just received in the War Office from a French Colonel, late military attaché at Constantinople, who, like the General Staff in 1906, said that a landing would be an extremely hazardous enterprise, since the Peninsula was strongly fortified and held by at least 30,000 troops. This officer recommended that the attack should be made on the Asiatic side as presenting the least difficulties.

The second and last attempt to force a passage by means of ships alone was made on March 18, and although our losses were considerable, the impression produced on the Admiralty authorities by the earlier reports of the action was that we should " go on within the limits of what we had decided to risk, till we reached a decision one way or the other." The question was discussed by the War Council on the morning of the 19th, and the First Lord of the Admiralty was then authorized to inform the Commanding Admiral that he " could continue the naval operations if he thought fit." What was to be done if he did not think fit is not recorded.

After this meeting a telegram reached the War Office from Sir Ian Hamilton, who had arrived at Mudros on the 17th, saying :—

> I have not yet received any report on the naval action, but from what I actually saw of the extraordinarily gallant attempt made yesterday I am most reluctantly driven towards the conclusion that the Dardanelles are less likely to be forced by battleships than at one time seemed probable, and that if the Army is to participate its operations will not assume the subsidiary form anticipated. The Army's share will not be a case of landing parties for the destruction of forts, etc., but rather a case of a deliberate and progressive military operation, carried out in order to make good the passage of the Navy.[1]

Lord Kitchener at once replied: "You know my views that the passage of the Dardanelles must be forced, and that if large military operations on the Gallipoli Peninsula are necessary to clear the way, they must be undertaken, after careful consideration of the local defences, and must be carried through."[2] Sir Ian regarded this telegram as a "peremptory instruction that he was to take the Peninsula," and on March 20 he intimated to Lord Kitchener that he "understood his views completely." He explained to the Dardanelles Commissioners that he did not regard the instruction as entirely depriving him of all discretion in the matter, and that if he "had chosen to say, 'This (the operation) is altogether an impossibility,' I might have said so, but I did not think so."

On March 23 he telegraphed :—

> I have now conferred with the Admiral[3] and we are equally convinced that to enable the Fleet effectively to force the passage of the

[1] Final Report of the Dardanelles Commission, page 12.
[2] *Ibid*, page 12.
[3] Admiral de Robeck, who had recently succeeded Admiral Carden.

Dardanelles, the co-operation of the whole military force will be necessary. The strength of the enemy on the Gallipoli Peninsula is estimated at about 40,000, with a reserve of 30,000 somewhere west of Rodosto. The unsettled weather prevailing in March introduces a dangerous, incalculable factor into the operation of landing a large force in face of certain opposition, but the weather next month should be more settled, and I am sanguine of the success then of a simple, straightforward scheme, based on your broad principles. I have already worked out the main features of my scheme, and I can communicate them, if you think it safe to do so. Practically the whole of my force will be required to effect what I have planned.[1]

The Admiral also telegraphed that he thought it would be necessary to take and occupy the Gallipoli Peninsula by land forces before it will be possible for first-rate ships, capable of dealing with the *Goeben*, to be certain of getting through, and for colliers and other vessels, upon which the usefulness of the big ships largely depends, to get through.

Three days later he reported :—

To obtain important results, and to achieve the object of the campaign, a combined operation will be essential. For the Fleet to attack the Narrows now would jeopardize the success of a better and bigger scheme and would, therefore, be a mistake.

This was followed on the 27th by a telegram giving more detailed reasons in support of a combined operation and saying :—

In my opinion, decisive and overwhelming results will be effected by the plan discussed with General Hamilton, and now being prepared. . . . The assumption underlying the plan originally approved for forcing the Dardanelles by ships, was that forts could be destroyed by gun-fire alone. As applied to the attacking of open forts, by high-velocity fire, this assumption has been conclusively disproved. . . . The analogy of the attack on the cupola forts at Antwerp by heavy howitzer fire is quite misleading, when applied to the case I have described. . . . The assistance of all naval forces available will, in my judgment, be needed to land the Army of the size contemplated, in the teeth of strenuous opposition.[1]

[1] Final Report of the Dardanelles Commission, page 13.

The expression of these views, the accuracy of which should have been obvious from the first, and had now been confirmed by an experience that could not be ignored, meant that the purely naval attack must be forthwith abandoned, but the Dardanelles Commissioners were unable to ascertain any precise date on which it was definitely decided that military action should be substituted. One reason for this was that after the meeting on the morning of March 19, when it was decided to tell the Commanding Admiral to continue his operations "if he thought fit," the War Council did not meet again until May 14, a period of nearly two months! The Prime Minister informed the Commissioners that in the interval "there were thirteen meetings of the *Cabinet*, at eleven of which the operations at the Dardanelles were brought up for report, and that they were on several occasions the subject, not merely of report, but of long and careful discussion."

This, however, was a very poor substitute for the constant and systematic supervision which the competent management of a great expedition requires. Operations designed to menace Constantinople had been proposed, some four or five months previously, as the best way of securing Egypt and as being likely to induce certain States either to join the Entente or to remain neutral. Later, in January, they had been sanctioned primarily for the purpose of giving assistance to Russia, and as no troops were available it had been decided to confine them to naval action alone. The advocates of the project thought that this action would suffice to force a passage without military aid, and, if it failed, could easily be broken off. But since that time political and military conditions had changed, both in the Near East and in other parts of the world, and even if the original arguments for striking at Constantinople had lost none of their weight, the execution of that policy had undoubtedly become much more difficult.

Independent naval action was now admitted to be futile, and as a result of the long warning given to the enemy all hope of effecting a surprise had vanished, while the garrison of the Peninsula had been increased and the defences multiplied and strengthened. Consequently, we required a much larger military force than when naval action was sanctioned some two and a half months earlier. Exclusive of the Russian army corps, which could not come into play until Constantinople had been reached, the strength of the Expeditionary Force amounted to only about 80,000 men, as against the estimated enemy strength of 70,000 men, and it must be assumed that, in case of necessity, the latter would be reinforced.

In their telegrams to London the two Commanders-in-Chief had certainly professed themselves to be sanguine of success, but they had also laid stress on the obstacles to be overcome, and each asserted that the whole of his available force would be required to carry the operation through. It was, indeed, quite clear, having regard to the conditions just described, that Sir Ian Hamilton would need a constant flow of drafts to keep his army up to strength, and more divisions as well, before he could complete his mission, even supposing that he could complete it at all. The provision of these drafts and reinforcements—an elementary feature common to all military operations—ought to have been faced by the authorities in London long before it was decided to plunge from a naval bombardment by a few battleships into "large military operations" which "must be carried through." Instead of suspending its meetings, the War Council ought to have been particularly active and had before it a complete appreciation of the military situation by the General Staff, specifying not only immediate requirements but also possible future developments with their probable effect on the conduct of the war as a whole, and giving a definite opinion as to whether the operation could, from a military standpoint, be properly undertaken or not. In short, it was essential, as the Dardanelles Commissioners reported, that before "land operations commenced the War Council should have carefully reconsidered the whole position. In our opinion the Prime Minister ought to have summoned a meeting of the War Council for that purpose, and if not summoned, the other members of the War Council should have pressed for such a meeting. We think this was a serious omission."[1]

An even more serious omission was that the Council never gave sufficient attention to the relation between the new campaign at the Dardanelles and that in progress on the Western Front. The orders to Sir John French, that his primary objective was to co-operate with the French armies in repelling the invasion of French and Belgian territory and in restoring the neutrality of Belgium, remained unmodified in any way. Sir John was left to drive the Germans out of Belgium and Sir Ian Hamilton was to seize and occupy Constantinople, neither officer being given any indication of the relative importance which the Government attached to their missions, while the question of whether we had or had not the resources sufficient for both undertakings also remained unexamined. The result was a continuous conflict of demands from the two theatres of war.[2]

[1] First Report of the Dardanelles Commission, page 43.

[2] *Vide* page 61.

Seeing that we eventually had to employ at the Dardanelles nearly 470,000 troops, or about six times as many as were allocated when the first landing was ordered ; that we lost about 120,000 men in killed, wounded and missing, besides suffering very heavy wastage from sickness ; and that the campaign had then to be abandoned as a failure, these omissions were surely as grievous as any that occurred at any period of the war.

With respect to what might have been the result if, subsequent to the bombardment of March 18, the naval attack had been at once pressed on, aided by such troops as were then on the spot, the Commissioners observed that whatever weight might be attached to the opinions of those in favour of adopting this course—Mr. Churchill, supported by the Prime Minister and Mr. Balfour, being foremost—

> it must be remembered that out of the sixteen ships which attacked the Straits on March 18, three were sunk and four were rendered unfit for further immediate action. Had the attack been renewed within a day or two there is no reason to suppose that the proportion of casualties would have been less, and, if so, even had the second attack succeeded, a very weak force would have been left for subsequent naval operations.[1]

For various reasons which need not be described here —though it may be said that most of them were due to lack of foresight and preparation at home—the inevitable result of hastily-prepared instructions—the actual landing of the Expeditionary Force could not be undertaken before April 25–26. During that night 29,000 men were disembarked at six landing places, part at Helles, the most southerly point of the Peninsula, and part at a point known subsequently as Anzac Cove on the western shore of the Peninsula, about fourteen miles

[1] First Report of the Dardanelles Commission, page 41.

north of Cape Helles. The operations, demanding as they did a series of landings on an open beach in face of a fully prepared enemy and, in some cases, the climbing of almost precipitous cliffs, proved to be a task of extraordinary difficulty which only succeeded owing to the remarkable endurance and resolution shown by the troops. The plan of operations subsequent to the landing was a combined advance by both forces from south and west. Heavy fighting ensued, especially at Cape Helles, where a determined effort was made to capture the commanding height of Achi Baba, but the resistance was such that at the end of ten days, on May 5, our troops had forced their way forward for only about 5,000 yards from the shore. Opposite them lay the Turks, who since their last repulse had fallen back about half a mile upon previously prepared defensive positions. When the attack was resumed on May 6 some slight progress was at first made, but not as much as was hoped, and on the 9th, after describing the third consecutive day's fighting, Sir Ian Hamilton said :—

> I might represent the battle as a victory, but actually the result has been failure, as the main object remains unachieved. Our troops have done all that flesh and blood can do against semi-permanent works, and they are not able to carry them. More and more munitions will be needed to do it. I fear this is a very unpalatable conclusion, but I see no way out of it.

The following day he telegraphed :—

> The only sound procedure is to hammer away until the enemy gets demoralized. Meanwhile, grand attacks are impracticable, and we must make short advances during the night and dig in for the day until we get Achi Baba. I then hope to be able to make progress without this trench method, but Achi Baba is really a fortress. If two fresh divisions organized as a corps could be spared me I could push on with good prospects of success, otherwise I am afraid it will degenerate into trench warfare with its resultant slowness.

He was informed by Lord Kitchener that one division would be sent, and arrangements had already been made to reinforce him with a division and other troops from Egypt and with an additional French division.

It may be recalled here that owing to the restricted width of the Peninsula there was practically no facility for the manœuvre of troops on shore. Hence all attacks had to be frontal, and the maximum number of troops that could be used in them was governed not by the number that could be made available but by the limits of the ground over which the attacks were delivered. The reinforcements just mentioned were useful enough in some ways, but the Peninsula became no wider and the hostile entrenchments no fewer, and it was now certain that the operation would be a much slower and more costly task than the War Minister had hoped, or the Commander-in-Chief had expected. The troops had suffered heavy losses during disembarkation and the subsequent fighting; the positions they held, consisting of hardly more than a fringe, were, including the beaches, commanded by shell-fire; and, in general, instead of being able rapidly to drive the enemy back and seize the heights which dominated the defences of the Narrows, the troops found themselves confronted by formidable fortifications and entanglements, the capture of which could only be gained by the same deliberate methods of trench warfare as those employed on all other battle fronts. It was in these circumstances that the War Council met on May 14, after two months' inaction, to decide what was to be done.

The point had been reached when the Expedition could no longer be considered by itself. The commencement of the second battle of Ypres, three days before the

Gallipoli landing took place, accompanied by the use of poisonous gas for the first time, was a reminder that the Western Front could be neglected only at our peril. On another part of that front a great offensive had just been started by the French, and the disappointing results of our co-operation at Festubert made it clear that the demands of the armies in France were likely to increase rather than decrease. There were also requirements in Egypt, Mesopotamia, and elsewhere which had to be met. Finally, a Russian reverse in Galicia had recently begun, and it seemed likely that the Russian army corps which was to be available near Constantinople, if and when we succeeded in forcing the Dardanelles, would not now be forthcoming.

The War Council therefore had to consider whether in view of these conditions the Gallipoli operations ought to be continued, and it had, of course, to take into account what effect the abandonment of the Expedition might have upon British prestige in the East, and upon the Balkan States whose co-operation the Entente had for so long been endeavouring to secure. The tendency at the meeting was to send out sufficient reinforcements for a further effort, but nothing final was settled except that Lord Kitchener should ask Sir Ian Hamilton what force would be necessary to carry through his present operations to success. He was to base his estimate on the supposition that adequate forces could be provided.

The reply, dated May 17, was that—

> On the one hand there are at present on the Peninsula as many troops as the available space and water supply can accommodate. On the other hand, to break through the strong opposition on my front will require more troops. I am therefore in a quandary, because although more troops are wanted there is at present no room for them. . . . If the present condition of affairs were changed by the entry into the struggle

of Bulgaria or Greece or by the landing of the Russians, my present force kept up to strength by the necessary drafts, plus the army corps asked for on May 10, would probably suffice to finish my task. If, however, the present situation continues unchanged, and the Turks are still able to devote so much exclusive attention to us, I shall want an additional army corps, i.e. two army corps additional in all. I could not land these reinforcements on the Peninsula until I can advance another 1,000 yards, and so free the beaches from the shelling to which they are subjected on the western side, and gain more space, but I could land them on the adjacent islands of Tenedos, Imbros and Lemnos, and take them over later to the Peninsula for battle. This plan would surmount the difficulties of water and space on the Peninsula, and would perhaps enable me to effect a surprise with the fresh divisions. I believe I could advance with half the loss of life that is now being reckoned upon if I had a liberal supply of gun ammunition, especially of high explosive.[1]

Unfortunately, just at this time, when every hour was of importance, the political difficulties arose which led to the formation of a Coalition Government,[2] and Sir Ian Hamilton's telegram was accordingly held over till the new Ministry had been appointed, and no action was taken on it until June 7—a further delay of about three weeks! During the interval the War Council had its name changed to that of the Dardanelles Committee.

On May 28 Lord Kitchener submitted for the information of the new Committee a memorandum reviewing the situation and dealing with three possible solutions of it:—

(1) To withdraw.
(2) To seek an immediate decision.
(3) To continue to push on and make such progress as was possible.

The main advantage claimed for (1) was that it would "put an end to an operation the difficulties of which

[1] "Gallipoli Diary," Vol. I, page 231–2, and Final Report of the Dardanelles Expedition, page 24.

[2] Mr. Balfour becoming First Lord of the Admiralty in place of Mr. Churchill.

had been underestimated, which has already made a considerable inroad on our resources and which will make a very considerable drain on both our naval and military resources before it is brought to a successful conclusion. The disadvantages, however, of abandoning the expedition are very great. The actual tactical operation of withdrawing would be one of great difficulty and danger, involving certainly much loss of life, the loss of large quantities of stores and ammunition, and possibly causing a serious military disaster. . . . More permanent disadvantages would be the loss of all the advantages " which it was the original purpose of the expedition to secure ; " the abandonment of all hope of further co-operation from the Balkan States ; the surrender to Germany of Constantinople, and all she seeks to acquire by dominating Turkey ; the abandonment of one of the most important strategical positions in the world, which has been won by great gallantry and at great loss of life, particularly to our Colonial contingents ; and last, but not least, a blow to our prestige which would resound throughout every portion of our Eastern Empire, and create serious difficulties and dangers for us in every Moslem country."

Objection was also taken to the second course, as the men and munitions asked for by the Commander-in-Chief could not be spared to bring the operation to a rapid conclusion, and even if they could it was thought to be doubtful whether they would secure the result he anticipated.

The third course, however, has much to commend it. It avoids any immediate blow to our prestige ; it keeps the door open to Balkan intervention ; it ensures our hold on a strategical position of great importance, which rivets the attention of the Turks and in all probability limits active operations on their part against Egypt, or in Mesopotamia, or the Caucasus.

The only thing to be said against it is that it involves certain dangers, viz. the risk arising from German submarines and of gas, assisted by the prevailing north winds. There are furthermore, in my opinion, possibilities of the Turks not being able to maintain their resistance on the present scale. This would enable our troops to advance as well as to take advantage of any movement that Bulgaria or Greece may take in our favour.

On June 2 Sir Ian Hamilton telegraphed to the effect that, in his opinion, the Russian reverses in Galicia had set free 100,000 Turks; that already there were 80,000 in the Peninsula; and that he might have as many as 250,000 brought against him. His view was that we must obtain the support of a fresh ally, or else that the reinforcements to the full extent demanded in his telegram of May 17 should be made ready.

Lord Kitchener's memorandum of May 28 was considered by the Dardanelles Committee on June 7, when the following conclusions were reached :—

1. To reinforce Sir Ian Hamilton with the three remaining divisions of the New Army, with a view to an assault in the second week of July.

2. To send out certain naval units, which would be less vulnerable to submarine attack than those under Admiral de Robeck's command.[1]

These conclusions came up for Cabinet consideration on June 9, and after a "very hot discussion" as to whether the enterprise should be persevered in or not it was agreed that the three divisions should be sent.[2] It is not easy to understand what the first conclusion was intended to mean. Apparently the intention was not to go as far as Lord Kitchener's second proposition, but at least two members of the Committee thought that it authorized a "more energetic prosecution of the operations" than that implied in the third proposition. It was not well

[1] Final Report of the Dardanelles Commission, page 25.

[2] "The World Crisis, 1915," page 393.

conceived in another respect. The Committee could not possibly know whether the "second week of July" would be a suitable time for the "assault" to be made. That was a matter which should have been left to the judgment of the Commander-in-Chief, for besides possible interference on the part of the enemy there could be no certainty that the three divisions would be ready to fight by the date specified. As a matter of fact, it was not until the second week in July that the first division began to arrive, while the last of the three was then only leaving England.

Later in June Sir Ian Hamilton was asked by Lord Kitchener if he would like to have a fourth division, and then if a fifth should be sent. As a result of these communications the infantry of two territorial divisions were added, and the whole arrived by the second week in August.

In the meantime, while awaiting the Government decision and the arrival of the reinforcements, fighting had continued on both the Anzac and Helles fronts, and in the hope of extricating his troops from the trench warfare in which they were entangled Sir Ian Hamilton decided to use the bulk of his reinforcements for effecting a landing at Suvla Bay, 18 miles north of Cape Helles, and by a continued advance from that point and Anzac to secure the Sari Bahr heights. These operations also failed to yield the hoped-for results, the losses incurred were extremely heavy, and by the second week of August the Government found themselves faced with the same question as in May, namely whether the operations were to be continued or abandoned, and if continued, in what way?

The question was considered by the Dardanelles

Committee on August 19, but a final decision was not reached until December! The position at the time was that Sir Ian Hamilton had reported that the Turks had 110,000 rifles on the Peninsula to his 95,000, and that to give him the necessary superiority he required 45,000 drafts to bring his divisions up to strength and new formations totalling 50,000 rifles, or 95,000 in all. It had been agreed at an Anglo-French conference held at Calais in July that no offensive on a large scale should be undertaken on the Western Front until the spring of 1916, when it was hoped that all the Allies would be fully ready. Meanwhile the demands for men and munitions for that front would be reduced and the requirements of the Dardanelles and other theatres would be correspondingly easy to meet. Bulgaria was becoming definitely hostile, and was expected to declare herself on the side of the Central Powers any day. The Russian reverses on the Eastern Front were still continuing.

On the following day Lord Kitchener stated that, owing to the unfavourable Russian situation, he could no longer support the Calais agreement, and that the reinforcements asked for by Sir Ian Hamilton could not be sent as they had been promised to France, and must go there. He proposed to send to the Dardanelles only such men and munitions as could be spared without interfering with Joffre's offensive operations then being prepared in Champagne and Artois. This was agreed to, and on being informed of it Sir Ian Hamilton replied that he would make the best of the forces at his disposal, but that within the next fortnight he might have to relinquish either Suvla or Anzac and must also envisage the possibility of having to reduce his front still further.

More telegrams were exchanged, and on August 27 the Committee, after a long discussion, decided that it was impossible at present to formulate any line of future policy except that Sir Ian Hamilton must endeavour to hold the ground he occupied with the troops he had. Meanwhile he was to report what the prospects were, after the experience he had had, of " achieving our main objective of turning the Turks out," and what force he estimated would be required to effect this. He replied on September 2 repeating that he could not launch any " grand new attack " unless and until the additional formations of 50,000 men were sent out together with sufficient drafts to make his divisions up to strength, plus an additional 20 per cent. of drafts to be on hand ready to meet further wastage.

When this report came before the War Committee on September 3 Lord Kitchener stated that an unexpected offer of help had just been received from France. General Sarrail had recently been removed from his command on the Western Front by General Joffre, and the French Government, wishing to provide him with other employment, had asked him to advise them as to the operations in the East. Sarrail had accordingly worked out a plan for a landing on the Asiatic shore of the Dardanelles, and an advance thence in conjunction with resumed operations in the Gallipoli Peninsula. The French Government proposed to send four divisions from France and wished for their two divisions with Sir Ian Hamilton to be relieved by British troops so as to make up a total of six divisions for General Sarrail. Lord Kitchener said he would instruct Sir John French to send two of his divisions from France to carry out the relief.

On inquiry, however, it turned out that the French offer had been made without consulting General Joffre, who vehemently protested against it, and although he was not strong enough to resist the political pressure to provide Sarrail with a command, he succeeded in making it a condition that the divisions—British as well as French—should not leave France until the result of the approaching Champagne-Artois offensive had been determined. The second week of October was fixed as the earliest possible date when this would be known, and before then another element was introduced into the problem which eventually prevented the divisions from being sent to the Dardanelles at all.

Bulgaria had at last mobilized and, in conjunction with Austro-German forces then being made ready, evidently intended to attack Serbia. This brought up afresh the question of sending troops to the aid of Serbia, Greece alone being in a position to help. A condition of her intervention was, as early in the year, that she should be reinforced by 150,000 Entente troops, and as an encouragement to her to take action one British and one French division were at once ordered to Salonika from Gallipoli. While they were on their way, on October 5, M. Venizelos was dismissed by his king, and Greece, repudiating her treaty obligations to Serbia, once more declined to intervene. The Entente thus found themselves faced with a pro-German Greece instead of an ally.

This awkward situation led to a considerable difference of opinion between the members of the Dardanelles Committee as to what should be done. Some, like Mr. Churchill, pointed "to the Dardanelles as the master key to the problem, and to a fresh naval attempt to force the Straits as the sole chance of changing the attitude of Bulgaria and averting the destruction of Serbia."[1] Others, with equal pertinacity, and having no faith in the resumption of the naval

[1] "The World Crisis, 1915," page 474.

attack, pressed for direct assistance being supplied and in the shape of troops. Eventually, on October 6, after heated and confused discussions,[1] the Cabinet decided to refer the matter to the Admiralty and War Office staffs for opinion. The reply of the joint staffs, contained in a memorandum dated October 9, was to the effect that the dispatch of troops to the Balkans would be both useless and dangerous, and that the interests of the Entente in general would best be served by providing reinforcements for the renewal of military operations in Gallipoli. It was recommended that they should consist of six British and two Anglo-Indian divisions to be taken from France, and that in the first instance they should go to Egypt to be suitably re-equipped and reorganized.

This advice was as unpalatable to the advocates of a campaign in the Balkans as it was gratifying to the adherents of the enterprise in the Dardanelles, and when the memorandum came before the War Committee on the evening of the 9th it soon became evident that no agreement on the subject could possibly be reached. Both parties were, however, in favour of large reinforcements being sent to some place in the Eastern theatre, and as they would necessarily take several weeks to move it was argued that in the meantime the situation might so develop as to make agreement possible. This suggestion afforded a convenient basis for a compromise, and it was accordingly decided on October 11 that six[2] divisions should be withdrawn from France and sent to Egypt, and that their subsequent employment should be settled later. Seeing that the question of future operations had already been awaiting settlement for nearly

[1] "The World Crisis, 1915," page 476.

[2] Two Anglo-Indian divisions of this number were eventually sent to Mesopotamia.

two months, this " decision " was not very creditable to the War Committee and it was of little use to the military authorities, for until something definite was decided one way or the other the requisite arrangements could not be made for the employment of the divisions either in Gallipoli or in the Balkans. The outfit required for Gallipoli was totally different from that required for the Balkans, and vice versa.

These proceedings naturally raised afresh the question of evacuating the Gallipoli Peninsula altogether, and on the same day as the above decision was given Lord Kitchener telegraphed to Sir Ian Hamilton asking for his estimate of the probable loss which would be incurred if evacuation were ordered. Sir Ian, who had already declared evacuation to be unthinkable, replied that the losses would depend upon weather and so many other incalculable factors that it was impossible to say what they might amount to, but in his opinion " it would not be wise to reckon on getting out of Gallipoli with less loss than that of half the total force as well as guns, which must be used to the last, stores, railway plant and horses."[1] If we were very lucky, we might lose considerably less than this estimate.

On October 14 the Government decided to recall Sir Ian Hamilton and appoint General Sir Charles Monro in his stead to command all the forces in the Mediterranean. General Monro was instructed to report on the best means of removing the existing deadlock, and " whether, in his opinion, on purely military grounds, it was better to evacuate Gallipoli or to make another attempt to carry it." He was also asked to give his estimate of the loss which would be incurred by evacuation. He arrived at Mudros on October 27.

[1] " Gallipoli Diary," Vol. II, page 253.

In the meantime the possibility of being compelled to evacuate the Peninsula weighed heavily on the mind of the Government, and various officers were consulted on the subject, myself amongst the number. The advice I gave was that we ought to come away immediately. As to losses I could only admit that the operation would be attended with great difficulties and serious risks, but that it ought to be feasible and need not be disastrous provided the preliminary arrangements were carefully made and absolute secrecy was preserved. My reasons for recommending evacuation were explained in the following memorandum dated October 25, and addressed to the Chief of the Imperial General Staff, who had written to me at G.H.Q. in France asking for my opinion on the action which had been proposed by the Joint Staffs in their memorandum of October 9 previously referred to.

You asked me in your letter of the 23rd instant whether, if I were in your place, and if I were told that no major operations would take place in France before the end of January and possibly before the end of March, I would decide against taking any troops out of France either to serve in Gallipoli or Egypt.

The first essential is to settle the basic policy on which the war is to be conducted, i.e. to settle where the main decision is to be sought, and having settled this keep it in the first place, and subordinate everything else to it. It is of no use laying down a policy and then departing from it, while at the same time pretending to adhere to it. If it is to be departed from the departure should be recognized, and it must then be understood that the original policy no longer holds good.

You have already said in your paper of the 9th instant that the " only sure road to final and complete victory is the defeat of the German armies " ; that we should seek for a decision in co-operation with the French in France, and much more to the same effect. The First Sea Lord has also said that unless forces can be spared from Flanders and France without detriment to the situation in France, no other operation should be attempted. I quite agree, as you know, with these excellent principles. It seems to me that if you lose the war in the west, you will lose it the whole world over, whereas if you win it there you can then do as you like with the remainder of the world, although it is possible you may have to recapture some of your lost outlying territories, though I do not see why you should necessarily have to do this.

You say there are three courses open as to Gallipoli: to hold on, to evacuate, to take the Peninsula. As a matter of fact, you are in favour of a fourth course, that of taking the high ground overlooking the Straits. As regards the first course I can say very little because I do not know the local situation, but it seems to me that you may not be able to hold on now that Germany is in process of obtaining a through railway to Constantinople. We know perfectly well that there is no insuperable difficulty in breaking through a first line of defence. It has been done several times in this theatre during the past summer. It is the second and third lines which give the trouble. In the Gallipoli there is only the first line, and if the Germans send down there plenty of ammunition, heavy guns, and gas (probably of a new kind) I should say that the possibility of our Force holding on would be very doubtful. I should also doubt your being able to get reinforcements there in sufficient time to help. It seems to me therefore that there is considerable danger of your being driven off the Gallipoli before you are in a position either to hold on or to advance.

Assuming that you could get troops there in time it would still seem doubtful whether you would be able to advance. Of one thing you may be fairly assured, and that is you will not be able to get going there for several weeks. I take it that you will not receive Monro's report before the middle or end of next month, and it will certainly take some weeks to prepare the attack after the decision to attack has been made. It always takes the French and ourselves several weeks to prepare an attack here. As regards your proposal to be content with taking the high ground, it seems to me that you are almost as likely to be shot off that ground as you are off the ground where you now are. At any rate it would be a costly business to get this ground, and I cannot see that it would have any effect on the final result of the war, unless it be conceded that the possession of this high ground would keep fully engaged a large number of Turks who would otherwise be sent to Egypt and would have to be dealt with there.

But I should have thought that the Dardanelles Expedition was now no longer serving any useful purpose. Its object was to open up the Bosphorus and the Dardanelles, but with both Turkey and Bulgaria against us we can hardly hope to achieve that. Personally I should advise withdrawal, firstly, because if I do not withdraw I shall probably be driven into the sea before I can prevent it, and secondly, because I am serving no useful purpose where I am, beyond holding such Turks as it may be thought would otherwise be sent against Egypt. The troops withdrawn should be sent to Egypt and be there made into an efficient force.

The situation is a very anxious one for you, and it is easy for me, without responsibility, to preach. It is much more difficult for you to decide. But it is not your fault that the situation is what it now is, and honestly I believe that your best course would be evacuation. Withdrawal undoubtedly means a loss of men and material, though perhaps not so much as imagined, and whatever the loss may amount to it will be a definite loss. As soon as the withdrawal is completed you will know exactly where you stand, and against the loss, whatever it may be, you can place a certain though indefinite loss—that of daily wastage ; the possibility of a total loss of everyone now on the Peninsula ; and a definite gain, i.e. the numbers successfully withdrawn.

About the middle of October the French Government decided to send to Serbia's assistance the divisions previously intended to be employed under General Sarrail in the Dardanelles, and they asked us to co-operate as strongly as possible. Relying on the advice of the General Staff that there was not the least chance of saving Serbia, and being reluctant to take any action that might still further jeopardize the position in the Gallipoli Peninsula, the British Government would not at first agree to co-operate. Later, as will be described in a subsequent chapter, they felt compelled to yield, and the four British divisions then under orders to proceed from France to Egypt were diverted to Salonika. This arrangement to employ in the Balkans all the British and French reinforcements ordered to the Near East was finally agreed to on October 31. The effect was, of course, to render the question of the Dardanelles more serious and pressing than ever, but some weeks were yet to elapse before it was finally settled.

On October 31 General Monro made his report in the following telegram :—

With the exception of the Australian and New Zealand army corps the troops on the Peninsula are not equal to a sustained effort, owing to inexperienced officers, the want of training of the men, and the depleted condition of many of the units. We merely hold the fringe of the shore, and are confronted by the Turks in very formidable entrenchments, with all the advantages of position and power of observation of our movements. Since the flanks of the Turks cannot be attacked only a frontal attack is possible, and no room is afforded on any of the beaches for the distribution of additional divisions should they be sent, nor is there sufficient space for the deployment of an adequate force of artillery. . . . In fact an attack could only be prosecuted under the disadvantages of serious lack of depth and of absence of power of surprise, seeing that our line is thoroughly dominated by the Turks' position. . . . It is, therefore, my opinion that another attempt to carry the Turkish lines would not offer any hope of success. . . . On purely military grounds, therefore, in consequence of the grave daily wastage of officers and men which occurs, and owing to the lack of prospect of being able to draw the Turks from their entrenched positions, I recommend the evacuation of the Peninsula.[1]

The General further recommended that the force should be temporarily sent to Egypt, as it " stands in need of rest, reorganization, and especially of training, before it can be usefully employed. The Corps and Divisional Commanders have done splendid work in the Peninsula, but they do not possess the opportunity or time, as they now stand, to make the force into a reliable fighting machine. Hence I think loss of prestige caused by withdrawal would be compensated for in a few months by increased efficiency."

[1] Final Report of the Dardanelles Commission, pages 53–54.

This opinion was strengthened by the bad state of health of the troops. In August, even when there was no serious fighting, the average net wastage due to sickness had amounted to 24 per cent. a month! In September the medical officer had reported that 50 per cent. of the men in seven battalions examined at Anzac had feeble hearts; that 78 per cent. of these had diarrhœa and 64 per cent. had sores on the skin. On the first three days of October over 1,800 sick were evacuated from one corps, and at times the total evacuations from all three places, Suvla, Anzac, and Helles, amounted to as many as 1,000 a day. At the end of October there was a notable decline in the sick-rate, but shortly afterwards the Corps and Divisional Commanders still had very little faith in their troops' powers of endurance, and reported that "with few exceptions none are at present capable of more than 24 hours of sustained offensive effort." It was a lamentable story, and in the history of the British Army there is no instance of such great and continued loss of life and health with so little justification.

Having got the advice of the experienced soldier whom they had specially sent out to advise them, the Government declined to be guided by it, and on November 1 Lord Kitchener telegraphed to General Monro asking whether the Corps Commanders were of the same opinion as himself.

Of the three consulted, two agreed with him and the third, while agreeing as to the "grave disadvantages of the position and the extreme difficulty of making any progress," was opposed to evacuation, mainly because of the adverse moral effect it would have in India, Persia, and Egypt, and of the many difficulties which would necessarily attend its execution.

General Monro himself repeated his opinion as to the necessity of evacuation, and as a rough estimate stated that his Corps Commanders thought a loss of 30 to 40 per cent. of personnel might be incurred. With this estimate he was inclined to agree.

The abandonment of the Expedition, upon which so much blood and money had been expended, was certainly not a course to be adopted without the most careful investigation and consideration. But the report of General Monro, coupled with the unhappy experiences of the past six months, and the recent decision to send the only available reinforcements to Salonika with the object of opening up an extensive campaign in the Balkans, should have been sufficient to convince the Government that abandonment was the only practical solution of the difficulty in which they were placed. They were not, however, yet prepared to face the confession of failure which abandonment involved, and before giving approval to it the Cabinet requested Lord Kitchener to go out to the Dardanelles in order to ascertain whether an alternative could be found.[1]

He left England on November 4, and the telegrams

[1] The Final Report of the Dardanelles Commission, pages 55–56 mentions two telegrams from Lord Kitchener to General Birdwood, whom it was intended at the moment to place in charge of the Expedition, General Monro being transferred to Salonika. The first, dated November 3, mentions certain arrangements for resuming offensive action and says: "I absolutely refuse to sign orders for evacuation which I think would be the gravest disaster and would condemn a large percentage of our men to death or imprisonment." The second, sent the following day, says: "The more I look at the problem the less I see my way through, so you had better very quietly and secretly work out any scheme for getting the troops off the Peninsula." These two contradictory communications are examples of the confusion and uncertainty which the mishandling of the operations entailed.

which afterwards passed between him and the Prime Minister show that he was greatly concerned as to the difficulty of defending Egypt in the event of an evacuation of the Peninsula, and so setting free the 120,000 Turks which hitherto had been held there. He accordingly returned to his old proposal for landing on the Asiatic coast in the neighbourhood of Alexandretta, so as to cut the Turkish railway communications with the south. This plan did not commend itself to the General Staff, and was ultimately rejected at a joint conference between representatives of the British and French Governments, held at Paris on November 17. On the 19th the Prime Minister informed Lord Kitchener of this decision, and asked for his opinion as to the evacuation of the Peninsula, in whole or in part, on the understanding that the Alexandretta project would not be sanctioned. He replied on November 22 that evacuation was inevitable, and recommended that it should be proceeded with at Suvla and Anzac, while Helles should for the present be held. He was disappointed that the Alexandretta project was not approved, as he thought that the defence of Egypt from Egypt itself might absorb such large forces as to prevent any serious offensive from being undertaken on the Western Front in the following spring.

On the same day as the above telegram reached London, the General Staff laid before the War Committee[1] a memorandum in which they also advocated evacuation, the requirements of the new campaign in the Balkans making it impossible to continue operations on the Peninsula, as they had recommended in their memorandum of October 9.

[1] The "Dardanelles Committee" had recently been replaced by this body.

It so happened that I was in London at the time, having been summoned from G.H.Q. in France to attend a meeting of the War Committee, and on the same day, November 22, I handed to the Chief of the Imperial General Staff a letter pointing out that although he had recommended on October 9 that the Western Front should be regarded as the principal front, G.H.Q. in France did not know whether his advice had been accepted, or what reinforcements they might expect to receive. In default of this information they could not discuss future plans with General Joffre. I therefore requested that the matter should be brought before the War Committee and a decision obtained. I added that until the Dardanelles question was settled one way or another " it will remain impossible to direct the operations, usefully and intelligently, either in France, Egypt or Gallipoli, and they will continue to be subject to those many vexatious and serious disadvantages which always attend the absence of a definite plan."

Most members of the Government were, by now, becoming satisfied that evacuation could not be avoided. Some, however, remained unconvinced, and disputed the soldiers' views regarding the great tactical difficulties of holding on to the Peninsula, and the strength of the attack which the Germans, in combination with the Turks, might ultimately develop against us. They argued that as it was admitted that withdrawal would almost certainly entail heavy losses, it would be wiser to accept the risk of remaining rather than voluntarily run away from a danger which, after all, might not arise.

The War Committee reassembled on the following day to consider what should be done, and in the end they decided upon complete evacuation. The matter was then referred, according to the custom of the time, to the Cabinet for approval.

At this meeting the desire of certain Ministers to effect Lord Kitchener's removal from the War Office was very prominent. When he left for the Dardanelles they had hoped that some pretext could afterwards be found for keeping him away from London permanently, and when his mission was terminated by the decision to evacuate, the question of delaying his return to England was at once raised. The first proposal made was that he should be asked to remain in the East so as to exercise a general supervision over the evacuation, and my opinion was taken as to the desirability of that step. There was only one answer. The operation—an extremely difficult one—must be under the direction of one authority only, otherwise nobody would know who was responsible for anything. If Lord Kitchener was to remain, then he must be appointed Commander-in-Chief in place of General Monro. If not so appointed, then the farther he was away from the Dardanelles the better, so that there might be no misunderstanding as to who was in charge. But the Government could not well order him, a Field-Marshal, to take the place of Monro, a Lieutenant-General, and therefore another expedient had to be found. After several unsuccessful attempts to evolve one, it was suggested that he should be asked to go as a temporary measure to Egypt, where his presence would be valuable when the moral effect of the evacuation was being felt. This suggestion, put forward by a Minister who shall be nameless, was warmly welcomed, and was conveyed to Lord Kitchener at the same time as he was informed that evacuation had been provisionally approved, and that (following the advice I had given), the method of carrying it out " must be left, of course, to the judgment of the Commander on the spot."

Lord Kitchener replied that he ought to be " back in England, as time is passing, and I can do no good here. I have arranged with McMahon (the High Commissioner) to quiet the effect in Egypt as far as possible." He started for England on November 24, and after paying a brief visit to the Italian front *en route* arrived back in London on November 30. He then tendered his resignation to the Prime Minister, which was refused, and resumed his duties at the War Office. It is literally true to say that more time was spent by Ministers at the meeting of November 23 in devising an excuse for keeping Lord Kitchener away from London, and in drafting a telegram for conveying it to him in a suitable form, than in coming to a decision on the question of evacuation.

The proposal to evacuate the Peninsula was discussed by the Cabinet on November 24, when Lord Curzon and several of his colleagues, " anxious at least that the opposite side should be heard, and fearful of a decision fraught with such fearful possibilities, pleaded for a few hours' consideration," and he undertook to " state the case to the best of his ability."[1] He did so in two memoranda dated November 25 and 30, and his arguments were replied to by Mr. Bonar Law in a memorandum circulated on December 4. Mr. Law recalled that the Government had decided to send out a military expert, General Monro, to report on the question of evacuation. That officer had reported in the strongest possible terms in favour of it, and of the three Generals whom he

[1] Final Report of the Dardanelles Commission, page 57.

consulted one alone was opposed to evacuation, the reason for his opposition being " entirely political." Not satisfied with General Monro's report, the Government next sent out Lord Kitchener, who was at first entirely opposed to evacuation, but on actual examination of the situation changed his opinion and expressed himself in favour of it. The General Staff at the War Office were also in favour of it. Mr. Law continued :—

It is the fact, therefore, that every military authority, without a single exception, whom we have consulted, has reported in favour of evacuation.

But this is not all. Some time ago the Cabinet unanimously came to the conclusion that the war could not be carried on by a body so large as the Cabinet. A War Committee was therefore appointed. The views of the military authorities came before this Committee, two of whose members, the Prime Minister and the First Lord of the Admiralty, were opposed in the strongest possible way to evacuation ; yet this Committee reported unanimously in favour of acting upon the advice of our military advisers. Their recommendation was brought before the Cabinet, with the result that on a matter to which delay must be dangerous and may be fatal, no decision has been reached. I hope that my colleagues will agree with me that the war cannot be carried to a successful issue by methods such as these.[1]

No stronger condemnation of the methods then pursued could possibly be pronounced, and it had the greater force in that it came not from a soldier or sailor but from one of the Ministers themselves. The continual delay was, as Mr. Law said, fraught with serious consequences. Between November 26–29 a blizzard of exceptional severity raged on the Peninsula, and 280 men were drowned in the trenches at Suvla and many more were frozen to death as they stood. Sixteen thousand cases of frost-bite and exposure had to be evacuated, 12,000 of these being from Suvla, where the positions

[1] Final Report of the Dardanelles Commission, pages 57–8.

were the most exposed, and 2,700 and 1,200 from Anzac and Helles respectively. On December 1 General Monro telegraphed pressing for a decision, and adding that unless evacuation took place soon the lateness of the season would render it altogether impossible.

Approval of the War Committee's decision still hung fire, one reason being that the naval command had been taken over by a new Admiral (Wemyss), who in a series of telegrams to the Admiralty strongly advocated a resumption of the naval attack. The difficulties of this were placed before the War Committee on December 2 by Admiral de Robeck, who had just vacated the command, and the final decision was, as before, reserved for the Cabinet. The result of the Cabinet meeting was that Lord Kitchener telegraphed to General Monro that the

Cabinet has been considering the Gallipoli situation all to-day. Owing to the political consequences there is a strong feeling against evacuation even of a partial character. It is the general opinion that we should retain Cape Helles. If the Salonika troops are placed at your disposal up to four divisions for an offensive operation to improve the position at Suvla, could such operations be carried out in time with a view to making Suvla retainable by obtaining higher positions and greater depth ? The Navy will also take the offensive in co-operation.

It is strange that Lord Kitchener should have sent this telegram, no matter how insistent the Cabinet may have been, to induce General Monro to go back on the opinion which he had previously expressed. He, Lord Kitchener, had seen the situation with his own eyes. He had reported on November 15 that " everyone has done wonders," and that " advances from our present positions are very difficult." Later, on the 22nd, he reported that " German assistance was now practically available, that this assistance would make our positions untenable, and that evacuation therefore seemed inevitable." Since then the situation had become worse rather than better, for the troops had suffered terribly from the bad weather, especially at Suvla. Moreover, we stood committed to co-operate with the French in the Balkans, where the operations were going against us; the divisions from France offered to General Monro had only just landed at Salonika; and how, in these circumstances, was it possible for them to be suddenly switched off to the Dardanelles?

Fortunately General Monro stood firm, and replied that the proposal to gain a more secure position at Suvla did not offer a reasonable prospect of success; that the divisions from Salonika could not possibly be ready before the bad weather set in; and that naval co-operation would be of little value owing to the unfavourable character of the terrain.

In this welter of personal animosities, conflicting opinions, and refusal to face facts, soldiers pressing for evacuation, Ministers making full use of their debating skill in arguing against it, and some of the sailors wanting to keep Helles, a decision was indeed hard to reach, as it always is when operations of war are directed by Councils or Committees. Eventually, on December 7 the usual compromise was made, the Cabinet deciding that Suvla and Anzac should be evacuated and Helles retained.

The Commanding Admiral persisted in advising a fresh naval attack, but was peremptorily told by the Admiralty that it could not be sanctioned, since its success was most doubtful, the losses were certain to be heavy, and the naval arguments against it were overwhelming. The evacuation ordered was at once proceeded with, and was completed on December 20. The same night the weather broke. A heavy gale blew, torrents of rain fell, water rushed through the trenches, and the landing stages were washed away by heavy seas.

There remained the question of Helles. The withdrawal from Suvla and Anzac had been marvellously successful, but withdrawal from Helles was not likely to be so fortunate, since the enemy was relatively stronger, and the invaluable element of surprise could not now be counted upon. On the other hand, there was nothing to be gained, and everything to be lost, by keeping a detachment at Helles now that Suvla and Anzac had been abandoned. My first act, therefore, on becoming C.I.G.S. on December 23, was to place before the War Committee a memorandum recommending that the Peninsula "should be entirely evacuated, and with the least possible delay." I pointed out that the troops were cooped up in a thoroughly bad position, where the wastage, heavy before, would become still greater; that they were perfectly well aware that the Expedition had definitely failed, and, having no hope of causing the enemy serious injury, would soon become dispirited; and finally, that we could not expect to win the war unless we paid greater attention to the necessity of concentrating our efforts in one direction at a time.

The War Committee accepted my advice, and on December 27 their action was confirmed by the Cabinet. The necessary orders were issued the same day, and by January 8 the whole force of about 40,000 men had been withdrawn. The only casualties were one man hit by a spent bullet, and three men accidentally injured when embarking. Nearly all the guns were brought away, but some 500 animals had to be left behind.

This fine achievement was rendered possible only by a combination of skilled organization and good fortune in the shape of calm weather. It remains to be said that between December 20 and January 7 the casualties amounted to 345 killed and 1,178 wounded. This was the price paid for remaining at Helles after Suvla and Anzac were abandoned.

Thus ended the Dardanelles Expedition—a wonderful example of gallantry and endurance on the part of the troops, and a calamitous display of mismanagement, procrastination, and vacillation on the part of the authorities in London. That the project had great merits was unquestionable, *if* it proved feasible in execution, but the " if " was uncommonly big, and was made the bigger by the merits being constantly pushed too much to the front, and the impediments being kept too much in the background, when the project was under discussion. It promised to yield political results of the greatest importance, and these naturally appealed the most strongly to Ministers. It was therefore the duty of the soldiers and sailors to see that naval and military considerations received proper treatment. They did not quite do this. They took, I submit, too narrow a view of their responsibilities, and there is no doubt that some of them viewed the project with considerable favour—until it was seen to be a failure.

Strategically, no less than politically, a blow at Constantinople was to be desired, since the fall of that city would exercise immense influence upon subsequent events, not the least of which was the opening up of communication with Southern Russia by the Black Sea. But it was essential, of course, that the attempt to deliver the blow should be made with such strength that failure would not occur, and that it should not imperil success in the principal theatre of war. These conditions were not fulfilled, and for the sufficient reason that we did not possess the means required to fulfil them.

At the beginning of 1915, the old regular army had to a great extent disappeared; the Territorial troops were needed to fill up the gap while the New Armies were being raised; the latter were still in their infancy and, as yet, but partially armed; and guns, munitions, and aircraft were equally wanting. It was impossible, in fact, to provide the means that might eventually be required for the Dardanelles unless we adopted a strictly defensive policy on the Western Front, and even then they might not prove to be sufficient. That would depend upon what the defensive requirements of the Western Front might be, and they, in their turn, depended upon whether Germany renewed the attack on that front, or continued the offensive on the Eastern Front. Paris and the Channel Ports must be held secure at all costs, quite apart from all arguments about the respective merits of Western and Eastern strategy.

In an appreciation of the general situation written by the First Lord of the Admiralty (Mr. Winston Churchill) on February 25, 1915, "which he used to argue from in the War Council," it was stated that[1] "There is no reason to believe that Germany will be able to transfer to the West anything like 1,000,000 men at any time." This was not the view of the French and British G.H.Q., as previous pages have shown, and it proved in fact to be quite erroneous. The German strength on the Western Front in January, 1915, was, according to von Falkenhayn, 1,500,000 men, while in February, 1916, at the beginning of the battle of Verdun, it amounted to 2,350,000 men, so that before any serious Russian collapse occurred the Western Front was reinforced by

[1] "The World Crisis, 1915," page 185.

850,000 men, and if the German High Command had stopped their offensive against Russia after the capture of Warsaw in August, 1915, they could easily have sent west at least another 250,000 men. This possibility of heavy reinforcements being brought to France was always uppermost in General Joffre's mind, and for good reasons, for if the enemy had forced a great battle on us in the autumn of 1915, before our munitions and New Armies were ready, the result might have been serious. At that period our vitals were not secure, and the success which at first attended the German offensive two and a half years later, in the spring of 1918, shows that they were not.

The conclusions reached by the Dardanelles Commissioners are contained in the following extract :—

> Viewed as a military enterprise which was undertaken not as a surprise, but after ample warning had been given to the enemy of the probability of a land attack, we are of opinion that from the outset the risks of failure attending the Expedition outweighed its chances of success. The conditions of the problem, so far as we can judge, were not fully investigated in the first instance by competent experts, and no correct appreciation of the nature and difficulties of the task involved was arrived at. . . . We think that the position which, in fact, existed after the first attacks in April and early days of May should have been regarded from the outset as possible, and the requisite means of meeting it considered. This would have made it necessary to examine and decide whether the demands of such extensive operations could be met consistently with our obligations in other theatres of war. In fact, those obligations made it impossible in May, June, and July to supply the forces with the necessary military drafts, gun ammunition, high explosives, and other modern appliances of war. We are of opinion that, with the resources then available, success in the Dardanelles, if possible, was only possible upon the condition that the Government concentrated their efforts upon the enterprise and limited their expenditure of men and material in the Western theatre of war. This condition was never fulfilled.[1]

---

[1] Final Report of the Dardanelles Commission, pages 85–86.

With regard to the claim sometimes made that the Expedition was justified on the ground that it held fast a large number of Turkish troops who would otherwise have been free to operate elsewhere, the Commissioners pointed out that in containing the Turkish force, estimated by Lord Kitchener at nearly 300,000 men, we employed a total of at least 400,000, our casualties amounting to nearly 120,000. The Expedition also involved a heavy financial expenditure, and the employment of a considerable naval force and a large amount of shipping. Taking these factors into consideration, the Commissioners did not think that, from a military standpoint, our gain in one direction compensated for our losses in other directions, though they thought that certain important political advantages were secured.[1]

The Turkish losses have become known since the Commissioners made their report, and they prove to be much greater than our own, the Turkish killed alone being more than double. The exhaustion of the Turkish armies in the Dardanelles undoubtedly facilitated the conquest of Mesopotamia and Palestine, which also took place subsequent to the report of the Commission. But, given more efficient strategical direction during the early stages of the war, the same results would probably have been obtained with a smaller total expenditure of effort against the Turks, and without the depressing consequences of failure.

[1] Final Report of the Dardanelles Commission, page 86.

CHAPTER IV

WAR ORGANIZATION OF THE GOVERNMENT

War Organization in 1914—Committee of Imperial Defence—General Staff—Offensive Sub-Committee—Formation of War Council—Dardanelles Committee—Independence of Indian Government in Military Affairs—My Memorandum on General Question of High Command—Formation of War Committee—My Memorandum on Relations between War Minister and General Staff—Lord Kitchener's Objections to it—Its Amendment and Subsequent Adoption—Mr. Lloyd George becomes War Minister—His Views on the New System—His Want of Sympathy with the Military Chiefs—Formation of War Cabinet, Imperial War Committee, and War Policy Committee—Duties of C.I.G.S. at War Councils—Soldiers as War Ministers.

PREVIOUS to 1914 very few people in the Empire had considered how the functions of High Command would have to be exercised should we become engaged in a great war, and those who had differed widely in their views. In ministerial circles it was assumed, rather vaguely, that the Government, being responsible to Parliament and the nation, would necessarily be supreme in the direction of naval and military operations as of everything else, but however admirable this might be as a theory it was of little worth unless the machinery for putting it into practice was ready for use when required, and its mechanism was understood by those responsible for working it.

For military purposes, and apart from the Cabinet,

the machinery available when the emergency arose consisted of the Committee of Imperial Defence and the General Staff. Of these, the former was merely a consultative or advisory body, and was never intended to be anything more than that. As its secretary told the Dardanelles Commission, its duties were "laid down in time of peace, and with a view to peace requirements." The natural result ensued. Immediately hostilities broke out the Committee, though not formally abolished, fell into disuse, and from August to November, 1914, the supreme control of the war was exercised directly by the Cabinet itself—a system which provided no security for quick military decisions, while it offered every inducement to political debate and delay. Referring to this period the Dardanelles Commission said[1] :—

> It must have been obvious from the first that it [the Cabinet] was far too numerous to control effectively the conduct of the war, more especially by reason of the fact that many of the Ministers presided over departments, which, in some cases, were very slightly and, in others, were in no degree concerned with warlike operations. It is to be regretted that this rudimentary fact was not recognized immediately after the outbreak of war. Thus, for four months, during which time events of the utmost importance were occurring, the machinery employed for designing and controlling the higher operations of the war was both clumsy and inefficient.

As to the General Staff—recently created for the express purpose of planning and carrying out military operations—the Cabinet either had no confidence in it or did not know how to use it, or they would not have summoned some eight other officers to assist them, on August 5,[2] in deciding upon the strategy to be followed. Moreover, the majority of these officers had

[1] First Report of the Dardanelles Commission, page 5.
[2] *Vide* Chapter II, page 53.

no status qualifying them either to give advice or to take executive action. Lord Roberts, about eighty years of age, had not been employed for ten years, and therefore was not in official touch with the situation. The Director of Military Operations could not advise over the head of his departmental superior, the Chief of the Imperial General Staff. Sir Ian Hamilton, recently Inspector-General of the Oversea Forces, was present in no particular capacity. Generals Haig and Grierson were concerned only with carrying out such orders as Sir John French might give them. Sir John was entitled to be heard regarding the place of concentration, but only to a limited extent regarding the troops to be employed. The latter was a question upon which advice should have been tendered only by the C.I.G.S., since it must be settled in relation to our requirements elsewhere, both at home and abroad, and of these he was the most competent judge. It was for him, and for no one else, to draw up plans of campaign for submission to the Government and, when these had been approved, to settle with Sir John French, as with all other British commanders throughout the world, any details that might call for adjustment. The necessity for working on some such system as this was, however, not yet realized. The warning given by Lord Salisbury in 1900 as to the unsuitability of our constitutional methods for war purposes had been unheeded, and it had occurred to no one in authority that the organization of peace would have to be completely changed.

The disposition of Ministers to seek counsel from several different officers instead of relying upon their selected adviser, the Chief of the Imperial General Staff, obtruded itself on subsequent occasions during the war, and it probably sprang from the same desire to have a variety of opinions from which to choose as that which had prompted Sir Henry Campbell-Bannerman to oppose the appointment of a Chief of the Staff in 1890, and Mr. Balfour to object in 1895 to the Commander-in-Chief being the sole military adviser of the War Minister. It can be understood that, feeling their responsibility, Ministers would be loath to place themselves unreservedly in the hands of a single soldier, but acceptance of the broad principle of unity of counsel need not prevent them from obtaining such other opinions as they might wish to have. It merely ensured that all opinions, from whatever source they might emanate, should be presented to them through one authoritative channel—the General Staff—so that they might be tested and criticized in relation to other plans and proposals. It meant, in short, method and efficiency, instead of the confusion and divided responsibility which inevitably result from duality of counsel and the separation of advisory from executive functions. To be of reliable value, advice must be the result of a careful scrutiny of all the factors involved, strategical, tactical, and administrative, and consequently it can only be furnished by the soldier who has at his disposal the personnel and information enabling him to make the scrutiny. Other soldiers may occasionally be right, but only as a matter of chance, and more often than not they will be wrong.

Another advisory body which the Government called into being on August 5 was one for dealing with operations directed against the German possessions in Africa and in the Pacific. It consisted of representatives of the Admiralty, War Office, Colonial Office, and India Office, the Inspector-General of the West African Frontier Force, " and others," and had an Admiral as chairman.[1] It was given the quaint and cumbrous name of " Joint Naval and Military Committee for the consideration of Combined Operations in Foreign Territory," and was more shortly known as the " Offensive Sub-Committee " of the Committee of Imperial Defence —another rather curious title. It held about a dozen meetings between August and November, and then disappeared from the scene at the same time as the first " War Council " was formed.

This Council was created " mainly for the purpose of curtailing the number of the members of the Cabinet who personally participated in the conduct of the War." Like the peace-time Committee of Imperial Defence, it was a committee of the Cabinet with some experts added, its members being the Secretaries of State for War, India, and Foreign Affairs, the Chancellor of the Exchequer, and the First Lord of the Admiralty. The Prime Minister was chairman. " Acting under Cabinet direction, keeping the Cabinet informed, and consulting the Cabinet before the development of any new policy, it investigated, discussed, decided, and took action in matters referred to it, the Cabinet always being ultimately responsible for the new policy."[2] After the formation of a Coalition Government in May, 1915, the War Council was re-named the " Dardanelles Committee," as its deliberations were chiefly in reference to the Dardanelles Expedition. Its functions did not differ materially from those of its predecessor, but the number of its members was increased to twelve.

I had little personal acquaintance with the work of either the War Council or the Dardanelles Committee, but, as is well known, neither of these bodies made appro-

[1] Official History, " France and Belgium, 1914," page 20.
[2] *Ibid.*, page 10.

priate use of the General Staff or of its Chief. In a general way, Ministers agreed that the best professional advice was necessary and ought to be obtained, but this advice was apparently understood by them to mean little more than the individual opinions of certain eminent soldiers, checked by the opinions of such other soldiers as the War Council, or individual Ministers, might choose to consult. The result was, as two Ministers informed the Dardanelles Commission: "The political members of the (War) Council did too much of the talking, and the expert members as a rule too little." Moreover, no attempt was made to define or to limit the respective functions of Ministers and professionals, and consequently, to quote the Dardanelles Commission again, these functions were differently understood by the professionals on the one hand and Ministers on the other.

> It was not the practice to ask the experts attending the Council to express their opinions.
>
> The experts themselves did not consider it their duty either to express any opinions unless they were asked to do so, or to intimate dissent, at the Council board, if they disagreed with the views set forth by the Ministers in charge of their respective departments.
>
> The chairman and ministerial members of the War Council looked to the naval and military experts to express their opinions if they dissented from the views put forward by the heads of their respective departments. As the experts did not express their opinions the Council was in technical matters guided wholly by the views laid before them by the Secretary of State for War and the First Lord of the Admiralty.[1]

In the circumstances it is difficult to see what else could have happened, and, as suggested in the preceding chapter,[2] the Commissioners were right in their finding that the experts did not adequately act up to the responsi-

[1] First Report of the Dardanelles Commission, page 10.
[2] *Vide* page 97.

bilities which, in virtue of their office, devolved upon them. They were not in the position of secretaries, expected to speak only when spoken to. They were not merely " technical advisers," as the frequent use of that phrase might seem to imply, and as some Ministers wished it to be understood. On the contrary, they occupied positions of the highest importance, with definite duties attaching thereto. The military expert, for example, was the professional head of the land forces of the whole Empire, so far as military operations were concerned, and it was his duty to speak for them and, in conformity with the instructions and approval of the Government, to plan, direct, and supervise their employment.

If the attitude adopted by the experts in connexion with the Dardanelles Expedition was in any way common to other campaigns, the control of the operations was bound to drift, as it did, more and more away from the experts and into the hands of Ministers. In the case of the Army special circumstances arose to accelerate that result. Besides the dispersion of the General Staff on the outbreak of war, its Chief, Sir Charles Douglas, was in failing health from the first, and on his death in October, 1914, he was succeeded by an officer who, coming from South Africa, was not in touch with the situation. Hence it was not surprising that Lord Kitchener, being inadequately assisted by the General Staff, accustomed for years past to settle everything for himself, and holding the rank of Field-Marshal, should take upon his shoulders work that ought to have been done by others. Scouting the feasibility of a limited participation in the war, and displaying wider vision and sounder judgment as to its development and duration than any other statesman or soldier in any country, Entente or belligerent, he at once commenced to make the British Empire into a military power of the first rank. To assume, in addition to this tremendous task, the duties of the C.I.G.S. was to undertake more than any one man could possibly perform. But had he not so acted and put the requisite life and energy into the proceedings, many things that required to be done might not have been done at all until too late. It would seem, too, that the C.I.G.S. accepted the position without either remonstrance or compunction, and therefore to that extent he had only himself to thank for being deprived of the powers which belonged to him. Something of the same kind might perhaps be said regarding the action of the First Lord of the Admiralty and his relations with the First Sea Lord, but on this point I prefer to express no opinion.

Into the apportionment of blame as between the two parties—Ministers and experts—for the irregular procedure which characterized the conduct of the war during 1914–1915, it would not be profitable, even if it were possible, further to enter. The demands of both equity and utility will best be met by saying that the irregularity arose first and foremost from the national apathy and impatience with which questions of war had too frequently been treated in time of peace, and from the neglect of statesmen, soldiers, and sailors alike to make a sufficiently close study of the principles by which the functions of High Command ought to be governed.

Proof of this was afforded by the fact that, in accordance with long-established custom whereby the Government of India controlled and directed all military operations based on that country, India was not only allowed but expected to make war on its own account. As already mentioned,[1] the Council of War held on August 5 decided " to urge the Government of India to send a division to capture Dar-es-Salaam," while later, the campaign in Mesopotamia was instituted and controlled by the India Office and the Government of India with, apparently, the full concurrence of the War Office.[2] For many years before the war all matters relating to the Army in India had been jealously retained by the India Office and Indian Government in their own hands, the military authorities in England exercising little more authority over them than over those of the self-governing Dominions, although 70,000 British troops, recruited and trained by the War Office, were permanently stationed in the country. With the exception of purely technical questions of a minor nature, and the informal exchange of intelligence, neither the Army Council nor the Chief of the Imperial General Staff could communicate direct with Indian army head-quarters. Such official correspondence as there was had to pass through the India Office, where it was dealt with as that department thought fit. In the early months of the war Lord Kitchener and the Commander-in-Chief in India used to exchange telegrams regarding military operations, but the practice was " discontinued on constitutional grounds."[3] These ring-fence methods may have been necessary and harmless in time of peace; for the purposes of war they were objectionable to the last degree. Effective co-operation between India and the rest of the Empire could not possibly be secured unless the various operations undertaken were dealt with as a

[1] *Vide* Chapter II, page 54.

[2] " Mesopotamia Campaign," Vol. I, page 72.

[3] *Ibid.*, Vol. II, page 30.

whole, and all instructions of the Government in regard to them were issued through one and the same channel, the C.I.G.S.

A system of this nature involved no undue interference with the functions of either the India Office or the Government of India, both of whom would be kept informed and be consulted on the questions with which they were concerned. Few people, however, seem to have thought about it, while the hands-off attitude of the Government of India was not conducive to arrangements being made either for using Indian troops or for centralizing the duties of supreme command. The result was that we began the war with a system which deliberately divided control between two different departments of State—War Office and India Office—and two different military head-quarters—London and Simla. Hence, India never knew from day to day what demands the Home Government might make upon her; the War Office never knew what help India could render or might need; and sometimes it was impossible for anyone to say whether a given question was the business of the War Office or the India Office, of the War Council or the Viceroy. These methods were referred to by the Mesopotamia Commission as follows :—

> The dual system under which London and Simla tried to conduct the campaign in Mesopotamia has obvious drawbacks. The chain of responsibility was greatly lengthened by the number of authorities, who had necessarily to be consulted, and who had a voice in the direction of affairs. . . . First, the General Officer Commanding on the spot in Mesopotamia, then the Commander-in-Chief in India, then the Viceroy, then the Secretary of State for India with his Military Secretary, then the War Council with the Imperial General Staff, and finally the Cabinet. Such a subdivision of authoritative control must weaken the sense of responsibility of each authority consulted, and it certainly has made it very difficult accurately to apportion blame

or credit. It was under the dual system that administrative failures took place during 1915 and early in 1916 in Mesopotamia, and it was not until London took over the sole charge that there was any marked improvement in the management of the campaign. The improvement and success since effected are a striking illustration of the all-importance of unity of control in time of war.[1]

Finally, in addition to the ministerial heads of the two fighting services and the Secretary of State for India, there were other Ministers who considered themselves qualified and entitled, as members of the Cabinet, to have a controlling voice in the operations undertaken. It thus came about by the end of 1914 that while the Secretary of State for War was aiming at decisive results on the Western Front, the First Lord of the Admiralty was advocating the seizure of the Dardanelles and Constantinople; the Secretary of State for India and the Indian Government were conducting a campaign in Mesopotamia; the Secretary of State for the Colonies was concerned with operations in various parts of Africa; and the Chancellor of the Exchequer was impressing upon his Cabinet colleagues the strategical advantages to be gained by transferring the main British military effort from the Western Front to the Balkan Peninsula and Syria. A more deplorable state of affairs can surely never have existed in the conduct of any war.

In conversations which I had with certain Ministers at G.H.Q. in France during the summer of 1915, the management of the war was frequently mentioned, and the feeling everywhere prevailed that improvement was greatly needed. But as Ministers had never systematically studied the subject they were at a loss to know where or how to begin, while the General Staff at

[1] Mesopotamia Commission Report, 1917, page 117.

the War Office, who should have been their mainstay, was, for reasons already indicated, not very helpful. In the month of June one Minister asked me to furnish him with suggestions in writing as to what should be done, and as there was then no likelihood of the Cabinet being reduced in numbers the only practicable plan was to continue to entrust the supreme direction of the war to a small section of it, delegating such Cabinet powers as were necessary. The memorandum containing these suggestions was as follows :—

The conduct of the war has hitherto suffered either from the want of adequate machinery for initiating military policy and giving effect to it, or from the failure of such machinery as exists to work efficiently.

Unfortunately our constitution does not contain such a highly efficient machine for the conduct and control of the war as that which obtains in Germany and Japan. It is necessary, therefore, to establish a makeshift arrangement, and as the Cabinet is obviously too large a body to deal with the matter efficiently, it is necessary to appoint an Inner Cabinet or War Council to which the Cabinet will delegate the requisite authority which constitutionally belongs to itself.

For such a system to work with success, individual members of the Cabinet who are not members of the War Council must recognize the necessity for sinking their individual views, and in the interests of the country loyally support the decisions to which the War Council may come. If every question of importance is to be again debated in full Cabinet, and if individual members of the Cabinet consider themselves at liberty to urge their particular views, nothing but confusion can result.

It is essential that the responsible military and naval authorities should be represented on the War Council. When speaking for their departments the Secretary of State for War and the First Lord of the Admiralty should not express their own views on purely military and naval questions, but those of the War Staff and General Staff. If they differ from the views of their responsible advisers, those views should not be suppressed.

The responsibility for co-ordinating the many and varied aspects of military policy rests with the Prime Minister, who is ex-officio

Minister of Defence. When conflicting views are expressed, as must necessarily often be the case, it is the duty of the Prime Minister to weigh the arguments and formulate the policy to be laid before the Cabinet. Only by the firm exercise of these functions by the Prime Minister can a consistent policy be assured.

A sound military policy cannot be properly formulated unless the General Staff at the War Office is placed in a position which ensures due consideration being given to its views. If no trained minds are brought to bear on the many questions that arise, the Cabinet will inevitably be influenced by those members who are the most persistent in pushing forward their views. These members may be the least qualified to express an opinion.

It is also necessary that those responsible for formulating military opinion should recognize that war is nothing but an instrument of policy, and that its conduct, while conforming to strategical principles, should also conform to the political object of the Government. The Government must therefore know its mind and what it is trying to accomplish, before its military and naval advisers can give the necessary advice.

Moreover, Commanders-in-Chief in the field must receive guidance as to the broader aspects of military policy before they can suit their operations to the political object. An uncertain policy will inevitably be reflected in the conduct of the operations. This aspect of the question is the more important when co-operation with allies is involved.

I recommended that the War Council should be composed of the First Lord of the Admiralty, Secretary of State for War, Foreign Secretary, First Sea Lord, and C.I.G.S., as members, the Prime Minister to be president. This was not an ideal arrangement, and the naval and military chiefs might preferably have attended the Council as advisers rather than as members. I was led to include them as members because at the time they were granted practically no status at all. With this exception, no better arrangement seemed feasible so long as the Cabinet retained its existing numbers and the right to exercise control over any matters that it might choose. A War Council of four Ministers and two professionals would at any rate be more suitable than the existing

Dardanelles Committee of twelve Ministers and no professionals.

Nothing was done to introduce this or any other fresh system until the autumn of 1915, by which time the situation both at home and on the various fronts had become serious. The war was still being conducted too much on the principle of maintaining "business as usual," and the time had now arrived for giving it that complete and unquestioned priority of place which from the first its effective prosecution had demanded. Further, it will be remembered that, within the Cabinet itself, dissensions, if not actual intrigues, had arisen, Lord Kitchener in particular being subjected to adverse criticism for the unsatisfactory manner in which it was alleged that the affairs of the Army were being managed.

Something had to be done, and as a means of providing a way out of the accumulating troubles it was decided to adopt an organization similar to the one I had recommended in the summer, and to replace the Dardanelles Committee by a "War Committee of the Cabinet" consisting of the Secretaries of State for War, Foreign Affairs, and India, the First Lord of the Admiralty, and the Minister of Munitions. The Prime Minister remained chairman. The reduction in the number of members by one-half was a welcome change, but on the other hand the Committee was accorded, if anything, less and not more power than its predecessor had enjoyed. All important decisions continued to be referred to the Cabinet for approval before action could be taken, and certain Ministers, who were not members of the Committee, were extremely jealous of their Cabinet rights and objected to give their approval to measures until the reasons for them had been fully explained. This entailed covering the same ground at least twice, and further delay was incurred by the difficulty of fixing a date and hour for the Cabinet to meet which would not interfere with the other duties which Ministers had to perform, either in Parliament or their respective departments.

During November the question of establishing a better system of war control, both British and Entente, was frequently discussed, either verbally or in writing, between myself and the authorities in London. At the end of that month Lord Kitchener summoned me to London to say that various changes were to be made, and that I was required to take up the post of C.I.G.S.

This proposal seemed unfair to the then occupant of the post, Sir Archibald Murray, who had only recently been appointed and was just beginning to secure for the General Staff the status and strength which it required. I said as much to Lord Kitchener, and added that, whilst anxious to meet his wishes, I was afraid I could not in any case be of much service unless the General Staff were permitted to carry out the duties which properly belonged to it. If this condition could not be granted I hoped that he would look elsewhere for a C.I.G.S. and permit me to remain where I was, in France.

In the course of our conversation, which lasted for nearly two hours, he assured me that no action of his should prevent the condition from being fulfilled, and he asked me to disregard the prevailing gossip that he insisted upon keeping exclusive control of everything in his own hands. On the contrary, he would be only too glad to rid himself of some of the work he had hitherto been compelled to do, if he could but find someone to relieve him of it. He described to me the tiresome and protracted discussions which took place in the Cabinet upon practically every question that came up for consideration, and the consequent delays experienced in obtaining decisions. He also referred to the hostility of some of his colleagues, who were continually endeavouring to thwart and discredit him in the eyes of the people, and were bent upon ousting him from the Cabinet at the first opportunity that offered.

No soldier could be aware, as I was, of the difficulties and personal animosities against which he was contending without wishing to assist him in surmounting them. It seemed desirable, however, before going to the War Office, that I should set down on paper for him to see what, in my opinion, the duties of the General Staff in future ought to be. He at once assented, and a memorandum was prepared and forwarded to him (with a copy for the Prime Minister) immediately after I returned to France. Two of the proposals contained in it were :—

All orders for the military operations required to put into execution the approved policy should be signed and issued by the Chief of the Imperial General Staff, under the authority of the War Council and *not* under that of the Army Council. . . .

The Secretary of State for War is responsible for the raising, maintenance, and equipment of the forces which the policy of the War Council makes necessary. This is of itself a task of great magnitude in the circumstances in which we are placed, and the Secretary of State for War can therefore be connected with actual military operations only on the same footing as any other member of the War Council.

To these paragraphs Lord Kitchener took exception, and wrote to me saying that he could not retain the responsibility of War Minister without full executive power, and with his functions curtailed to the feeding and clothing of the Army (the Minister of Munitions having recently taken over the other services of maintenance). Hence, if my proposals were accepted by the Government, as he thought they would be, he must cease to be Secretary of State for War. He might still continue to be a member of the War Council, and " in that case you may rely on me always to do my best to support you in carrying out the difficult task you will have before you."

There could, of course, be no question of resignation of the most trusted leader the nation then had, and as he was travelling through France on the day that his letter reached me at St. Omer, I went to Calais and from there accompanied him to Paris so as to discuss the points in dispute. His main contention was that the actions of the General Staff, as of all other public servants, were subject to parliamentary control, and therefore somebody must be answerable to Parliament for them. This duty could not be performed by any collective body of Ministers such as the War Council, but only by the Minister who was responsible for all other Army matters. He quite agreed that operation orders ought to be signed and issued by the head of the General Staff, and not as heretofore in the name of the Army Council and over the signature of the secretary, a civilian, but he considered that this should be done under his authority and not of the War Council as I had suggested.

I held to the opinion that there ought to be no intermediary between the C.I.G.S. and the head of the Government, but, constitutionally, Lord Kitchener's view was doubtless the more correct, and I decided not to press the point of procedure so long as he conceded the principle of my having direct access to the War

LORD KITCHENER LEAVING THE HOTEL CRILLON, PARIS, WITH SIR WILLIAM ROBERTSON.

Council. This he did, and the first of the two paragraphs was amended accordingly, while the second was expunged altogether. I took up the duties of C.I.G.S. on December 23, and during the time that we afterwards worked together Lord Kitchener showed a genuine desire that everything should go on as smoothly and helpfully as possible. So far as I am aware it did so.

My object in wishing to change the custom by which all military business of whatsoever kind was conducted in the name of the Army Council was simply to ensure that the drafting of operation orders should be vested, unhampered, in the hands of the General Staff. At the time the Council consisted of four military and four civil members besides the War Minister, and all had the right, if they chose to exercise it, to be consulted before any important orders were sent out. Having more than enough work of their own to do, they had no wish to become mixed up in that of the General Staff, and consequently they never were consulted except in so far as their respective departments were concerned—a custom which must of necessity be followed under any system. Therefore while they shared the responsibility for the orders issued, they knew, in fact, nothing about them and did not want to know anything.

The new system would have the further result of causing the General Staff at the War Office to be recognized as the supreme staff authority by the armies in the field—a matter of great importance. It would also bring the procedure at the War Office into conformity with that at the front, where the issue of operation orders was necessarily the business of the General Staff and of no one else. The sham control over the operations previously exercised by the Army Council would disappear, and, most important of all, the General Staff would be brought into closer touch with the Government and the War Council.

The change was eventually authorized in the following Order in Council dated January 27, 1916 :—

> The Chief of the Imperial General Staff shall, in addition to performing such other duties as may from time to time be assigned to him under the Order in Council dated the 10th August, 1914, be responsible for issuing the orders of the Government in regard to military operations.

The more important paragraphs of the memorandum sent to Lord Kitchener, as re-drafted after my conversation with him in Paris, were as under :—

General Head-quarters,
British Army in the Field in France,
5th December, 1915.

Dear Lord Kitchener,—You were kind enough yesterday to express your willingness to receive some observations of mine regarding the conduct of the war, with special reference to the status and duties of the Chief of the Imperial Staff.

For a long time past I have given careful and anxious consideration to this question. Both the history of past wars and our experience in the present war show that certain conditions are normally essential to the successful conduct of military operations, though there have, it is true, been isolated instances of commanders of genius who have triumphed in the absence of these conditions.

These conditions are :

(I) There should be a supreme directing authority whose function is to formulate policy, decide on the theatres in which military operations are to be conducted, and determine the relative importance of these theatres. This authority must also exercise a general supervision over the conduct of the war, and must select the men who are to execute the policy on which it has decided. Its constitution must be such that it is able to come to quick decisions, and therefore as regards the conduct of the war it must be absolute.

The War Council should be capable of performing the functions of this supreme authority, provided it is relieved of responsibility to the Cabinet as a whole as regards the conduct of military operations, and that it has real executive power and is not merely an advisory committee.

The War Council will frequently find itself in a position similar to that of a commander in the field—that is, it will have to come to a decision when the situation is obscure, when information is deficient, and when the wishes and the powers of our Allies are uncertain. Whatever these difficulties may be, if and when a decision is required it must be made. If it is deferred success cannot be expected; the commander concerned will have a grossly unfair burden placed upon him; and in fact the absence of a decision may be little less than criminal because of the loss of life which may be entailed.

(II) In order that the War Council may be able to come to timely decisions on the questions with which it has to deal, it is essential that it should receive *all* advice on matters concerning military operations through one authoritative channel only. With us that channel must be the Chief of the Imperial General Staff. It is his function, so far as regards military operations, to present to the War Council his reasoned opinion as to the military effect of the policy which they propose, and as to the means of putting this approved policy into execution. The War Council are then free to accept or reject the reasoned advice so offered.

Advice regarding military operations emanating from members of the Cabinet, or of the War Council in their individual capacity, or from any other individual, should be sifted, examined, and presented, if necessary with reasoned conclusions, to the War Council by the Chief of the Imperial General Staff before it is accepted by the War Council.

(III) All orders for the military operations required to put into execution the policy approved by the War Council should be issued and signed by the Chief of the Imperial General Staff, under the authority of the Secretary of State for War, *not* under that of the Army Council. Similarly, all communications from General Officers Commanding regarding military operations should be addressed to the Chief of the Imperial General Staff. In fact, the same procedure is required in London as obtains in the field—the War Council being in the position of the Commander-in-Chief of the whole of the Imperial Land Forces, and, with the War Office Staff, constituting the Great General Head-quarters of the Empire.

(IV) The adoption of this system by which communications regarding military operations are issued and received by the Chief of the Imperial General Staff will greatly expedite the dispatch of business, and will help to preserve greater secrecy than now prevails.

Instances have occurred in the war of the contents of the most important documents becoming public property within a few days. Than this nothing could be more harmful to the conduct of the war. It would be for the Chief of the Imperial General Staff to give orders as to the reproduction and distribution of these communications, and he would of course be responsible for seeing that the Secretary of State for War and the War Council receive at all times full information of all that they should know.

(V) The Chief of the Imperial General Staff must be free to devote his entire time to the duties above indicated, and have sufficient leisure to think quietly out the many difficult problems which are continually arising, and also to keep himself thoroughly fit in mind and body. He must therefore be relieved as far as possible of War Office routine duties. To do this the Assistant Chief of the Imperial General Staff should become a Deputy Chief of the Imperial General Staff with authority to represent, as and when necessary, the Chief of the Imperial General Staff in all Army Council business.

(VI) The number of General Officers Commanding with which the Chief of the Imperial General Staff should deal should not exceed the number which experience shows to be possible—about half a dozen.

For this it is necessary that a General Officer Commanding-in-Chief should be appointed to the command of the Home Forces or those in Great Britain, as may be deemed best, his position being similar to, say, that of the General Officer Commanding-in-Chief in France, except that the present system of administration need not be disturbed. He would also be responsible for Home Defence, the troops for this purpose being allocated, of course, under instructions issued by the Chief of the Imperial General Staff as in all other cases—*vide* Para. (III).

I need not go more fully into my reasons for the above proposals, as I am sure they will be obvious to you. It is of paramount importance in war that there should be a definite plan of operations, and that that plan should be carried out with promptness and decision. It is impossible that this should be so if the War Council is itself compelled to listen to conflicting advice, and to decide between the merits of rival experts. It is equally impossible that this should be so if the War Council has to submit its plan for the conduct of the war to the approval of the whole Cabinet. The War Council is now conducting military operations in a number of separate theatres of war, and has control of large reserves which may be thrown into one theatre or another.

France has no reserves left, therefore the decision as to the future conduct of the war by the Western Allies rests in great measure with the War Council. It is vital then that it should possess the machinery both to come to timely decisions and to have its decisions executed.

My proposals seem to necessitate some modifications of the Orders in Council which lay down the constitution of the Army Council and the duties of the Chief of the Imperial General Staff. If that is so those Orders should be amended for the period of the war. They were never intended, I suppose, to meet a situation such as now exists, and they certainly do not meet it.

I hope you will not think that I have any desire to make a bargain for myself, but I feel strongly that I cannot serve the War Council, my King, or country, as Chief of the Imperial General Staff unless the above conditions are fulfilled. It is my conviction that the system by which the war has been conducted hitherto has been such as to make victory very difficult indeed, if not impossible. Having no faith in it I could not do justice to it, and therefore if my proposals cannot be accepted you would be better advised to select an officer who sees in the existing system a possible means of bringing this war to a successful conclusion. . . .

The direction of the war became much more effective as a result of the introduction of the above measures, but in some respects military responsibility continued for some time longer to be divided up between different State departments, and was by no means centralized in the War Office alone. The old custom which permitted the India Office, Colonial Office, and Foreign Office respectively to wage little wars on their own account in India, the Colonies, and the Protectorates, calling upon the War Office for advice or assistance, or both, when they could no longer do without them, was allowed to survive long after its destruction was due. The campaign in Mesopotamia was a case in point. Not until it was nearly a year old was the Imperial General Staff called upon to give an opinion in regard to it, and not until the spring of 1916, when it seemed likely to end in disaster, was responsibility for its direction definitely transferred to that Staff.

Military questions regarding Persia and the Persian Gulf were also dealt with by the India Office, and the Government looked to the same department for advice on matters connected with the defence of India. In the Sudan, again, operations were conducted by the Sirdar, as authorized by the High Commissioner, who in his turn received the instructions of the War Committee through the medium of the Foreign Office. The awkwardness of these roundabout methods was manifested on several occasions during my first year of office as C.I.G.S., as no doubt it had often been before.

One example may be quoted. The Sirdar desired to undertake a certain operation in Darfur for which the time was limited, and therefore a quick decision was needed. But he had to refer his proposal for the approval of the High Commissioner, who submitted it to the Foreign Office, who could not decide it until a military opinion had been obtained from the War Office. Lord Kitchener, after consulting the General Staff, promptly took such action as enabled a timely decision to be given, but machinery of this sort was obviously much too cumbersome for the purposes of war, whatever its merits might be in time of peace. Had the Sirdar been in direct communication with the General Staff, the question could have been settled in a few hours instead of taking, as it did, three or four days.

On another occasion the India Office disapproved of certain military dispositions which the Indian authorities were making for frontier defence, and the General Staff were asked for their views respecting the instructions which the Secretary of State for India proposed to send to the

Government of India on the subject. Having no responsibility for the operations for which the dispositions were designed, and feeling imperfectly informed on matters of detail, I replied that I was not competent to give an opinion, but that for what it was worth it differed from that of the India Office. The War Committee was accordingly asked to decide between the two of us! In this case there was no urgency, but there might have been, and the system of having two State departments responsible for the same duty was obviously bad.

Shortly after the General Staff had taken over control of the campaign in Mesopotamia, I suggested to the War Committee that the principle of centralization should be extended to all theatres and possible theatres of war. This was especially to be desired in the case of Persia and India, which were closely bound up with Mesopotamia, and the need for unified military control was the greater because political responsibility in regard to Persia was already divided between two departments, the Foreign Office and the India Office. Not wishing, however, that Ministers should think that the General Staff were striving to seize more power than they could appropriately exercise, I explained when putting the suggestion forward that the difficulties and risks of making important changes during the progress of a great war were considerable, and that "in view of the many questions involved other than military I am not prepared to press that the responsibility for advising the War Committee upon all military operations should devolve upon myself." This was not the point I had in mind so much as the necessity for placing the responsibility for each theatre in *one* department, and not in two as there was an inclination to do. I therefore stated the case, and left the matter entirely in the hands of the Committee, my concluding observations being :—

Speaking without full knowledge of the political and administrative questions involved, it does not seem that there would be any insuperable difficulties in arranging for unity of direction in all theatres by the C.I.G.S. The responsibility for the actual conduct of operations must, in any case, rest with the commanders on the spot. The functions of the Imperial General Staff would be confined to seeing that the commanders in the field understand and act in conformity with the decisions of the War Committee, that operations in all theatres are co-ordinated, and that the resources of the Empire are distributed amongst them in the most effective and economical manner. This need not involve interference with the functions of either the Foreign Office or India Office. In the spheres in which they are chiefly interested these departments would be kept informed and would be consulted at all stages just as the Foreign Office is now informed and consulted as to the operations in Europe, in which its co-operation forms a very essential part of the machinery for the conduct of the war, or as the Colonial Office is informed and consulted as to the campaigns in East and West Africa in which it is directly interested. The only important change necessary is to bring commanders in all theatres into direct communication with the Imperial General Staff.

For many obvious reasons it is desirable that, in war, all the military forces of the Empire should constitute one Imperial Army, and as such receive the instructions of the War Committee from the Imperial General Staff. If the Committee decide to adopt this principle, the departments concerned can consult together and settle the details.

The Committee decided to make no change, but as no more campaigns were started in countries lying outside the existing sphere of General Staff control no particular harm resulted. Moreover, it gradually became the established practice in all departments to consult the General Staff on military questions as a matter of course, and to be guided by their opinion. In this way the necessary co-ordination could be, and was, ensured.

When, in June, 1916, Mr. Lloyd George became War Minister, the system set up at the end of 1915 appeared to be not so satisfactory to him as it had been to his predecessor. He seemed to be particularly suspicious of the Order in Council, which he apparently thought had unduly increased the powers of the C.I.G.S., and at the expense of his own. In reality it did not. It merely entrusted a certain duty—the issue of operation orders—to one department of the War Office (which was no less subordinate to the War Minister than any of the others) instead of pretending to assign it to the Army Council as a body.

A short time before he left the Ministry of Munitions for the War Office Mr. Lloyd George spoke to me about the working of the new system, and in order to explain it I sent him a letter which was much the same as that which I had written to Lord Kitchener in December. In reply he acknowledged the value of the change made by the Order in Council, and said that no War Minister was likely, and certainly not himself, to wish to alter it during the war.[1] On the other hand, he drew attention to certain considerations which he thought had been overlooked in my letter, namely, that the War Minister was ultimately responsible to Parliament and the country for all War Office matters, and he developed this principle at some length so as to show how, in his opinion, it should be applied in practice. He added that he did not think that our respective views regarding the relations between the War Minister and the C.I.G.S. were really very different, if at all, and he believed that on the basis of my letter and his reply thereto an effective co-operation could be secured. "After acting with you for six months on the War Committee I feel no doubt that you and I could work in complete harmony for the common good."

[1] In 1918, when Prime Minister, Mr. Lloyd George altered it. See page 232.

This was very gratifying to learn, and I hastened to assure Mr. Lloyd George in a subsequent letter that there had been no intention on my part to disregard the considerations to which he had referred, and I expressed the hope that the further explanation now sent to him would make things quite clear.

In another respect Mr. Lloyd George's letter was not so encouraging. After saying that the position of the War Minister in relation to the Government on the one hand and the War Office on the other, must be much the same as the First Lord of the Admiralty in relation to the Government and the Board of Admiralty, he went on to observe that the partnership between the civilian and the expert at the Admiralty had won and maintained for us the command of the sea, and he could have wished that our land operations had been attended with an equal measure of success. Up to the present time our fifty divisions on the Western Front had barely (and not always) held their own against the German thirty divisions. While fully agreeing as to the inefficiency of the system by which the war had been conducted previous to the resuscitation of the General Staff, he remarked that no conspicuous military victories had been produced during the six months that the new arrangements had been in force. Perhaps it was too early to expect good results from them, and he hoped that a substantial victory would yet justify them.

It occurred to me that the " partnership " quoted had not, in point of fact, always been either successful or happy, in the initiation of the Dardanelles expedition for example. But I was concerned with the Army, not the Navy, and the aspersion cast upon it disclosed in the new War Minister a want of sympathy with commanders in the field whom it was his duty to support by every means in his power. I therefore asked his leave to point out that :—

It is less than a month that we have had in France as many as the fifty divisions you mention, and for want of heavy guns and ammunition and for other reasons we have necessarily been on the defensive. Troops acting on the defensive are bound to lose ground now and then, and in course of time to lose the war. That is why all soldiers and sailors hate it, as by it alone they can never hope to win. Even our superior Fleet has not prevented the bombardment of our coast towns. Taking everything into consideration, I maintain that our officers and troops have done marvellously well, not only during the last six months but since the beginning of the war. It must be remembered that we went into the war with a superior Navy, which for years previous had received the full support of the country. On the other hand, our Army was totally inadequate to meet the demands made upon it, as had long been foreseen by soldiers would be the case. We began the war with a force of only six regular divisions, fourteen imperfectly trained and poorly equipped territorial divisions, and with no heavy artillery worth mentioning. We are now commencing to make good the deficiencies, and to have a reasonable chance, which we have not had before, of showing that we can fight as well as the Germans can. What the actual result will be I shall not attempt to prophesy. No one can be sure of success in war, especially when dependent upon New Armies. France tried them in 1870 and failed, and the New Armies of the Northern States of America took some four years before they could defeat the numerically inferior troops of the South. The difficulty is increased when fighting with allies. But whatever the result may be I am quite sure that no officers could have risen to the occasion better than ours have done in expanding from an Army of twenty divisions to one of seventy divisions, to say nothing of heavy artillery, etc. No Army could have done more than ours to make itself efficient, and I have the fullest confidence in the commanders and staff in France as I have in the brave British men who have so patriotically come forward to fight for their country under the most adverse conditions. They thoroughly deserve all the help, trust, and sympathy which people at home can give, and needless to say these are the most valuable when the most needed.

I may say here in connexion with the comparison

which Mr. Lloyd George saw fit to make between the two services that, after becoming Prime Minister, he more than once remarked that the staff work at the Admiralty was not as good as it was at the War Office, and he suggested that I should advise the First Sea Lord how to improve it, on the lines of the War Office system. Knowing how extremely objectionable to the naval authorities any such action would be, I asked that the Deputy-Chief of the General Staff should be sent in my stead to talk matters over informally with the Admiralty Staff, if the latter were agreeable. They were quite pleased to receive him, and the information he gave regarding Army methods was, I understood, of some assistance.

The change in Mr. Lloyd George's opinion with respect to the quality of the work done by the General Staff was probably due to the better knowledge he acquired of it while head of the War Office. Copies of all communications which passed between the General Staff and Commanders-in-Chief were shown as a matter of course to the War Minister, but they were not circulated to other Ministers. Mr. Lloyd George had therefore not seen them before coming to the War Office, and knew little about the kind of work that was being carried on. It was a revelation to him, the instructions regarding the actual operations being especially attractive. When he left the War Office to become Prime Minister he gave directions that these instructions should continue to be sent to him—a practice for which there was no precedent so far as I am aware, and for good reasons. It unavoidably led to secret plans being seen by far too many people, some of whom, such as the numerous secretaries, paid and unpaid, who thronged the precincts of No. 10 Downing Street, had no concern with them beyond sheer curiosity and the desire to enhance their own importance by gaining information denied to others.

Of the results of Mr. Lloyd George's six months' reign at the War Office there is nothing of much interest to record, for he was connected with no measure having any special influence on the course of the war. As will be explained later, he placed before the Cabinet a recommendation of the Military Members of the Army Council for extending and simplifying the principle of National Service, and gave to it his full support. But on becoming Prime Minister, about a fortnight later, he dropped it, and declined to carry it into effect until the German offensive of March, 1918, compelled him to do so. He displayed but little sympathy towards the various Commanders-in-Chief, with the exception of General Maude, the only General who could yet produce a decisive victory, and he listened with sceptical impatience to my explanations of the difficulties with which these officers had to contend. He preferred his own strategical ideas to those of the General Staff, and of administrative work, which seemed to bore him, he left as much as possible to be done by the Under-Secretary of State, Lord Derby. He was, in fact, so much occupied with political activities, especially during the two or three weeks which preceded Mr. Asquith's resignation, as to devote considerably less than undivided attention to the affairs of the Army.

On becoming Prime Minister he replaced the traditional Cabinet of about a score of members by a War Cabinet of five. Under his presidency these assumed unrestricted control over the whole war business of the nation, and, having no special departments of their own, they could give their full time to that duty. The constitution of this new body was discussed at a breakfast at Lord Derby's house, at which Mr. Lloyd George, Lord Carson, Lord Derby and myself were present, at the time when the Premiership was about to change hands. In its final shape the organization was the work of Mr. Lloyd George, and it was a great improvement on the old system. The original members were Lords Curzon and Milner, Mr. Bonar Law, Mr. Arthur Henderson, and the Prime Minister as chairman.

In 1917 two other bodies were brought into being: the "Imperial War Committee," which admitted of the oversea Dominions being represented, and the "War Policy Committee of the Cabinet," which was formed of members of the War Cabinet, and dealt with the conduct of the operations and war policy in general.

It will be seen from the foregoing account that although the body responsible for the supreme management of the war underwent from time to time important changes in personnel and size it was throughout composed entirely of Ministers, the military and naval chiefs attached to it always acting as advisers and executive agents and never as members. The merits of this system can hardly be questioned—at least as far as the Army is concerned. The conduct of a great war covers many activities of a non-military character, which, as part of the general national effort, demand careful and competent treatment, and this the professional head of the Army, the C.I.G.S., has not the time, even if he has the knowledge, to give, his hands being more than full with his own special duties.

In 1914–1918 these duties were particularly onerous, for the British operations covered a much wider area than those of any other country. France and Russia fought for the most part on two fronts only, Austria on three, and Italy, save for comparatively small detachments, on but one. Germany at one period had five campaigns on her hands simultaneously: on the Eastern and Western Fronts, in Serbia, in Rumania, and in Palestine, but geographical conditions enabled all of these except the last, in which few German troops were employed, to be closely connected with the central point of direction and supply. The British General Staff had to direct the operations of seven wars: on the Western Front, on the Gallipoli Peninsula, in Palestine, at Salonika, in Mesopotamia, and in East and West Africa, for the evacuation of the Gallipoli Peninsula was not completed until after the Salonika campaign had begun, and the conquest of the Cameroons was still incomplete when the campaign in East Africa had started. These seven campaigns were waged in three continents under great differences of climate and topography, and each therefore required different equipment and different organization. A watchful eye had also to be kept on the north-west frontier of India, the western frontier of Egypt, the hinterland of Aden, and other doubtful territories.

Besides being unusually onerous, the duties to be performed were in some respects wholly novel, in that Great Head-quarters had never before in any war been permanently located at the seat of Government,[1] nor had the Chief of the General Staff been required, as I was, to give to the Government a daily account of his stewardship and be cross-examined thereon. Nor did

[1] The attachment to Great Head-quarters in the field of the civil head of the Government, as in the case of Germany in 1870, has little or no analogy to the British organization of 1914–1918.

the system obtain in any other country, save one. Only in France, and not until the war was nearly three years old, was a Great Head-quarters formed at the capital and a Chief of the General Staff appointed (first General Pétain and afterwards General Foch) to carry out duties similar to those which devolved upon the C.I.G.S. of the British Army.

At 11 a.m. on practically every day of the week, except Sunday, I was required to attend the meeting of the Cabinet, War Committee, War Cabinet, or whatever the ministerial managing body might at the moment be called, in order to report the events of the past twenty-four hours ; to predict, when requested, what they might be during the next twenty-four ; and to elucidate or justify such General Staff recommendations as awaited Government sanction.

The First Sea Lord (later known as the Chief of the Naval Staff) was not called upon to make such lengthy statements and explanations as myself. He had less to talk about, and naval phraseology was less easy for Ministers to understand. Theoretically our respective statements were supposed to be made at the beginning of the meeting, so that we might get back early to our offices. But they were often postponed because some unexpected question had cropped up which, in the opinion of those present, must be disposed of before anything else was discussed. In this category would be such items as the publication of a politically objectionable newspaper article ; an awkward question in the House of Commons which had to be answered the same afternoon ; anxiety as to the staunchness of an Ally or the attitude of a Neutral ; fear of industrial troubles ; and sometimes criticisms of military matters gleaned by Ministers during a visit to the front, or received in a letter from a constituent, or heard at a dinner-table on the previous evening. When at last the agenda paper was reached, the business in hand might take a long time to settle, or, when settled, the Prime Minister might ask me to remain in case I should be wanted in connexion with some other subject to be considered. Thus it came about that I seldom left the meetings before 1.30 p.m., and serious encroachments were accordingly made upon the time available for the dispatch of other work to be done—such as the consideration of high strategical problems, concerted action with the other allied armies, principles of training, instructions to Commanders-in-Chief, distribution of troops, and so on.

As can be imagined, it was not always easy at these meetings to give just the information which Ministers wished to have, for the subject under discussion might be largely technical or for some other reason be impossible to explain off-hand to the satisfaction of a body of men having no practical experience in military affairs. The majority of Ministers realized this, and refrained from pushing their inquiries unduly far. Others, though few in number, were less easy to satisfy. Ignoring the uncertainties and human frailties with which operations of war are so often attended, they would complain that answers to their questions were not sufficiently precise, and would try to pin me down to more definite statements than circumstances permitted of being made. War is not a matter either of arithmetic or logic. There are in it so many probabilities and improbabilities that neither the military expert nor anyone else can say, with any pretence to reliability, what will actually happen. All he can do is to give his convictions and with them Ministers ought to be content.

Again, just as the lack of visible progress on the Western Front led to the belief that some new form of strategy was needed, so the daily recurring list of casualties repeatedly gave rise to the suggestion that something was wrong with our tactics. For instance, in 1916 I had more than once to meet the ministerial argument, put forward with great ingenuity, that to shoot down the enemy from behind cover must surely be a less costly as well as a more simple method of waging war than to advance across the open and so get shot down oneself. It was apparently thought that defensive action alone would bring victory, and would bring it more cheaply than would the offensive policy of which most soldiers appeared to be so fond.

In reply to tiresome heresies such as these I would recall the demoralizing effect upon troops which prolonged defensive tactics inevitably have ; urge that, although the attacker might at first be the heavier loser, it was the defender who would certainly lose most in the long run, once his physical and moral powers began to break down ; and that, as in the conduct of any business, civil no less than military, without offensive action, without initiative, success could never, in point of fact, be achieved. But the Ministers to whom I refer would shake their heads, condemn the so-called process of " attrition " as being merely the unintelligent application of brute force, and maintain that there must be some way of securing victory without engaging in too much of that hard fighting, which, unhappily, all wars involve—especially when the combatants are counted, as in 1914–1918, by tens of millions of men. The appalling losses suffered by the defending British armies in France in March–April, 1918, and by the defending German armies six months later, showed how fatuous these defensive notions were.

The longer concrete evidence of coming victory was delayed the harder it became for the General Staff to keep the direction of the war on right lines. Especially was this the case during 1917, and it was mainly caused by the fact that certain members of the Government brooded too much over our own difficulties and losses, and took too little credit for those that were being suffered by the enemy. Mr. Lloyd George, in particular, would unfairly belittle British military efforts as compared with German, and the attempt on my part to put the other point of view, and to look at things through German eyes, would be met with the reply that the same sort of thing had been said many times before, and that we were still as far from winning the war as ever. The daily communiqués issued by G.H.Q. on the Western Front were frequently criticized in this sense, and as often as not the enemy's account of the fighting would be accepted as the more correct version of the two. That the enemy would naturally so draft his communiqués as to present his own position in the most favourable light and ours in the worst was seldom realized.[1] In all great wars similar dissatisfaction and impatience may be expected to manifest themselves, and responsible soldiers must be prepared to accept them as

[1] It is of some interest to quote Ludendorff on this subject: "It has been said that my communiqués were unreliable. They were indisputably truthful, and they were framed in accordance with our duty to the army, the people at home, and our Allies. . . . Losses of ground were mentioned if they affected the general situation, but not until no harm could be done by doing so. Nobody could expect me to communicate our losses in guns and prisoners to the enemy, not even the German who thinks so objectively. . . . Suspicion of the reports from G.H.Q. went at times so far as to cause them to be compared with enemy reports."—"My War Memories," page 710. The experience of the German General Staff, was, it will be seen, not unlike our own.

part of the burden which, in the absence of definite success, they will have to bear.

Reverting for a moment to the suggestion previously made that the C.I.G.S. ought to confine himself to military duties, it may be admitted at once that this is sometimes rather difficult to do. For example, if the war be prolonged political controversies are bound to arise, as they did in every belligerent country during 1914–1918, and although the C.I.G.S. may not personally care two straws which political party is in power, or who is its leader, he will be more than human if he does not lean towards the one which is the most likely to give to the Army what he is seeking to obtain for it—say, a greater share of the national man-power resources.

Public opinion, again, may place him on a higher pedestal than he is accustomed to occupy in peace-time, and may look more towards him and less towards the political chief to show the way to victory. He may be told by public men in high positions that the country is weary of the way in which the war is being conducted by the "politicians"; that it will support whatever measures he, the soldier, may say ought to be adopted; and that the one thing for which it longs is a *man*, a leader, who will plainly say what should be done.

When to these conditions we add the desire to do what is believed to be best for the nation's welfare, plus an element of personal vanity—from which no man is entirely free—it will be seen that the path of the military chief is rather more difficult to tread than might at first be supposed.

There is the further fact that the careers of Army officers now lie almost entirely in the hands of Ministers, and not as at one time in those of the Sovereign. This may be a necessary system, but officers holding high rank cannot be expected to forget that by displaying no political tendencies one way or the other they may ultimately find themselves without friends in any political party and be suspected equally by all. For myself, I consistently endeavoured to give political matters as wide a berth as possible, but I was frequently drawn or pushed towards them against my wishes.

Another dilemma often encountered was how far I could rightfully go in trying to meet ministerial proposals which were militarily unsound, and which, if opposed, might impair those good relations with Ministers which it was essential to maintain. In peace-time differences of opinion may be allowed to slide without great harm being done, as it may be possible to adjust them at a more convenient season. In war, compromises are much more dangerous ; errors and omissions can seldom be rectified (the enemy will see to that) ; and men's lives are at stake. In war, too, things do not proceed on the smooth and simple lines of peace, and I, at any rate, often found it very difficult to make a choice between acquiescing in a course of military action which seemed undesirable, and saying outright that I could be no party to it.

A Minister once tired to persuade me that the duty of a professional adviser begins and ends with giving his advice, and that after it has been considered by the Government, the instructions of the latter should be obeyed without further remonstrance, the adviser being absolved from all responsibility for the consequences. The question had arisen owing to my declared intention not to remain C.I.G.S. if the War Cabinet persisted in making the British military representative on the Supreme War Council independent of the British General Staff—a system not followed by any other country represented on the Council. It was, in fact, both preposterous and dangerous, and as it affected the issue of orders to Commanders-in-Chief and the dispositions of the armies, it admitted of no compromise.

While still under discussion, the Minister mentioned came to my room at the War Office with the object of finding a solution acceptable alike to the War Cabinet (or rather to the Prime Minister) and to myself. To illustrate his argument he asked, " What would happen if Rawlinson, an Army commander, received an order from Haig, his Commander-in-Chief, and declined to obey it because he did not agree with it ? " I suggested that the case was not like my own, since Haig, not Rawlinson, must be presumed to be the best judge of the right military thing to do. On the other hand, if Haig received from his civilian superiors, the Government, a military instruction which he considered to be unsound or impracticable it would be his bounden duty to ask that it should be entrusted to someone else, for no one, King, Minister, or Parliament, could absolve him from the responsibility of seeing that the lives of his men were not thrown away in a military operation which he, a soldier, believed to be bad.

My position was similar. I was more than a mere adviser. I was the professional head of all the British armies, as Haig was of those in France. They looked to me, as did the whole Empire, to see that they were not asked to do impossible things, and were not in any way placed at a disadvantage unnecessarily. They might (and unfortunately did) suffer from the dual system of responsibility just mentioned which the War Cabinet desired to set up, and therefore I had to tell the Minister that, while anxious to meet his wishes, I must put duty to the Empire first and duty to his colleagues in the

Government second. Whether I was right or wrong in this action others can judge. The effect of it upon myself was the forfeiture of the post of C.I.G.S., which I had naturally hoped to retain until the war was finished and victory had been won.

The war afforded no confirmation of the view sometimes expressed that the War Minister ought to be a professional soldier. On the contrary, Lord Kitchener's occupation of the post showed that the appointment of a soldier, especially if of very senior rank, must necessarily be attended, both at Government head-quarters and at the front, with certain disadvantages which it is desirable to avoid. The country undoubtedly gained far more than it lost by having Lord Kitchener at the head of the War Office, and most people will agree that no one else could have raised, or would have thought of raising, the great armies without which, humanly speaking, victory could not have been secured. But Lord Kitchener was an exceptional man, and the precedent is not one that can usefully be followed as a rule. Whatever may be the case in other countries, with us it clearly seems best that the War Minister should be selected from the political and not from the military ranks.

It is not technical knowledge that a War Minister requires for the discharge of his responsibilities, but the ability to obtain this information from his military colleagues, and to apply it appropriately when dealing with questions of policy and administration which call for his direction and decision. As regards operations, it is not for him to draw up plans of campaign, to expound them to the Government, or to control their execution. These duties are for the Chief of the General Staff, and although the Minister has the unquestionable right to be regarded by that Staff as the responsible head of the Army, he, in his turn, should be careful to recognize the line beyond which his interference in the domain of the military experts becomes an impediment rather than an aid to success.

CHAPTER V

UNITY OF COMMAND

Various Suggestions for Co-ordinating the Entente Operations—My Report on the Need for Improvement, October, 1915—Further Memorandum of November 5, 1915, on the same Subject—French G.H.Q. Proposals—Joint Allied Standing Committee formed—My Third Memorandum on the Subject, February, 1916—Inter-allied Conferences—Unification of Command at Salonika and on Western Front, 1917—Further Consideration of Question by General Staffs at Paris—Rapallo Conference—Formation of Supreme War Council, with Technical Advisers—Renewed Discussions at Versailles—Objections to Generalissimo—Solution proposed by the Military Chiefs—Ministers decide to form an Executive Committee—My Objections to British Method of carrying out this Decision.

BY the autumn of 1915 the Entente armies had become engaged in five different campaigns in Europe, besides several in Africa and Asia, each of which was being prosecuted more or less independently of the others and on no good system for securing effective co-ordination of the whole. The Dardanelles Expedition, for example, had been commenced by Britain without obtaining the whole-hearted co-operation of France, which could not be secured because the enterprise was opposed by General Joffre. France, on her part, had, in order to meet the recent invasion of Serbia, started a campaign in the Balkans in which Britain had consented to share only with reluctance and to a limited extent. On the Western Front, where the French Army was large, the

British Army (at first) very small, and the Belgian Army maintained from French sources, it was tacitly agreed that the strategical employment of all three must primarily rest in the hands of General Joffre. But with the exception of this local and purely military understanding the operations were without any central control, either as to conception or execution; the probable action of the enemy was inadequately studied and not always foreseen; and when measures to meet it had eventually to be taken, hurried conferences, panic-decisions, incomplete preparations, and conflicting aims were the natural result.

Sundry remedies were propounded by means of which the political and military activities of the several nations might be united in one supreme authority, the first being put forward in October, 1915, by Lord Selborne (then a member of the Cabinet). He proposed to entrust the direction to an Allied Council composed of a Minister, a soldier, and a sailor, nominated by the British and French Governments respectively. This was intended to be a preliminary organization, to be followed later by one including representatives of Russia and Italy. The Council was to be given a suitable staff, and to sit at Paris or, alternatively, to meet twice a week, once at Calais and once at Dover.

Being summoned from France on several occasions about this time to attend meetings of the Cabinet or War Council when the various campaigns were under consideration, I had an opportunity of learning something about the unsatisfactory position which prevailed. Instability of purpose on the part of both the British and French Governments was becoming more marked every day; discontent and disappointment at the absence of conspicuous success were turning into a feeling of bewilderment and despair ; and, in general, there seemed to be a real danger that the war might be lost unless more business-like methods for conducting it were introduced.[1] The urgent need for them was particularly emphasized by the fuss and friction which attended the negotiations between the two Governments respecting the commencement of the Salonika campaign, and on October 31, after returning to France from the conference held in London at which General Joffre had threatened to resign his command if the plan he had proposed were not agreed to by the British Cabinet, I sent the following memorandum to the C.I.G.S. :—

For months past we and the French have been at a great disadvantage because of the absence of co-ordination in the conduct of the war. No real progress will ever be made until this disadvantage is removed. Nothing could have been more pitiable than our proceedings of the last month. Germany suddenly sends about a dozen divisions into the Balkans (the only disposable forces she has), and we immediately become panic-stricken and helpless. Troops are rushed off there by the French without any proper reflection as to what may be the result, and now the British are sending troops there mainly to ensure the safety of those already sent. The pity of it is that, as Germany is now on the down grade, we can have every hope of winning through if we but keep our heads, make a plan for finishing the war, and stick to it.

Our General Staff (at the War Office) are unanimously of opinion that this plan should be based on seeking a decision in the west, and they consider that it is neither useful nor sound to start a campaign in the Balkans. Theirs may be a good plan or it may not. Apparently several members of the Cabinet think it is not, and it certainly is not being given the best chance of succeeding. If, then, it is not in favour, what is the alternative plan ? The French General Staff have none,

---

[1] Mr. Churchill wrote in June, 1915 : "The lack of any real co-ordination in the exertions and plans of the Allies has been evident at every stage ; and this must be reckoned as one of the chief causes leading to the failure of the campaign of 1915."—"The World Crisis, 1915," page 405.

for finishing the war, so far as I can gather. They do not deny, in fact I understand them to admit, that the Western Front remains the principal theatre, but at the same time they persist in sending troops away to the Balkans. . . .

The original proposal understood to have been put forward by the French Government was to send 150,000 men, on condition that the Greeks came in. The Bulgarian army was then inside its own frontiers. On the 27th instant, the Bulgarian army then being at Uskub, the Serbian army in process of being enveloped, and the Greeks having declined to come in, General Joffre's staff proposed sending a minimum of 250,000 men. On the following day the same staff proposed 150,000 men, without any explanation of the reduction. These very different plans do not give us much confidence in their soundness, and in the opinion of British G.H.Q. in France the Balkan operations have been imperfectly examined by the French, their many difficulties slurred over, and their probable consequences left out of account.

For good or for evil we are now committed to co-operate in them "energetically," and therefore must make the best of them. But we should nevertheless try to prevent in future a recurrence of the hurried fashion in which they have been undertaken. To succeed in this we require to have a plan agreed upon between ourselves and the French covering operations all the world over.

The French seem to assume that the troops now under orders *will* suffice to open and maintain communication with the Serbian army, and that Greece and Rumania *will* come in.[1] But, remembering Antwerp and Gallipoli, supposing these things do not happen? We say we will withdraw, but shall we be in a position to do so? Covering a railway is no different from covering anything else. We are at war, and war is a matter of fighting. The railway to Uskub can only be opened and kept open by fighting, and if we lose in the fighting shall we be able to withdraw, and dare we withdraw, even if we are able? These contingencies must be faced and provided for.

We may put what we like into written agreements, but we cannot get away from the fact that we have started a Balkan campaign, and we should at once arrange with the French how it is to be carried

[1] These were the objects for which the Salonika campaign was undertaken, the rôle of the Anglo-French contingent being to keep the Uskub railway open to the south.

out. The situation there may soon be quite different from what it is now, and more troops will almost certainly be needed besides those already agreed upon. Every possible development should therefore be considered and worked out beforehand by the staffs in consultation, otherwise we shall have a repetition of the jumble, cross-purposes, and friction of the past month. . . .

It is necessary that we should have a more dominating control over matters. Our stake is as great as the French stake; we have now a great Army in the field; our Navy is all-powerful; we are finding the greater part of the money; our General Staff is as competent as the French General Staff to show the way to victory; and therefore we ought to take a much greater share in the planning of operations than we have taken hitherto. In my opinion, based on a good knowledge of French G.H.Q., we ought not to allow ourselves again to be drawn aimlessly and hurriedly into operations of which we disapprove —that is, unless we are to leave supreme control of the operations in French hands, and do merely what they ask us to do.

I assume that this is not intended, and if I am right the French should be asked at once to say who are their representatives in the matter—General Joffre and his staff, or the War Minister and his staff? Their representatives and ours should be placed in definite and constant touch (they can easily meet at Calais whenever necessary). They should formulate a general plan upon which we can work, and not merely follow the German lead as in the past; this plan to be approved by the joint Governments, who should refrain from agreeing to any other until they have before them the considered opinions of the combined staffs. . . .

This memorandum was followed by one sent direct to the Prime Minister, and containing a more comprehensive survey of the whole position. Its preparation was not, strictly speaking, the business of the General Staff in France, but having regard to the urgency of the case I decided to send it in. Ministers had not had, so far as I knew, any complete statement of the kind before them since the war began, and without it plans for the future could not usefully be considered. It would at least show how matters were viewed by the General

Staff on the main front, and afford some indication of the directions in which more effective co-ordination was needed. With the memorandum I sent the following letter :—

6th November, 1915.

DEAR MR. ASQUITH,—

Before I left England on Tuesday last Lord Kitchener asked me, as a result of some long conversations we had together, to write him a paper giving my views on the conduct of the war, stating fully and freely what measures should, in my opinion, be taken in order to win. He particularly told me to hold nothing back. I have just finished the paper, and as he has left the War Office temporarily I send it to you, as there is no time to lose.[1]

The paper trespasses on the domain of your chief military adviser —Sir A. Murray—and therefore I feel considerable hesitation in sending it to you, as it is desirable you should receive advice from the responsible officer only. On the other hand, it may be useful to you, at any rate as regards the nature and effect of operations on this front, and if you can agree to treat it as personal, no harm should be done by sending it. As a matter of fact, I believe Sir A. Murray would agree with it.

Another reason for sending it is that I feel so strongly that we *can* win through if only we decide what is the right thing to do, and then resolutely stick to our decision and refuse to be diverted from it by the many specious temptations which always beset those responsible in time of war. . . .

I remain,

Yours truly,

W. R. ROBERTSON.

To the Rt. Hon. H. ASQUITH, M.P.

The memorandum itself, which the Prime Minister ordered to be printed and circulated to the Cabinet, read as follows :—

MEMORANDUM ON THE CONDUCT OF THE WAR.

By Lieutenant-General Sir W. R. Robertson.

1. The war may end either in the defeat of the Central Powers, in the defeat of the Entente, or in mutual exhaustion.

The object of the Entente Powers is to bring about the first of these

[1] Lord Kitchener had just left England for the Dardanelles.

results, which can only be attained by the defeat or exhaustion of the predominant party in the Central Alliance—Germany. Every plan of operation must therefore be examined from the point of view of its bearing on this result. If it is not, it will have a false basis, and will accordingly lead to false conclusions.

2. Obviously the most effective method of attaining the end we desire is to defeat decisively the main German armies, which are still on the Western Front. If it can be proved that this is either impossible or more difficult of attainment by direct than indirect means, it is then right to have recourse to subsidiary operations, provided always that they lead to the defeat or exhaustion of our chief enemy.

3. It follows that the first questions we have to ask ourselves are :—

Is the defeat of the German armies by direct attack possible? If not, can we bring about this defeat by indirect attack? What is the bearing of each of the various campaigns to which we are committed upon one result or the other?

4. Leaving minor colonial operations out of account, we are now waging war in four theatres—Mesopotamia, in the Dardanelles, in the Balkans, and in France.

5. The campaign in Mesopotamia does not help us towards our end, but neither does it employ troops which can conveniently be used, owing to climatic and other reasons, in the Western theatre, nor does it cause an appreciable drain upon our resources in munitions. Provided that these conditions continue, and that the campaign does not detrimentally affect our financial position, it is justifiable to exploit the success gained in this theatre to the fullest extent, in view of the relief which the occupation of Baghdad may give to the general situation in the East.[1]

6. The operations in the Dardanelles and in the Balkans are presumably intended to contribute to the defeat of the Central Powers. They must therefore be considered in relation to the main operations of the Entente. Their justification and the amount of force which should be devoted to them depends upon the answer to the question —Is the defeat of the German armies by direct attack possible?

---

[1] This statement ought to have been greatly modified, but I was not then aware of the defective arrangements made for carrying out the campaign. It confirms, by the way, the suggestion made more than once in this book that outside opinion is not to be depended upon in these matters.

7. Briefly, the history of the war on the Western Front up to the end of November, 1914, is one of effort on the part of the French and ourselves to prevent the enemy from turning our left flank. In this we were successful, the German offensive was definitely broken, and a defensive line was established from Switzerland to the English Channel. The enemy then transferred his attacks to the Eastern Front, and devoted his energies in the West to the strengthening of his position by every means which skill and artifice could devise, until it was only possible to penetrate his defences when an enormous quantity of high-explosive shell was available to batter the trenches and the wire obstacles in front of them. The effect of this was to create conditions without precedent in war. There were no data available on which the amount of force required to break the enemy's front could be calculated, and this could only be arrived at by experiment. The failure of the German efforts in the West, an exaggerated estimate of the effect of our naval blockade, and faith in the result of an offensive in the spring, which was not founded on an accurate idea of the amount of force required to pass from defence to attack, produced in England a general feeling of optimism and expectation of an early and successful end to the war.

8. On the other hand, the long wait during the winter of 1914–1915, during which we were recovering from the exhaustion of the campaign of the previous autumn, were reorganizing our forces, embodying our reinforcements, and collecting sufficient guns and ammunition to make attack possible, caused a feeling of impatience in certain minds. This apparently led to the attempt to seek an easier solution to the problem by indirect attack through the Dardanelles. The failure of this operation, combined with the repeated and unsuccessful attempts of the French and ourselves to break completely through the enemy's front in the West, have produced a more than corresponding feeling of depression and dissatisfaction.

9. There may be some excuse for this feeling in so far as the Dardanelles are concerned, but there is none as regards the position on the Western Front, and such depression and dissatisfaction as may exist are largely due to an altogether false idea of what may be anticipated from any given attack. Each successive offensive of the Allies in the West is regarded as a failure unless it produces a decisive result. But the decisive defeat of 2,000,000 men on a front of 400 miles can only be brought about by prolonged effort, and cannot in the most favourable circumstances be the consequences of one battle.

10. In war our own difficulties and dangers loom large; those of the enemy are apt to be forgotten. Because the naval blockade did not produce the effect expected of it last winter it has none the less been very real and effective. Because the Allied attacks in the West have not completely broken through the German defences they have not been failures. The drain upon German resources caused by the operations in the West has been great and continuous. An appendix [1] attached to this paper gives a comparison between those resources last January, when they reached their maximum development, and at the present time; by this comparison the value of the operations of the last nine months can best be judged.

11. Since April last the initiative on the Western Front has been uniformly in the hands of the Allies. They have attacked whenever they chose, and whenever the lengthy preparation required could be completed and the necessary store of ammunition had been accumulated. Each attack has produced greater results than the preceding one, the last ending in the capture of 30,000 prisoners and 120 field and heavy guns, a greater loss than German arms have sustained in any battle at any time since Jena. The statement given in the appendix clearly proves that in comparison with population the drain upon our resources has not been great, while that upon German resources has been very severe.

12. We have at present eleven New Army divisions available as reinforcements, the Germans have no new formations to bring into the field. We are now beginning to receive the heavy guns required adequately to support an attack on a large scale, and there is good prospect that within the next few months we shall receive the number of these proportionate to our strength in infantry. For the first time since the commencement of the war the supply of munitions on an adequate scale is assured. Hitherto our power to assist the French in their attacks, and the extent of front on which we have been able to attack, has been limited chiefly by the number of guns and the quantity of ammunition at our disposal. We have not yet made the maximum effort of which we are capable. We are creating an army during the war, and we are exceedingly fortunate in having the time to do this. Our old divisions are full of recruits; our new and territorial divisions lack training and experience; the army as a whole lacks cohesion. The personnel is magnificent, and events have shown that, given training and experience, both new and territorial divisions

[1] Not reproduced here.

will be equal to any call likely to be made on them. But the creation of an army is a slow business, which demands great effort and great patience. It took Wellington eight years to make the army which won Vittoria and entered Paris.

It is not of course possible to say that the next great attempt which we and the French may make will succeed in breaking through the enemy's successive lines, but judging from past experience there is a reasonable certainty of obtaining such a measure of success as will add greatly to the cumulative effect of past successes.

13. It is sometimes argued that if we cannot be certain of driving back the enemy in a decisive battle, the only way for us to end the war is to kill off Germans, which can be better done by awaiting attacks than by undertaking costly attacks ourselves. This contains a half-truth. It is quite possible that we may end the war by exhausting Germany's supply of men rather than by inflicting decisive defeat on her armies, but we have no guarantee that the enemy will attack us if we sit still. Germany has possession of Belgium, of ten French provinces, and of Poland. She is obviously convinced that she is not likely to increase materially these gains for the present or she would not have embarked on her Balkan enterprise in preference to dealing with her chief enemies. If we remain inactive we leave Germany free to employ her resources in extending her gains so that she may have still more booty with which to bargain at the Peace Conference. On the other hand, Germany cannot afford to have her front broken because it is not possible to measure the extent of the disaster which this might entail, and because her future depends largely on her power to maintain the morale both of her armies and of her people. Time and again both we and the French have been near enough to making a break to frighten her badly, and to cause her to put out her utmost efforts against our attacks. It is in the early stages of a battle that the attack suffers proportionately heavy loss. If complete success is achieved and the line is broken, the losses of the defeated must at least approximate those of the victor. If the success is partial, the enemy's efforts to ward off disaster cause him losses which go far to adjust the balance. In the recent battle our losses on the Loos front amount to about 33 per cent. of the fighting strength of the 175 battalions engaged. So far the preliminary German casualty lists, which are never complete, have been published for 65 battalions which were engaged in the battles of September and October. Their losses amount to 60 per cent. of fighting strength.

14. There is, then, no reason to despair of success by means of direct attack on the Western Front ; on the contrary, the prospects of ultimate victory are good. We are only justified in not concentrating our full resources on the Western Front if we find an easier road to success in a subsidiary theatre. That possibility will now be considered.

15. The object of the Dardanelles Expedition was to open up communication with Russia through the Bosphorus, to force Turkey to make peace, and to bring in the Balkan States on our side. This object cannot now be achieved, and the force in the Peninsula has no longer any prospect of contributing, directly or indirectly, to the defeat of Germany. In fact, the operations are now without an object. At most they occupy a number of Turks, some of whom might eventually be used against Egypt, while the upkeep of the force entails a heavy drain upon the resources which ought to be used against our chief enemy. Withdrawal from the enterprise is therefore the best course, provided it is possible and does not produce a condition of things elsewhere which might necessitate the employment of a larger force than is served from the Peninsula.

16. The recommendation as to the possibility of withdrawal must come from the commander on the spot, but it is hardly conceivable that a considerable proportion of the force could not be got off, while by remaining there is a very serious danger that we may lose the whole. Communication between Austria and Bulgaria by way of the Danube has already been established, and we may expect any day to hear that the Nish-Adrianople railway is in the enemy's hands. In a few weeks at most Germany will be able to keep the Turks supplied with ammunition, heavy guns, and possibly gas.

Experience has taught us that, given sufficient guns and ammunition, any front system of defence can be broken. It is the depth of the enemy's defences and the power of bringing intact reserves up quickly to occupy rear lines which make attack difficult on the Western Front. There is no depth in the Gallipoli defences, and therefore the chances of resisting a determined attack, supported by adequate artillery and the employment of gas (probably of a new kind), appear to be small.

17. A reasonable prospect of such a success as would enable us to increase the depth of our defences in the Peninsula might afford some justification for remaining, on the grounds that we would then avoid an open confession of failure and its effect on Egypt and India. The chances of such a success must also be determined by the commander on the spot, but since this success would not contribute to the object

Further, it should be remembered that we need to have as many troops as possible in France so as to have ample opportunities for giving the training which is so much needed ; to be able to find frequent reliefs for troops in the trenches and thus to reduce wastage ; and to be able constantly and relentlessly to wear down and exhaust the enemy by minor attacks.

24. There is still another reason against depleting the forces in France. The Germans have recently transferred ten divisions from the Eastern to the Western Front, we and the French are in process of sending away ten (including the two Indian divisions). Our relative superiority over the enemy will therefore be reduced for a time to the extent of nine corps, since the new divisions will not all be assembled for many weeks, and then require long training before they are fit to be used. We may hope that this alteration in strength is not sufficient to cause us to fear that the enemy can gain any far-reaching success. There is, however, always the possibility that the enemy may seek to clinch a victory in the Balkans by attempting to gain a local success in the West. There are already some indications that he may be preparing for some such coup. The French were unduly optimistic about the prospects of their last offensive, and are now depressed because it did not give them all they expected. That is the French nature : it will recover as it has in the past, but it is very important on all grounds that we should not at the present juncture give the enemy the opening he is seeking. If Flanders is unsuited for big movements of troops during the wet season, there are many parts of our own and the French front southward from the La Bassée Canal on which battles have been fought in the past during the winter, and there are no climatic reasons why this should not be the case again.[1] These facts should be carefully weighed before deciding on any further weakening of the Allied forces in France.

25. The one touchstone by which all plans and proposals must be tested is their bearing on our object in the war. If it is agreed that the main theatre of war is on the Western Front, then in order to be strong there we must be prepared to take risks elsewhere. It is a commonplace of war that local commanders and local authorities exaggerate the importance and dangers of the immediate situation with which they are concerned. It is the function of the higher direction to keep clearly before it the main issue and the broad prin-

[1] The battle of Verdun began the following February.

ciples of the conduct of war, and to refuse absolutely to be drawn away by any specious plans of local urgency from the course on which it has deliberately determined to proceed.

26. It is not sufficient to be clear as to the object of the war and to have settled where our main effort is to be made ; we must also have the machinery for putting these decisions into practice. One grave defect in the conduct of the war up to the present day has been the lack of this machinery. We are now conducting four distinct campaigns, and we hold in England large disposable reserves. It is essential in these circumstances that there should be one military authority responsible for advising His Majesty's Government regarding military policy in all theatres. The officer selected for this all-important part must be trusted by the Government to carry out his duties without interference, and if he cannot be so trusted he should be replaced. Experience has shown that in a war of the magnitude of the present one it is undesirable to combine in one person the functions of supreme military adviser and of War Minister. In our case it is especially undesirable to combine these functions, because we are engaged in the stupendous task of raising large armies during the progress of the war.

27. We must also have efficient machinery for determining the general policy which will guide the military authorities. Unless this is forthcoming it is futile to look for success, no matter how good the work of the naval and military advisers may be. If, as is sometimes said, the British system of government is unsuited to the conduct of war, then it must be amended for the period of the war. It is not possible to carry on war in an efficient manner if each of a considerable number of men has authority to make plans, to endeavour to convince his fellow-members of the soundness of his views, and to search for those who are prepared to carry out his plans. To what extent the principle of collective Cabinet responsibility should and could be delegated to a small body is a question which is outside the scope of this paper, but there is no doubt that, so far as the conduct of naval and military operations are concerned, prompt decision and prompt action are required, and for these a small responsible body is essential.

28. Once established, this authority must make itself felt, and it is of the first importance that it should set itself to restore confidence in the country. This paper has endeavoured to show that there is no justification for the wave of depression which appears to prevail

in many quarters. Morale is a vital factor in war, and we find that depression at home is beginning to be reflected in the Army in France. That Army is now largely composed of officers and men who are ignorant of what must be expected in war, who are therefore confronted with strange conditions in circumstances of great difficulty, who read the papers, think for themselves, and are in close touch with feeling at home. If every wild story which comes from France is believed, if the public are consequently looking for imaginary disasters, if the enemy is credited with superhuman wisdom and efficiency, if our successes are belittled and our failures exaggerated, the effect on the prosecution of the war may be disastrous. What is required is a clear and reasoned appreciation of the task in front of us, of our power to meet it, and equally a clear and reasoned appreciation of the enemy's task and of his difficulties.

29. We also need to take hold of the war as a whole to a much greater extent than we have done in the past. Our stake in the war is as great as that of the French, we have now a great Army in the field, our Navy is all-powerful, financially we are the dominant partner. The supreme military authority at home ought to be in direct and constant touch with the supreme military authority in France, and we should insist on the effective co-ordination of our plans and those of the French. The other Allies may be invited to join later, but the immediate necessity is effective co-operation between ourselves and the French, and we must be satisfied that proposals made by the French are based on sound reasoning, and are in agreement with the main Allied plan of operations. Victory is assured to us if only we make a reasonable and appropriate use of our superiority in men, money, munitions, and ships. We cannot make this use unless we have a carefully considered, complete, and accepted plan upon which both countries can base their action.

5th November, 1915.

The same question was dealt with in a memorandum prepared by French G.H.Q. for an allied military conference held during the first fortnight of November at Chantilly. It stated that :—

Under existing conditions co-ordination of the efforts of the Allied Powers should be attained from a military point of view if the programme agreed upon by the Commanders-in-Chief is carried out punctually, but that co-ordination depends at present upon no alteration in our combinations being necessitated by the enemy's initiative. Now, in order that we may not be taken by surprise, the Allies must provide for eventualities, that is to say, they must foresee possible action by the enemy and study beforehand the measures which it may be necessary to take in order to oppose designs.

It must be recognized that up to the present the Powers of the Quadruple Entente have not carried out this preliminary study in common. For example, the German attack on Serbia has caused us to come to decisions under the pressure of events because we had not considered this eventuality in time. It is indispensable that a method of conducting operations which is so prejudicial to our general interests should be changed. The understanding between the Powers must include every sphere of activity, military, naval, financial, economic and industrial. It is true that it is not the duty of the Commanders-in-Chief of the Allied Armies to study all these problems. They should confine themselves to a common study of such military problems as may arise, consider the most appropriate solutions, and present them for the approval of their respective Governments. . . . The existing organization, which consists of periodical meetings, interchange of telegrams or of liaison officers, does not permit the Commanders-in-Chief to arrive at a general agreement on all these questions. It should be possible to create for this purpose a permanent organization at the head-quarters of one of the armies of the Quadruple Entente, which should include an accredited representative of each of the Allied armies. (This representative might be the Military Attaché, provided that he is freed from all other duties.) The body so organized should examine, on the initiative of its President, all problems with which the Coalition may be faced, and should communicate the reports or proposals drawn up in common to the respective Commanders-in-Chief. On the basis of these reports, Commanders-in-Chief should address their proposals to their respective Governments and prepare the action agreed upon by the Coalition.

What importance, if any, the two Governments attached to these memoranda, I cannot say, but at a conference of British and French Ministers held at Paris on November 17 it was agreed to form a "Joint Standing Committee to co-ordinate the action of the Allies in regard to the war," and the British Government was asked to draft rules for its composition and procedure. The rules were duly drawn up, and they provided that the Committee should consist of the Prime Ministers of the countries concerned, and of such other Ministers as were required according to the subjects to be discussed. Such expert advisers as were required were also to attend, and there was to be a permanent secretariat. The Committee was to be merely advisory in character, and its conclusions were made subject to the approval of the respective Governments before action upon them could be taken. Russia and Italy were to be invited to nominate representatives. The project did not materialize, but as the Committee was to have neither executive powers nor permanent composition it could not in any case have been of much use.

Considerable progress now began to be made, however, in a military sense by the cultivation of closer relations between the principal head-quarters, and by holding more frequent conferences, under the presidency of General Joffre, for dealing with operations on all fronts. Unfortunately, the value of the conferences was diminished by the absence of a suitable representative from Russia. Other armies were represented by their Commanders-in-Chief or Chiefs of the General Staff, but, owing to distance, Russia was mostly represented by an officer permanently attached to French head-quarters and he, not being employed at the front or in a high position, could not speak with the requisite knowledge and authority.

In February, 1916, soon after assuming the duties of C.I.G.S., I laid before the War Committee a memorandum renewing the suggestion made in November that Britain ought to take a more prominent part in determining the general policy to be pursued. When the British

Army was very small we could not well avoid playing a subsidiary rôle, but by 1916 it had become much greater, and the time had arrived for taking a less modest view of our resources and abilities than we had hitherto done. To a daily increasing extent the Entente countries were looking to us to furnish them with financial, shipping, and other forms of assistance, and it was only right that the grant of these should be made conditional upon our views being accorded greater weight in the Entente councils. Moreover, a period of stress was coming, as it comes in every war, to the belligerents of both sides, to meet which courage and determination were required, and it was necessary that we should supply that firm and consistent guidance of which some of the Allies stood in need. Signs of irresolution were already appearing. France was beginning to run short of men, and was feeling the heavy strain which she had so heroically borne during the past eighteen months. Russia was suffering from want of organizing power, and was inclined to follow some "will-o'-the-wisp," such as the conquest of Constantinople, rather than the practical aim of defeating the enemy and regaining her lost provinces. Italy's whole-hearted co-operation was open to doubt so long as she did not declare war against Germany, and there were points of friction between her and France and Serbia in connexion with the Adriatic.

German diplomacy had been actuated by four main objects: to bring in neutral states so as to augment her reserves of men; to create dissension between the different members of the Entente with the object of breaking it up; to create internal troubles in the outlying territories of the Entente so as to cause the latter to disseminate their forces; and lastly, to check their supplies of food, raw material, and munitions of war.

In order to counter these aims it was necessary that the diplomacy of the Allies should have corresponding objects in view. Certain suggestions were made in the memorandum as to what these objects might be, and the matter was then left to the War Committee to decide. The final observations submitted were :—

> Whether on closer examination the fields of action which I have suggested above prove to be ripe for development, or whether there are others in which our interests can be more readily advanced, I am convinced that the Allies should come as soon as possible to an agreement as to the general policy to be adopted ; that this policy should, in strict harmony with naval and military preparations, be offensive in nature ; and lastly, and most important of all, that every effort should be made to ensure unity of control in foreign policy by measures similar to those recently taken to bring about a like result in military strategy. This I hold to be the essential point, and such suggestions for the action of diplomacy as I have ventured to submit have been made solely with the object of pointing out where, from a military point of view, such action appears to be most needed, and of enabling the War Committee to come to an early decision. With my limited knowledge of what is and what is not possible I cannot do more than offer suggestions.

I do not recollect what decision, if any, was reached when this paper came before the War Committee, but whatever it may have been matters continued to go on much the same as before.

The necessity for ensuring more unified action was next mentioned at an allied military conference held at Chantilly a month later, when some anxiety prevailed as a result of the fighting then taking place round Verdun, and it was further emphasized at an Allied ministerial conference held at Paris on March 27. This was attended by representatives of all the Allies, and was referred to by M. Briand, the presiding Minister, as marking a new development in the management of the war, and as a proof of the determination of the Entente Powers to adopt and follow a common and concerted policy. Hitherto, he said, the enemy had been able to act against the Allies separately, as he might choose. In future there would be opposed to him one policy, one army, one front, and the chief task of the conference was to decide how the resources of the Allies could most effectively be utilized in carrying out the general offensive campaign then about to begin.

From this time onward conferences between the Entente Ministers, who were usually accompanied by their professional advisers, were held at fairly frequent intervals, but from a military standpoint the advantages derived from them were not great, and in a General Staff paper of June 1 the need for improvement was again brought to notice. The conferences were assembled on no kind of system either as to time, place, or purpose, while all attempts to regularize them failed because so many people were concerned that it was impossible to make arrangements to suit the convenience of everybody. When arranged, they had more than once to be deferred, adjourned, or abandoned altogether, because some unforeseen event, such as the sudden irruption of political troubles at home, made it undesirable for the Ministers of one country or another to be absent from their posts. Again, the number of people present rendered the preservation of secrecy and the prompt dispatch of business impossible. It was seldom that less than a score would attend, and when all countries were represented the number might amount to as many as a hundred, made up of Prime Ministers, Ministers for Foreign Affairs, Army, Navy, Munitions, and Finance, Ambassadors, Commanders-in-Chief, and other technical delegates, secretaries, assistant secretaries, and interpreters. No body less suitable to be entrusted with the supreme management of the war could have been devised.

At a conference held at Rome early in 1917, and attended by the customary large number of delegates, it was agreed to place the British contingent at Salonika under the orders of General Sarrail, the same conditions being observed as when the French contingent was employed under the British commander in the Dardanelles Expedition. In the following month the newly formed War Cabinet agreed at a conference at Calais to extend the system by placing the British armies in France under General Nivelle, who had recently succeeded General Joffre. This was a temporary and local arrangement designed to apply only to the joint operations about to be undertaken on the French and British fronts, and did nothing to ensure permanent co-ordination and direction of the Entente operations in general. Being, for this and other reasons, a defective arrangement, and having received from the Government no notice of the intention to adopt it until suddenly presented at ten o'clock in the evening, Sir Douglas Haig and I felt compelled to object to it.

As General Nivelle did not produce the expected victory, British Ministers were not disposed for the moment to make any further experiments in unifying the command, and so far as they were concerned the subject was dropped. The General Staffs of the two countries, however, discussed it at Paris in May, 1917, when considering the effect of the Russian collapse and the entry of America into the war, and the idea was mooted of forming an inter-allied staff. It came to nothing and the result could hardly have been otherwise, for an inter-allied staff without an inter-allied Commander-in-Chief, or Generalissimo, is not a logical organization. Staffs do not of themselves command or direct anything. They are the medium through which a Commander-in-Chief exercises his will, and at the time there was not the least possibility of Ministers agreeing to the appointment of any such officer. Sir John French and General Joffre had already been superseded in the chief command of their respective armies. General Nivelle was on the point of being superseded. Sir Douglas Haig had been made subordinate to him, and was not held in high esteem by the British Prime Minister. General Foch had been removed from the command of the French armies of the North, and afterwards employed on unimportant duty. In fact, not one of the principal military leaders of the time was regarded by Ministers as a sufficiently capable leader to whom the supreme command of the Allied armies could be entrusted.

The above narrative shows that the necessity for co-ordinating the management of the war was fully appreciated both by Ministers and soldiers long before so-called unity of command became a political catchword at the end of 1917. The necessity was admitted by everybody. The difficulty was to determine the method by which co-ordination could be effected. It has always been so in every war in which allies have been engaged, and the problem was particularly awkward in the Great War because of the large number of countries concerned, the size of their armies, and the distances by which some of the latter were separated one from the other. German accounts of the war show that the Central Powers had their trouble in the matter just as the Entente had theirs. The Bulgarians were offended because the Austrians treated them less as allies than as auxiliaries of inferior standing, while the Austrians complained of the attitude of the Bulgarians and their insatiable greed for territory.

Relations between Austrian and German head-quarters were also subject to friction, and it was not until the Austrian armies had been routed by Brussiloff in 1916 that formal unity of command was definitely placed in German hands.

The question next came up for consideration at the Rapallo Conference[1] in November, 1917, after the Italian reverse at Caporetto, when it was decided "with a view to the better co-ordination of military action on the Western Front," to form a "Supreme War Council." It was to be "composed of the Prime Minister and a member of the Government of each of the Great Powers whose armies are fighting on that front. The extension of the scope of the Council to other fronts is reserved for discussion with the other Great Powers." Its "mission" was "to watch over the general conduct of the war. It prepares recommendations for the decision of the Governments, and keeps itself informed of their execution and reports thereon to the respective Governments."

The war plans drawn up by the competent military authorities of the different countries were to be "submitted to the Supreme War Council which, under the high authority of the Governments, ensures their concordance, and submits, if needs be, any necessary changes."

Each Power was to delegate one permanent military representative whose "exclusive function" it would be to act as "technical adviser" to the Council. These representatives were to receive from the Government

[1] The delegates were the Prime Ministers of Italy, France, and Britain, assisted in each case by one or two other Ministers and the Chiefs of the General Staffs.

and competent military authorities of their respective countries " all the proposals, information and documents relating to the conduct of the war," and to " watch day by day the situation of the forces and of the means of all kinds of which the allied armies and the enemy armies dispose."

Mr. Lloyd George proposed that the Council should sit in London, hoping that by this means British influence would be more effectively secured. French Ministers were equally eager that the Council should meet in Paris, and they were supported by the Italians. In the end it was settled that the Council should be located neither at London nor at Paris, but at Versailles. This account of what occurred in the selection of a place may serve to explain what may hitherto have been a puzzle to some people.

The establishment of the Council filled a much felt want, in that it systematized the meetings of Ministers, helped to secure co-ordination of national policies, and to expedite the dispatch of ministerial business in general. On the other hand, as its members consisted entirely of Ministers the Council was a civil and not a military body, and therefore was not qualified to ensure either the " better co-ordination of *military* action " (the ostensible purpose for which it had been created), or the " concordance " of war plans, or to make " any necessary changes " in them.

No less objectionable was the appointment of military representatives to advise the Council over the heads and independently of the Chiefs of the General Staff, who alone possessed the requisite knowledge of conditions enabling them to give the advice. Such an arrangement must inevitably be attended with confusion, and it had the further defect that these so-called technical advisers had no responsibility for carrying out the plans which they might induce the Council to adopt. As compared with the Chiefs of the General Staffs, who were, quite properly, charged with both duties, they were in the happy position of the man who can say, " Heads I win, tails you lose." The point of view of the man who is responsible for giving effect to the advice which he tenders, and feels that he must stand or fall by the results achieved, is very different from that of the man who has no such responsibility. As a rule it is fairly simple, in war as in peace, to say what one would like to do. It is quite another matter to do it, and for that reason advisory and executive duties are best united in one and the same person.

When the Rapallo Agreement was communicated to the Army Council they pointed out to the War Cabinet that by Letters Patent they exercised the powers and authority of a Commander-in-Chief in regard to all questions connected with the Military Forces. They therefore assumed that the " technical advice " given by the British military representative to the Supreme War Council would be given on their behalf, and that he would, like all other military officers, receive his instructions from them. The War Cabinet replied that they did not question that he was subject to their jurisdiction, but they counted on the good will of the Council in making a success of the new scheme, and they wished it to be understood that the military representative would have " unfettered discretion as to the advice he offers."

To this the Army Council replied that while desirous of co-operating cordially in the development of the work of the new body, they felt it their duty to say that delay and ill-defined responsibility would arise from the powers granted to the military representative, that these evils might tend to alienate the confidence of the forces under the Council's control, and in other ways might jeopardize the effective prosecution of the operations. In order to minimize them they asked that the C.I.G.S. should as heretofore attend the meetings of the Supreme War Council, and give to it such military advice as it might need. They also asked that the military representative should not tender advice without first informing them of the nature of it. No attention was paid by the War Cabinet to these submissions so far as I can remember. The C.I.G.S. attended the meetings of the Supreme War Council, but the system of dual counsellors was nevertheless set up.

The contention that the " technical advisers " ought not to advise or otherwise act independently of the supreme military authorities of the armies to which they belonged was recognized as being sound both by France and Italy, and by America also when she subscribed to the scheme. The French Prime Minister went so far as to propose nominating the Chief of the General Staff, General Foch, as his representative, but Mr. Lloyd George insisted that this could not be allowed and that the General, on becoming a "technical adviser," must relinquish his French staff duties. M. Painlevé gave in to this demand, but a fortnight or so later, when M. Clemenceau became Prime Minister, the arrangement was cancelled. General Foch retained the post of Chief of the General Staff, and General Weygand, his subordinate, was appointed " technical adviser." Similarly, the American representative, General Bliss, was, so far as one could judge, given no more authority to speak for the American Army than the American Commander-in-Chief, General Pershing, deemed fit. With Italy the position was much the same, and consequently in each of the three cases prime responsibility for advice and execution ultimately rested in one and the same officer. The British Government alone divided responsibility by giving their representative on the new Council a position independent of the British General Staff.

Effective co-ordination could only be secured in one of two ways: by the joint action of the Chiefs of the General Staff, or by the employment of a Generalissimo. Mr. Lloyd George had no belief in the former system, and he dare not, or would not, adopt the latter. Speaking in the House of Commons on November 19, a few days after the Rapallo Conference, he stated that he was "utterly opposed" to the appointment of a Generalissimo, as it "would produce real friction, and might really produce not merely friction between the armies, but friction between the nations and Governments."[1]

The above is a summary of the main events, as known to me at the time, which led to the introduction of the new form of supreme control in military affairs. But according to M. Painlevé,[2] protracted negotiations took place between the British and French Governments about which I knew nothing. Just as the War Cabinet had decided earlier in the year, without first ascertaining the views of either the Secretary of State for War or the C.I.G.S., to place the British armies under General Nivelle, so did they decide, again without hearing the opinion of their responsible advisers, to establish the new system of command which, even if every possible pre-

[1] "Hansard," November 19, 1917, page 896.

[2] "Comment j'ai nommé Foch et Pétain," page 240 *et seq.* M. Painlevé was War Minister from March to September, 1917, and Prime Minister September to November, 1917.

caution were taken, would still be very difficult to carry into effect. The first I heard of it was in a telegram received from London when visiting General Cadorna's head-quarters, where I had gone after the Caporetto disaster in order to ascertain what the situation was and what assistance was required. On arrival at Rapallo a few days later to take part in the conference then assembling it at once became evident that, as at Calais, the Prime Minister had already made up his mind to push the project through. As I had had no proper opportunity to consider it, I was not in a position to express any opinion about it, and I accordingly stayed away from the sitting of the conference at which it was discussed.

M. Painlevé says that three months before the conference he proposed to Mr. Lloyd George and Lord Milner that an inter-allied General Staff should be created, with General Foch as its chief, this step to be regarded as a preliminary to the later appointment of General Foch as Generalissimo. Mr. Lloyd George, while agreeing with the proposal in principle, said that as he and Lord Milner were alone in supporting it, due patience must be exercised until public opinion in England could be prepared to accept the change.

On September 25, shortly after becoming Prime Minister, M. Painlevé again discussed the question with Mr. Lloyd George, on this occasion at Boulogne, where a meeting was being held to consider the extension of the British front in France. It was then agreed, apparently, that the new staff should be formed as early as possible, and that General Foch should be given command of the allied reserves until such time as English opinion would admit of his being definitely made Commander-in-Chief of the two armies. In this way the complete unification of command was to be reached in two stages, the first being the formation of the inter-allied General Staff which the Generalissimo, when appointed, would require. To attempt, for the moment, to achieve more than this would, Mr. Lloyd George thought, be to go further than the country and Parliament would permit. It was arranged that the French Government should draw up a scheme as a basis for subsequent discussion in London. Of these proceedings I was told nothing, although present at Boulogne. The conversation was conducted, says M. Painlevé, between him and Mr. Lloyd George "*seul à seul.*"

M. Painlevé's account of the difficulties which he experienced in preparing the promised scheme in such a manner as to satisfy both parties would be amusing, were the matter not so serious. His French colleagues desired that the control over the British armies to be vested in the staff over which General Foch was to preside should be as complete as possible, and they complained of the vague way in which the scheme was drafted. "What exactly were the powers of the new organization?" they asked. "What was the use of giving General Foch command of the reserves alone? Was not that merely to add a third authority to the two already existing (Haig and Pétain), and so further divide responsibility instead of centralizing it?"

Having so altered the draft as to satisfy his colleagues, M. Painlevé arrived with it in London on October 8 to find further trouble awaiting him there. British Ministers were naturally as reluctant to part with the control over their armies as French Ministers were desirous of acquiring it, and while the latter wanted the scheme to be made more precise, Mr. Lloyd George asked that it might be kept general, or he would not be able to accept it without considerable qualifications.

After three days of "*discussions ardues*" a scheme was agreed to in respect of main principles, but, as is often the case in such matters, the two Cabinets failed to agree about the details, and these had not been entirely adjusted when the battle of Caporetto occurred and so brought up the question for final settlement. Apparently the scheme formed the basis of the organization approved at Rapallo under the name of Supreme War Council.

As indicated by its title, M. Painlevé is chiefly concerned in his book with showing that if his advice, concurred in by Mr. Lloyd George, had been acted upon General Foch would have been nominated Generalissimo months before the German offensive in March, 1918. He may, however, have exaggerated a little in representing Mr. Lloyd George as being entirely in agreement with him, and as declining to accept a Generalissimo only because of the opposition which the appointment might meet with in the country, Parliament, and the Army. At any rate, the real attitude of Mr. Lloyd George differed considerably from the account which M. Painlevé gives of it.

In the first place, there was his well-known desire to bring the military chiefs more and more under ministerial control. Only for a brief interval—at the Paris conference of May 4 and for a special reason—did he display any distinct willingness to accord to the military chiefs that freedom of action to which, in virtue of their responsibilities, they were entitled. Secondly, there was his insistence at Rapallo that General Foch, as head of the "technical advisers," should cease to be Chief of the French General Staff, so as to become the servant of the Supreme War Council alone. Thirdly, not once did Mr. Lloyd George, during my time as C.I.G.S., express any admiration for General Foch's qualifications either as a commander or a counsellor, while there were occasions when he seemed to hold quite a contrary opinion about them. Lastly, there was his statement in Parliament as late as November 19, after the Rapallo Conference, that he was "utterly opposed" to the appointment of a Generalissimo.

The next effort to solve the difficulty was made at the historic meeting of the Supreme War Council held at Versailles between January 30 and February 2, 1918. As a result of being thrown on the defensive, the attention of the French and British military authorities had for some time past been directed to the provision of strategical reserves available to reinforce any part of the allied fronts, the chief problem being how best to constitute and command them. On my initiative a conference had been held at French G.H.Q. in order to see what could be done, and on several occasions the subject had been discussed between the General Staff at the War Office and British G.H.Q., but without anything definite being settled. One difficulty was that the two Commanders-in-Chief, Sir Douglas Haig and General Pétain, feared that their authority might be unduly interfered with if the reserves were in any way placed under a separate authority, and they maintained that such assistance as might mutually be required could best be arranged between themselves without the intervention of a third party, according to the custom which had hitherto prevailed. This view was not convincing even in regard to the Western Front, while it had no application at all to the Italian Front.

On January 24, the question was dealt with in a memorandum prepared by the "technical advisers," and a day or two before it came up for consideration by the Supreme

War Council Mr. Lloyd George asked me to say what ought to be done. My reply, given in a memorandum dated January 30, was to the effect that as general reserves were certainly necessary, they ought to be provided. Further, that they ought to be controlled by an authority superior to both the French and British Commanders-in-Chief, for no matter how close co-operation between these officers might be, circumstances might so develop as to render the intervention of such an authority imperative. For instance, one Commander-in-Chief might be attacked and call for help, while the other might quite reasonably expect to be attacked himself later, and in that case the former might not feel justified in giving his colleague the help requested. Both of them would naturally feel bound both by their duty to their country and to their troops to take a local rather than a general view of events.[1] Or again, both fronts might be attacked simultaneously, in which case it might be necessary to effect a retirement on one front, or submit to heavy losses there, in order to provide more troops for the other. Many other cases could be quoted in which superior authority ought to step in and assess the relative importance of the different parts of the front, and have the power to issue such instructions to the Commanders-in-Chief as would best ensure the success of the operations as a whole. It was also necessary to make arrangements for sending further reinforcements to the Italian Front.

As to the possibility of this " superior authority " taking the form of a Generalissimo, there were many difficulties, political, military, and constitutional, in the

[1] This is exactly what happened some seven weeks later, when General Pétain felt unable to meet to the full the requests made by Sir Douglas Haig.

way. The feelings of the troops had also to be considered. If there were any great outstanding General whom everybody would be willing to follow, and who would satisfy the various Governments concerned, then perhaps a Generalissimo would be a possibility, but, as already explained, there was no such man. In the circumstances it seemed to me that the duties of High Command could only be exercised, under the instructions of their respective Governments, jointly by the Chiefs of the British and French General Staffs, as it had been, for example, in the case of the dispatch of reinforcements to Italy the previous autumn. What we wanted was not so much new machinery as an improvement in, and more definite recognition of, the existing machinery. As to America, Belgium, and Italy, all that seemed possible for the moment was that they should be represented on the High Command by officers of sufficient authority to make the views of their Governments and Commanders-in-Chief known, and to keep them informed of what was happening.

Constituted as above, the High Command would not attempt to replace Commanders-in-Chief, but would only perform those duties which must necessarily devolve upon superior authority and could not be performed by officers in command of one section of the front only. Commanders-in-Chief would, as heretofore, jointly draw up plans for all possible contingencies so as to ensure co-operation between their armies, and, broadly speaking, they would be allowed a free hand in carrying them out. It was, however, essential that the High Command should approve these plans.

This represents the gist of the advice I gave to the Prime Minister. The system proposed was far from being perfect, but it was thought to be preferable to either of the two alternatives that had been suggested—the appointment of a Generalissimo (which nobody yet regarded as a possibility),[1] and the creation of some other kind of authority under the Supreme War Council, and which eventually materialized in the form of an "Executive Committee." On the following day Sir Douglas Haig, General Foch, and General Pétain expressed their concurrence in the proposals I had made, and it was arranged that General Foch should lay them before the Supreme War Council. This was done in general terms during the afternoon sitting on February 1, some discussion took place, and an adjournment was then made for tea in order to give time for a definite scheme to be drafted. The draft was prepared by French Staff Officers under General Foch's supervision, the first three paragraphs reading as follows :—

1. *En vue d'assurer la co-ordination des opérations militaires, conformément aux directives des Gouvernements, sur tout le front s'étendant de la Mer du Nord a l'Adriatique, il est crée une Direction Supérieure de la Guerre.*

2. *Cette Direction comprend les Chefs d'État-Major Généraux Françaises et Anglais, ainsi que des Officiers Généraux réprésentant l'Italie, l'Amérique et la Belgique. Elle siège a Paris.*

3. *Cette Direction arrête les Plans ayant trait à la conduite générale des opérations, d'accord avec les Commandants en Chef, l'initiative de ces Plans pouvent être prise par la Direction ou par les Commandants en Chef.*

The remaining paragraphs dealt in detail with the duties of the Direction in regard to the constitution and employ-

[1] In further confirmation of this may be quoted a remark said to have been made by Mr. Lloyd George on March 23, 1918, at a dinner given by the American Ambassador in London : "If the Cabinet two weeks ago had suggested placing the British Army under a foreign General, it would have fallen. Every Cabinet in Europe would also have fallen, had it suggested such a thing."—"The Life and Letters of Walter H. Page," Vol. II, page 366.

ment of the reserves. Owing to the hurried manner in which it had to be prepared the scheme was not quite appropriately worded, and, moreover, it was not at all the kind of scheme that Mr. Lloyd George had in view. He wished to see the reserves controlled in some way by the Supreme War Council. Signor Orlando also suggested that control should be entrusted to the " technical advisers " of the Council. Eventually the meeting was adjourned until next day, M. Clemenceau asking those present to think the matter over with a view to the preparation of a fresh draft.

Knowing that the Prime Minister wished to extend the executive powers of the Council, whereas the scheme submitted by General Foch would, if accepted as it then stood, tend to curtail them, and being ready to agree to almost any scheme rather than see the conduct of the operations pass into the hand of a polyglot committee, I prepared the same night a new scheme, but keeping to the principle that control over the reserves must be exercised by the Chiefs of the General Staff. This I sent to the Prime Minister with an explanatory minute early next morning before the Council reassembled. The two documents were as under :—

PRIME MINISTER.

I have now had an opportunity of more closely considering the scheme put forward by the French Staff to-day for the control of the general reserves on the allied front, and am of opinion that it goes unnecessarily far. In its place I enclose a Note giving what I consider to be the simplest and most practical and constitutional system to ensure adequate control of these reserves, which would not interfere with the Supreme War Council system, but merely provides executive means which that Council does not possess.

2. As regards the alternative proposals which you wish to have considered, namely, that the control of the general reserves should be vested (*a*) in the Supreme War Council ; or (*b*) in representative

General Officers of the allies attached to the Supreme War Council under the presidency of General Foch, they appear to me to be identical in principle in that they place executive power in the hands of a new body—and one not under ministerial control. I may note that General Weygand already acts under the orders of General Foch and reports to him daily. The only difference therefore in this respect in the two schemes would be that General Foch would in (*b*) be recognized as a member, while in (*a*) he would not.

3. If it were decided to adopt (*b*), I am inclined to think that General Foch's powers might gradually become very like those of a Generalissimo. Either (*a*) or (*b*) would, in short, probably work to the entire satisfaction of the French, for in addition to General Foch's position (on the Executive Committee) he has at his disposal the whole of the machinery of the French War Office and is in direct touch with the French Minister of War.

4. With us the case is different. No British officer in France who is not a Member of the Army Council and in direct touch with that body can have the necessary information as to the state of the troops, the supply, munition, and medical situation and other questions essential to the effective control of military operations. On these points I feel that both the Secretary of State for War and the Army Council should be consulted, as they affect vitally the principles of command and administration of our troops in the field.

5. There are also constitutional questions to be considered. As to these I speak with diffidence and lack of knowledge, and suggest it is necessary you should consult the Secretary of State for War before deciding to adopt either of the two alternatives. I do not quite see how a British Commander-in-Chief can be made, constitutionally, to obey the orders of an allied body, or indeed of anyone except the Army Council and the Secretary of State for War—a Minister of the Crown. If the C.I.G.S. were made a member of the Versailles body, as is proposed in the case of General Foch, this difficulty could be more easily surmounted perhaps.

W. R. ROBERTSON,
C.I.G.S.

PARIS,
1st February, 1918.

NOTE ON CONTROL OF THE GENERAL RESERVES.

1. It is decided to establish a Higher Control in order to ensure that the general reserves available on the whole front from the North Sea to the Adriatic may be employed in the most effective manner.

2. This Higher Control will consist of the British and French Chiefs of the General Staff. When the British Chief of the General Staff cannot be present he will be represented by a British General Officer. Representatives of the American and Belgian Armies will be attached for the purposes of keeping their Commanders-in-Chief and Governments informed as to the situation in regard to reserves. When America has a larger force available this arrangement will require review.

3. The functions of the Higher Control will be :—

(*a*) To form general reserves. Instructions will be issued by each of the two Chiefs of the General Staff to their respective Commanders-in-Chief in accordance with the general situation and with the plans approved by the Supreme War Council. The troops composing the general reserve will remain under the orders of their respective Commanders-in-Chief but are at the sole disposal of the Higher Control and are not to be engaged by the Commanders-in-Chief without its sanction.

(*b*) To supervise the arrangements for movement of the general reserve. In order to assure the timely movement of the general reserve the Commanders-in-Chief will make all necessary arrangements for their transportation and concentration. These arrangements will be submitted to the Higher Control for its approval.

(*c*) The employment of the general reserve. The general reserve will be employed by the Commanders-in-Chief in accordance with instructions issued by the Higher Control.

4. If the Italian Government is prepared to appoint a General Officer to the proposed Higher Control, the same procedure as above will apply to Italy. If their constitution does not admit of this, then the only course is to attach an Italian representative to the Higher Control, without executive functions, to keep the Italian Commander-in-Chief informed of the views of the Higher Control as to the possibilities of reinforcing the Italian front or of Italian troops reinforcing the Franco-British front.

PARIS,
1st February, 1918.

What value was attached by the Prime Minister to these proposals I cannot say, but when the Council reassembled he produced a scheme of his own of an entirely different character, and this, subject to certain minor alterations, was eventually adopted in the form of a Resolution. It read as follows :—

RESOLUTION IN REGARD TO THE CONSTITUTION AND CONTROL OF A GENERAL RESERVE.

(1) THE SUPREME WAR COUNCIL decides on the creation of a general reserve for the whole of the armies on the Western, Italian and Balkan Fronts.

(2) The Supreme War Council delegates to an Executive composed of the Permanent Military Representatives of Great Britain, Italy, and the United States of America, with General Foch for France, the following powers to be exercised in consultation with the Commanders-in-Chief of the armies concerned :—

(*a*) To determine the strength in all arms and composition of the general reserve, and the contribution of each national army thereto :

(*b*) To select the localities in which the general reserve is normally to be stationed :

(*c*) To make arrangements for the transportation and concentration of the general reserve in the different areas :

(*d*) To decide and issue orders as to the time, place, and period of employment of the general reserve ; the orders of the Executive Committee for the movement of the general reserve shall be transmitted in the manner and by the persons who shall be designated by the Supreme War Council for that purpose in each particular case :

(*e*) To determine the time, place, and strength of the counter-offensive, and then to hand over to one or more of the Commanders-in-Chief the necessary troops for the operation. The moment this movement of the general reserve, or of any part of it, shall have begun, it will come under the orders of the Commander-in-Chief to whose assistance it is assigned :

(*f*) Until the movement of the general reserve begins, it will, for all purposes of discipline, instruction, and administration, be under the orders of the respective Commanders-in-Chief, but no movement can be ordered except by the Executive Committee :

(3) In case of irreconcilable differences of opinion on a point of

importance connected with the general reserve, any Military Representative has the right to appeal to the Supreme War Council.

(4) In order to facilitate its decision the Executive Committee has the right to visit any theatre of war.

(5) The Supreme War Council will nominate the President of the Executive Committee from among the Members of the Committee.

TRIANON PALACE, VERSAILLES.
Feb. 2, 1918.

I took no part in the discussion at this second meeting, as the Council had heard me the previous evening support the totally different scheme submitted by General Foch. Further, I had that morning, as just explained, given the Prime Minister a written statement of my views, and I remembered that only the day before he had very strongly resented my expressing opinions to the Council that were contrary to his own, when, as in this case, I had already made them known to him.[1]

It was with considerable surprise therefore that I read the account he gave to the House of Commons on February 19 when describing what had passed at the conference: "Everybody was free to express his opinions, not merely Ministers but Generals. The Generals were just as free to express their opinions as the Ministers . . . I want the House, again at the expense of repeating myself, to recollect that this passed the Versailles Council without a single dissentient voice so far as all those who were present are concerned, and as far as I know it was completely accepted by every military representative present."[2]

General Foch, who also remained silent, so far as I recollect, must have felt, as I did, that the scheme was unsound, but he may have hoped that, as President of the Executive Committee, he would in course of time convert it into

[1] This passage refers to the objection I had raised to Mr. Lloyd George's Palestinian strategy—*vide* Vol. II, page 287.

[2] "Hansard," February 19, 1918.

something more practical. Meanwhile it conferred upon him a considerable degree of control over the British armies without in any way impinging upon his control over the French armies, and therefore he could afford to accept it in preference to the different one which he had proposed the day before.

Neither Italy nor America was much affected by the scheme. The former was herself receiving the assistance of ten Anglo-French divisions, and for the present she was not likely to be asked to send troops to other fronts. America had as yet but a comparatively small force in the country, and, as already mentioned, her representative on the Executive Committee would exercise just as much power as the American Commander-in-Chief might allow, and no more than that.

The Resolution was approved by the War Cabinet on February 4, and was then passed to the Army Council for action. The Council in reply reminded the War Cabinet that, constitutionally, they were responsible for the safety and welfare of the Army (which were directly affected by the question of reserves), whereas the Executive Committee had been given such powers that it could disregard the Council and interpose between them and the Commanders-in-Chief. Further, that the system by which Commanders-in-Chief were to receive orders both from the Council and from the Executive Committee must cause confusion and complication in the conduct of the operations. The Council therefore maintained that the constitution of the Committee would not only place Commanders-in-Chief in an impossible position, but would also deprive the Council of the responsibility entrusted to them under the Constitution of the Realm, and that any such abrogation of that responsibility would be a violation of the trust reposed in them. After further discussion and correspondence the War Cabinet decided to get over the constitutional difficulty by making the British representative on the Executive Committee an Army Councillor.

On February 7, being compelled to leave London for a few days, I wrote to the Prime Minister :—

Believe me, I have every wish to fix up a satisfactory and workable arrangement with respect to the reserves. In fact, I have been in communication with Haig, Pétain, and Foch on the subject for some weeks past, because the principle is, in my opinion, unquestionable. The only point in question is the method, and I trust that may soon be decided.

On return to London on February 11, I received from Lord Derby, War Minister, under cover of a private letter, the Note which follows and which he said had been agreed to by the Prime Minister and himself. He expressed the hope that I would support it when considered by the Army Council that afternoon.

10 DOWNING STREET,
WHITEHALL, S.W.1.

1. The C.I.G.S. to hold office under the same conditions and with the same powers as every Chief of the Staff up to the appointment of Sir William Robertson.

2. The C.I.G.S. to continue to be the supreme military adviser of the Government.

3. The Military Representative at Versailles to be a Member of the Army Council.

4. The Military Representative at Versailles to be in constant communication and consultation with the C.I.G.S., but to be absolutely free and unfettered in the advice which he gives as a member of the Board of Military Representatives sitting at Versailles.

5. When that advice is formulated it is to be submitted to the C.I.G.S. for the purpose of advising the Cabinet thereon.

6. When it is necessary to summon a Supreme Council, either to decide upon a plan of operations or to settle differences that may have arisen between the various Commanders-in-Chief, or between any

one or more of the Commanders-in-Chief and Versailles, or for any other purpose, the C.I.G.S. to accompany the Ministers delegated to attend the Council for the purpose of advising them as to the decisions to be taken, after hearing what the Military Representatives and the Commanders-in-Chief have to say from their respective points of view.

7. As prompt decisions may have to be taken as to the sending of reserves to one part or other of the battle front, and time lost in referring to London may be fatal, full powers must be given to the Military Representative in accordance with principles already settled to give the necessary orders in respect of divisions included in the General Reserve.

8. The C.I.G.S., even when not accompanied by a Minister, to have the right to go to France to consult in person with any one or all of the Military Representatives of the Supreme Council.

9. The Military Representative at Versailles to be Sir William Robertson and the C.I.G.S. to be Sir Henry Wilson.

D. LLOYD GEORGE.

Naturally I was surprised to find that the two Ministers had decided, without giving me any previous intimation, to appoint another officer to the high post which I had occupied for more than two years, but the decision itself caused me no surprise. As subsequent chapters will show, it had frequently been my unpleasant duty during 1917 to object to military enterprises which the Prime Minister wished the Army to carry out, and this opposition had doubtless determined him to try another C.I.G.S. whose strategy would coincide more closely with his own. On the point of supersession therefore there was nothing to say, and I said nothing.

The question of taking up the appointment at Versailles was on another plane. I believed that the system which the Prime Minister desired to set up in order to give effect to the Resolution was fundamentally bad, and, holding that opinion, my acceptance of the post could lead to nothing but harm. I accordingly replied to Lord Derby as follows :—

You will remember that at a meeting on the 6th instant the four Military Members present advised you that, in order to give effect to the intention of the Supreme War Council with respect to the formation and control of the allied general reserves, the Army Councillor holding the appointment of C.I.G.S., who is fully acquainted with the resources and needs of the British military forces, is the proper officer to be delegated as British Military Representative on the Executive Committee at Versailles. After careful consideration I am convinced that there would be no difficulty in making such arrangements as would permit of the British C.I.G.S. carrying out the duty without interference with essential duties at home.

I am still unable to see any other practical and workable system, for the reasons given in the various papers submitted to yourself and to the Prime Minister during the last fortnight, as well as for those put forward by Army Councillors at the meetings recently held. I need not further refer to them except to say that it is impossible in practice to separate action in connexion with general reserves from action concerning innumerable other matters which go to make up "military operations"; and that the decision of the War Cabinet leaves, as before, the issue of orders affecting military operations in the hands of two different authorities—one the C.I.G.S. and the other the British Military Representative at Versailles. The fact of my remaining an Army Councillor does not in my judgment remove this defect.

It seems to me absolutely necessary that the General Staff officer who is to give orders regarding the reserves in question must be in constant and direct touch with the various departments of the War Office—the Great Head-quarters of the Imperial Military Forces—and be directly served by, and in close touch with, the Intelligence Branch of the General Staff. Only the C.I.G.S., residing normally at the War Office, can be in this position, and for an officer who is not in that position to attempt to interfere with the employment and location of reserve troops under the British Commanders-in-Chief in France, Italy, and the Balkans, upon the right use of which final victory depends, would inevitably lead to confusion and perhaps to disaster. So strongly am I convinced of this that I am compelled to say that I cannot undertake the very great responsibility involved. I say this with the deepest regret because I am keenly desirous of doing my utmost to assist His Majesty's Government in their very difficult task of winning the war, but on reconsideration I feel sure that you will see that it is asking too much of me to carry out and perpetuate a system which the A.G., M.G.O., D.C.I.G.S., and myself consider to be fundamentally defective.

In conversations which took place during the next two days Lord Derby showed that he was now desirous I should remain C.I.G.S., and on February 13 he handed me a copy of a note which he had addressed to the Prime Minister proposing that this should be done. Sir Henry Wilson was to continue to act as the British representative on the Executive Committee, and the position between myself and him was to be "practically the same as between General Foch and General Weygand." On being asked whether these arrangements were agreeable to me, I at once accepted them without qualification of any kind. As in the case of France, they left in the hands of the C.I.G.S. unquestioned authority over the employment of the Army, and did not divide it between two officers as was done in the Prime Minister's Note.

This arrangement was not accepted by the Prime Minister and there was never the least probability that it would be, for it completely vitiated his object of securing the services of a second adviser. Thinking that a verbal explanation might help the Cabinet to realize the defects of his proposed system, I asked to be allowed to make one. Only the Prime Minister and one other member of the Cabinet had been at Versailles, and the remaining members had no full knowledge of what had been said there.

Summarizing the proceedings of the past fortnight as above described, I repeated that the only workable method was for the C.I.G.S. himself to be a member of the Executive Committee which the Supreme War Council had decided to set up, and that presented no special difficulty. The Prime Minister's proposed system was objectionable because, unlike that adopted by all other allied armies, it divided up responsibility for the operations between two different officers, and this had been the cause of my repeated requests to keep responsibility centralized. Whether I remained C.I.G.S. or left that post and joined the Executive Committee mattered not at all. The important thing was that there should be a good system of command, and that the War Cabinet should have a C.I.G.S. whose advice they could trust and accept. Unless they had this confidence in me I could be of no use to them either in London or Versailles, and would be ready to make way for anyone else they might wish to appoint.

The following morning I was informed that the post of C.I.G.S. had been offered to Sir Herbert Plumer,[1] and that in the event of his accepting it I would be offered the command of the British Army in Italy. He declined it, and on the 16th the Prime Minister again asked me whether I would agree to his Note of February 9, and retain the post of C.I.G.S. A week earlier I would not have hesitated to say "Yes," as I was then intent only upon trying to make the best of such arrangement as the Government might select. Since then, however, the position had been entirely changed by the Prime Minister's decision to employ a new C.I.G.S., and there was the further point that I was determined not to continue in the post unless the full powers which belonged to it were retained. For Ministers to take advice regarding the management of the war from one Army Councillor, myself, in London, and from another, the British representative on the Executive Council, in Versailles, was a hopeless arrangement, and as the Prime Minister insisted that this must be done and that the

[1] Why this was done, when Sir Henry Wilson had already been selected for the post, I do not know.

British representative must be "absolutely free and unfettered" in the advice he gave, I had no alternative but to refuse his offer. After taking an hour to think the matter over, I sent the following letter :—

16th February, 1918.

DEAR PRIME MINISTER,—

I desire to express my thanks for the appreciative words you saw fit to say to me this morning. I have considered the appeal you made to me to endeavour to acquiesce in the system of controlling the reserves, by which the C.I.G.S. is not on the Executive Committee. Indeed I have considered the same question over and over again during the last fortnight. I deeply regret to say that my conscience will not allow me to depart from the views I expressed to the Cabinet on Thursday last, and in the various papers you had previously seen.

It is a matter of real concern to me that you cannot see your way to adopt the method I have ventured to advise for carrying out your policy in this matter, for I still feel that the method you have decided to adopt must prove unworkable and dangerous. Believe me, it is with the deepest regret that I cannot send you any other reply to your kind personal appeal.

Yours sincerely,
W. R. ROBERTSON.

The same evening the official Press Bureau issued a notice that the Government had accepted my resignation as C.I.G.S., but from what has been said it will be seen that the statement was not quite correct. Having been instructed some days before to vacate the post of C.I.G.S., I was not in a position to resign it.

The Executive Committee completely broke down as soon as put to a practical test, and on March 26 it was replaced by a Generalissimo, General Foch, who retained that post until the end of the war. Further reference to the subject is made in the closing chapter.

CHAPTER VI

THE WESTERN FRONT, 1916

Situation at End of 1915—My Recommendations as to Future Plans—Plans recommended by Allied Military Conference at Chantilly—Proposals of Imperial General Staff—Formally approved by the War Committee, but never really supported by certain Members of the Committee—Battle of Verdun—Second Allied Military Conference at Chantilly—Views of Imperial General Staff on General Situation on June 1—Battle of the Somme—Its Results—General Staff's Review of Situation on October 26—My Memorandum on the Prospects of Victory—Change of Government—Memorandum supplied to Mr. Lloyd George regarding Matters requiring Immediate Attention.

THE situation with which the British authorities were confronted towards the close of 1915 was briefly as follows :—

On the Western Front the operations of the year had terminated in what was practically a stalemate—and one which, as at the end of 1914, left large tracts of Entente territory in the enemy's possession. On the Eastern Front, Russia had suffered severe defeats, losing heavily in men, material and morale, and it was doubtful whether or when she could sufficiently recover to take again an effective part in the war. Italy was unable to make headway in expelling the Austrians from their positions beyond the Isonzo, and had not yet declared war against Germany. Serbia had just been overrun, her troops driven out of the country, and the Anglo-French army sent to her assistance was opposed by strong forces in front, had an uncertain neutral (Greece) on its flanks, and was left with the unprofitable mission of defending Salonika. The Gallipoli Expedition had been abandoned as a failure, except that the troops at Cape Helles still awaited the decision of the Government as to whether they were to stay there or come away. On the western border of Egypt the Senussi tribesmen had established themselves within striking distance of the Nile Valley. On the east Turkish troops were in possession of the Sinai Peninsula, and threatened the communications through the Suez Canal. In Mesopotamia an Anglo-Indian detachment of about 20,000 men was besieged by Turkish forces at Kut-el-Amara, and there was little chance of relieving it. In East Africa, British territory was invaded, and British prestige at a low ebb.

So far as responsibility for it rested with Great Britain, this unsatisfactory state of affairs may be mainly ascribed to the fact that the British Government had not yet considered and agreed upon a comprehensive war policy by which *all* operations undertaken could be strictly determined. Moreover, certain Ministers still held fast to the belief that victory could never be won—or only at prohibitive cost—by straightforward action on the Western Front, and that it must be sought through indirect lines of attack elsewhere. Strategy of this kind would, it was argued, place the enemy at a disadvantage, and enable a favourable decision to be secured with comparative ease and rapidity. Referring to the wide dissemination of force brought about by these erroneous notions, the officer [1] who held the post of Director of Military Operations from the beginning of the war to December, 1915, and who was therefore acquainted with

[1] "Experiences of a Dug-out, 1914–18," by Major-General Sir C. E. Callwell.

the way in which questions of military policy were decided during that period, tells us that :—

> Some statesmen are ever, unconsciously perhaps but none the less instinctively, gravitating towards the line of least resistance. This peradventure, accounts to some extent for the singular attraction which operations in the Near East, or Palestine, or anywhere other than on the Western Front, always seemed to present to certain highly placed men of affairs. The idea that the actual strategical position in these somewhat remote regions was such as to constitute any one of them the line of least resistance from the Entente point of view, was based on a complete misreading of the military situation. That theory was founded on the fallacy that the Western Front represented the enemy's strongest point. It was, on the contrary, the enemy's weakest point, because this front was from its geographical position the one where British and French troops could most easily be assembled, and it was the one on which a serious defeat to the enemy necessarily threatened that enemy with a grave, if not an irretrievable, disaster.

The task of the General Staff was to correct the mistaken strategy by which the prosecution of the war was so seriously hampered, and to bring the various divergent enterprises within the narrowest possible limits. It was not an easy task, and some of the commitments were bound to have a detrimental effect on the operations for a long time to come, no matter what remedy might be applied. The narrative will show, too, that Ministers more than once insisted upon secondary campaigns being expanded rather than curtailed, some in one direction and some in another. These particular Ministers would reject with impatience, if not with ridicule, such counsel as was opposed to their own strategical conceptions, and regarded as lacking in "imagination," those who suggested that the road to success lay not in starting fresh campaigns, but in a steady perseverance with those plans which, after careful consideration, had been deliberately selected as the best to adopt. Fortunately, there were other Ministers who, realizing the danger of a repetition of previous errors, were anxious to hear what the responsible military authorities had to say, and, as far as practicable, to act upon the advice which they gave. What the views of these authorities were, and what advice they tendered as to the policy which ought to be adopted, will now be described.

One memorandum on the subject was that sent by me from G.H.Q. in France to Mr. Asquith on November 6, and reproduced in the preceding chapter.[1] It was followed on December 2 by one sent to the C.I.G.S., who was then engaged in reviewing the situation afresh and wished to have my observations as to what our war policy should be. Summarized, the suggestions forwarded and the reasons for them were to the following effect :—

When, towards the end of the summer of 1915, the Central Powers found themselves numerically inferior to their adversaries in the West, and with insufficient forces to achieve complete victory in the East, they naturally looked round for some means whereby their relative striking power on at least one of the two main fronts could be increased. There were three ways by which this could be done :—

(1) By destroying such parts of the Entente forces as were exposed to defeat.

(2) By inducing the Entente to detach troops from the main fronts to other theatres.

(3) By adding to the forces on their own side.

All three objects were attained by the Balkan campaign : Serbia was crushed ; ten Anglo-French divisions, of which more than half came from France, were sent to the Balkans ; and Bulgaria declared herself on the side of the Central Powers.

[1] *Vide* page 196.

There was also a chance that both Rumania and Greece would join them. The former was cut off from communication with Great Britain and France except through Russia and was ruled by a German Prince, while the King of Greece might be influenced by his German wife. Should these two countries follow Bulgaria's example the forces of the Central Powers would be augmented by a total of about fifty-six divisions. These would constitute a valuable reinforcement, numerically at any rate, and although it was unlikely that they would be employed on the Western Front, or could be made sufficiently mobile to advance far across the Eastern Front, they could be utilized to "contain" considerable Russian forces on the southern section of the latter front. Some thirty or forty German divisions would thus be set free for an offensive in the North, or to assist in making a bid for decisive victory in the West.

These seemed at the time to be fair deductions to draw from the enemy's recent operations in the Balkans, and more likely to prove correct than to see in them, as some people did, the intention to embark on a policy of territorial conquest in the Near and Middle East; while of the two main fronts there were good reasons why the Western should be chosen for offensive action in preference to the Eastern. Russia was a land of vast extent, in which there were few natural obstacles against which an army could be penned and compelled to surrender. It contained few if any really vital points, and assuming that the Russian armies could be supplied either through Archangel or through Vladivostok, Dalni, and Fusan, the occupation of no area in European or Asiatic Russia need necessarily involve the collapse of her armed resistance.

In France the position was different. There the

theatre of operations was of limited extent, and topographical conditions and neutral frontiers offered many opportunities to the strategist. Paris, for instance, was little more than fifty miles from the German line on the Oise, and its capture would be one of the most effective ways by which the Central Powers might hope to bring the war to an end. Other strategical points of obvious importance were the Channel Ports linking France with England, and Creil, thirty miles from the German line, the main railway junction connecting Paris and the south with Flanders and the north.

An offensive against Italy was, of course, not impossible, but its object, as in the case of the Balkans, would be of a secondary nature such as the gain of territory and the punishment of what Germany regarded as treason to the Triple Alliance.

The general conclusion therefore was—

that France still remains the main theatre both for Germany and ourselves, and that German efforts are directed to obtain a sufficiency of force with which to seek a favourable decision in that theatre. The question for us is: What are we to do? In theory, it is understood, we still regard the West as the main theatre, but in practice we act otherwise. It is folly to say or to write that the West is the dominant theatre, if day by day and week by week we send, or propose sending, troops away from the West just because the enemy appears to menace other parts of our possessions. The fact is we have no plan of our own for winning the war, or at any rate if we have we do not adhere to it. We are chiefly intent on countering, or attempting to counter, German movements. No more fatal or disastrous policy could be pursued than this. Since Germany entered on her Balkan campaign we seem entirely to have lost our mental balance, and have wasted time and power in proposing and discussing various military expeditions without any consistent and proper regard to any main plan. One, if not the chief, reason for this is loss of faith in some quarters in the feasibility of achieving success in the West. This crippling doubt should be faced, and we must ask ourselves the question: Can we end the war quicker or more successfully than by attacking with our utmost strength in the West ?

No amount of argument can alter the fact that we can only end it successfully by defeating or exhausting the Austro-German armies, and the defeat of Germany will almost certainly bring with it the defeat of Austria, while the defeat of Austria would by no means necessarily entail the defeat of Germany. . . .

Since we and the French cannot find outside France a theatre suitable for offensive operations against the German armies, and as we must necessarily provide a large force to defend that country, the only valid argument against our being as strong as possible on the Western Front is that it is hopeless to attack the entrenched lines which have there been established between Switzerland and the Channel. If this attack is held to be hopeless, it follows that we have no alternative but to make peace as soon as we can, unless the Government are satisfied that our resources are such as will enable us to wear out and finally to exhaust the Central Powers by blockade.

But is it hopeless ? In the battles of last September we achieved important tactical successes but failed in our object, which was to break through the enemy's lines. The main lessons of these attacks, as of all previous attacks, are that, given adequate artillery preparation, or some form of surprise such as a gas attack, there is no insuperable difficulty in overwhelming the enemy's troops in the front line and in support, but that there is the greatest difficulty in defeating the enemy's reserves which have not been subjected to the strain of a long bombardment and come up in good order fresh from their billets to meet our troops at a time when they are somewhat exhausted and in the confusion unavoidable in a modern battle.

The great tactical problem with which we have to deal, and which we have for long been constantly considering, is the one which has faced commanders in every battle, namely, when, where, and how to bring up the reserves in order to defeat the enemy's reserves ? The conditions of trench warfare and the absence of a flank at which to aim have greatly increased the difficulty of doing this, but have they necessarily altered the principles of command in battle ? Those principles are that sufficient force should be employed to exhaust the enemy and force him to use up his reserves, and that then, and then only, the decisive attack which is to win victory should be driven home. In Champagne, at the beginning of 1915, the French successfully carried out a wearing-down attack and drew in large enemy reserves, but neither we nor they were then strong enough to follow this up with a decisive blow. In September both we and the French attempted to carry out the decisive attack without having first drawn in the enemy's reserves, with the result that we saw the enemy denuding the parts of his front on which he was not being attacked in order to meet us at the points where we were attacking. There seems to be no doubt that if we had been able previously to mount a powerful attack against some part of the front subsequently weakened, the chances of our success would have been much greater than were those of the attacks we actually did launch, and which were very nearly successful. In our next offensive we need to go back to first principles, and to decide with the French what is the maximum force we can employ to exhaust the enemy's reserves, and what we can make available for the subsequent decisive attack. . . .

There are therefore no grounds for considering that the prospects of a successful offensive on the Western Front next spring are anything but good, if we and the French consistently continue to harass and wear down the hostile troops by minor enterprises, artillery bombardments, and such like methods, and if the strength of these troops is not materially increased in the meantime. In order to prevent this it is essential that Germany should continue to be relentlessly pressed on the Eastern Front during the winter, and that every effort should be made to enable Russia to take a strong offensive in the spring simultaneously with our attack. If, on the other hand, the Germans reinforce the West by troops from the East we shall, if we concentrate our efforts in the West, be in a position to meet them with our maximum available strength, while we may hope that Russia will succeed in delivering decisive blows in the East. Hence, from every point of view it is essential we should be as strong as possible in the West.

A few days after this memorandum was written a conference was held at Chantilly, under the presidency of General Joffre, to consider what the plans for 1916 should be. It was attended by representatives of all the Entente armies, including the British Commander-in-Chief and myself. The following conclusions were reached :—

Les représentants des armées alliées sont unanimes à reconnâitre que la décision de la Guerre ne peut d'obtenir que sur les théâtres principaux, c'est-à-dire sur ceux où l'ennemi a maintenu la plus grosse partie de ses forces (front russe, front franco-anglais, italien).

La decision doit être recherchée par des offensives concordantes sur ces fronts. Tous les efforts de la coalition doivent donc être tendus pour donner à ces offensives leur maximum de puissance au double point de vue des effectifs et des moyens materiels.

Les résultats décisifs ne seront obtenus que si les offensives des Armées coalisées sont prononcées a des dates suffisamment rapprochées pour que l'ennemi ne puisse transporter ses réserves d'un front sur l'autre.

Other paragraphs dealt with the dates when the offensives should begin on the different main fronts, and with measures for rendering mutual assistance in the event of attack by the enemy. With regard to secondary theatres the conclusions were :—

Les conférents sont unanimes à reconnâitre qu'il ne faut employer sur les théâtres secondaires que le minimum de forces possible, et que les troupes qui se trouvent en Orient paraissent, dans leur ensemble, suffisantes pour parer aux besoins :—

Région de Salonique

Les membres conférents, a l'exception des représentants de l'Armée Britannique, estiment que le corps expeditionnaire franco-anglais doit être maintenu dans la région de Salonique.

En toute hypothèse, quelle que soit la décision prise par les gouvernements, les membres conférents estiment à l'unanimité que l'organisation de la défense de Salonique doit étre effectuée d'extrême urgence.

En ce qui concerne la presqu'île de Gallipoli les conférents sont unanimes à en demander l'évacuation immédiate et complète.

Quant à la défense de l'Egypte, dont l'importance pour la suite de la guerre ne peut étre contestée, les conférents estiment unanimement que cette défense doit être assurée en tout état de cause, mais en y consacrant le moins de forces possible.

These conclusions were communicated to the Governments concerned, and on December 16, about a week after the conference took place, the Imperial General Staff submitted the further review of the situation mentioned on p. 241. It was entitled " The future conduct of the War," and was noteworthy as being the first com-

FRANCE, BRITAIN, RUSSIA, ITALY, AND SERBIA REPRESENTED AT THE WAR COUNCIL AT FRENCH GREAT GENERAL HEAD-QUARTERS AT CHANTILLY.

From left to right, in front : General Porro, Sir John French, General Joffre, and General Jilinski. Back row : Sir Henry Wilson, Sir William Robertson, and the Serbian Military Attaché.

prehensive document of its kind which the War Office had presented to the Government since the war began some sixteen months before. It dealt exhaustively with the various factors affecting the choice of a definite war policy ; discussed the possibilities of opening up new lines of attack instead of continuing to seek a decision on the Western Front ; and it specified the alternatives from which a selection could be made.

Assuming that Holland would remain neutral, and omitting a landing on the Belgian coast as merely amounting to part of a scheme for an offensive on the Western Front, the alternatives considered were :—

(1) A landing near the head of the Adriatic so as to co-operate with an Italian offensive across the Isonzo, and then move on Budapest. A difficult operation, which was thought to offer little prospect of penetrating far into Austrian territory.

(2) A landing in Asia Minor, say at Alexandretta, so as to co-operate with a Russian advance through the Caucasus. This was considered to be an " immense undertaking," the time required for preparation would be long, we should be fortunate if we gained decisive results within a year, and when we had gained them it would only be against the Turks. Meanwhile, half a million of British and Russian troops, and as many more at least as wastage, would have been withdrawn from the war against Austria-Germany.

(3) An advance through the Balkan Peninsula to and beyond the Danube. This was regarded as a still more formidable enterprise, and was also condemned as unsound. " It would not only not promise any adequate results as against the Central Powers, but might very possibly ruin our chance of ultimate victory."

As a general argument against undertaking these or

other new main operations, the War Committee was reminded that the enemy's central position and excellent communications enabled him to mass troops on any of his fronts and move them from one front to another far more rapidly and securely than we could. Consequently, if any large Entente forces were taken away from the existing fronts to share in a campaign elsewhere—which could not be done without the enemy's knowledge—he could either launch an attack against the front so weakened, or transfer the necessary forces from that front in ample time to meet the new attack. If he took the latter course, he could either attack the Entente troops with superior numbers while they were in the early stages of developing the fresh attack, or he could occupy a fortified position on the new line of advance and make it as formidable as the lines were in France.

Had the Entente been strong enough to hold the enemy fast on the existing main fronts, and in addition could have thrown in a large army against him elsewhere, the possibility of gaining an advantage by opening a new line of attack would have been much increased. But there was no chance at present of such an army being found. France could not hold her own front without assistance. Russia had ample men, but being short of war material could put only a small proportion of them into the field. Italy might possibly spare a detached force, without entirely abandoning the offensive against Austria, but would naturally be reluctant to uncover her own frontier for the sake of supplying troops for employment elsewhere. The Serbian army would not be of much value for an indefinite time. As possible allies there remained Greece and Rumania, but they were equally likely to join the Central Powers, and it would be foolish, especially after the Dardanelles failure and the downfall of Serbia, to base any plan of campaign upon the expectation of receiving active help from either of them.

Hence Great Britain alone could be said to have disposable troops for employment in a new direction, and even they were comparatively few in number. Including the Dominion forces, we had in Europe and Egypt a total of 72 divisions, of which 13 were second-line territorial divisions and some of the divisions of the New Armies were as yet far from being ready to take the field. When ready, not less than 13 would, it was considered, be needed for Home Defence if the forces on the Western Front were reduced to a strictly defensive rôle, since this would leave the enemy free to withdraw troops for the invasion of Great Britain should he wish to do so. It was further estimated that 28 divisions would be required to help the French to make the Western Front secure, unless and until Russia could bring far heavier pressure to bear against the enemy on the Eastern Front than she had done for some months past.

After meeting these demands, amounting to at least 41 divisions, and adding to them the 5 divisions recently sent to Salonika and 8 others considered to be necessary for the defence of Egypt, the 18 surplus divisions would obviously not suffice for operations on a great scale in a new theatre, while operations on a minor scale would not meet the object in view—the gaining of decisive results against Austria-Germany. If, on the other hand, the surplus divisions were placed in France more of them would become available, because if there were any serious dangers of her own defences being broken through, Germany would not be likely to detach troops for the purpose of invading Great Britain, and therefore we could be satisfied with fewer divisions for Home

Defence. In other words, by having our full strength on the Western Front, Great Britain would be automatically protected, and at the same time stronger forces could be assembled for offensive action than in any other theatre. It was calculated that, after making allowance for various uncertainties as to when divisions would be ready, we could have in France by the spring a minimum of 42 and a maximum of 59 divisions, whereas for an offensive in the Balkans, for example, the minimum would be 15 and the maximum 29 divisions.

Besides the question of troops there were other factors to be taken into account before deciding to start a new campaign. The provision of sea-transport was already imposing a heavy strain on the mercantile marine, and with the limited number of ships available it would take many months to convey a large army by sea to a new theatre, while the task of maintaining it there might later prove to be impossible. There was also a limit to the power of the Navy to escort the transports conveying troops and the vast quantities of stores required for their maintenance; to open, administer, and guard new bases; and to carry out all the multifarious duties devolving on it. Special types of equipment and land-transport would also be needed, and these would take a long time to procure even if they could be obtained at all.

With respect to the assertion that the enemy's defences on the Western Front could never be effectively breached, the memorandum pointed out that by means of adequate preparation on their part and inadequate preparation on ours, the Central Powers had gained important advantages at the outset which the armies in France could not possibly have prevented, and which, as in all such cases, would take the Entente a long time to counteract. Chiefly owing to our unreadiness, and to the lack of unity of control, the efforts of the Entente had necessarily been piecemeal, and some of their strength had been wasted in the vain endeavour to accomplish secondary objects without sufficient means, in the Dardanelles for example. Despite all this, the Entente Powers were now attaining to an approximate equilibrium of force, and the ability to employ the whole of it simultaneously. By next year they would be capable of developing a marked superiority of force, and of using it in a manner which would impose a much greater strain upon the enemy's power of resistance than any to which it had been subjected hitherto.

In the autumn just past, even though Russia was failing and Italy was tied to her own frontier, the enemy had been reduced to the defensive on both main fronts, and in the West he barely escaped a serious defeat. The dominating advantage of interior lines hitherto enjoyed by him would disappear when he lost his power to throw reserves from side to side at will. When he was " all out " on the defensive, and was hard pressed by superior forces, his sting would be drawn and success against him at any one point might well be the prelude to disaster.[1] Judging from what had occurred in the autumn there seemed to be no good grounds for supposing that the Entente Powers would not be capable of exerting this pressure in 1916, if they developed their full strength, determined to apply it simultaneously against the Austro-Germans, and agreed to act on a generally-accepted plan.

The enemy's line extending from the North Sea to the Mediterranean could not be effectively turned on either flank. The attempt to turn it by way of the Dardanelles had just been abandoned; the Balkan

[1] This was a remarkably accurate forecast of what actually happened in 1918.

approach was even more impracticable ; and the northern flank was quite impossible. Consequently the only alternative to direct attack was what the memorandum described as a policy of investment. The possibility of gaining victory by it depended mainly upon the power of the Entente to make the investment complete, to outstay the enemy financially, and to deprive him of the food and other supplies necessary for the maintenance of his resistance. Having regard to the interests of neutral states, it was considered doubtful whether the investment could be made complete, and in any case so many troops would have to be dispersed defensively along the investment line that no strong general offensive would be possible at the same time. If the Balkan States had joined the Entente, or remained strictly neutral, investment would have been easier to accomplish. As matters stood, the footing which the Central Powers had recently secured in the Balkans placed them in a strong position in regard to food and certain other requirements, and also, perhaps, in some degrees as regards reserves of men. On the whole, the conditions were not deemed favourable to success by investment, and at the best it would be a long and wearying process.

With these considerations before them, the General Staff came to the conclusion that " a strong, vigorous, simultaneous and sustained pressure by all the Allies on existing main fronts, as early as possible next spring, is not only a reasonable plan but practically the only one offering any reasonable prospect of defeating the armies of the Central Powers next year. If no effort be spared in preparation, and if the execution be carried out whole-heartedly, the prospects of success are considered at least sufficient to justify the attempt." As concentration of strength was the essence of the plan, existing commitments in secondary theatres were to be reduced to a minimum and every available division was to be sent to France by the following spring.

As to the probable action of the enemy, it was thought that he would hold the Italian front defensively, try to induce us to detach troops to the East, and mass as strong forces as possible for an offensive either against France or Russia, which could be timed to anticipate the offensive of the Entente. If this forecast proved to be correct (as in fact it did), the situation would be suitably met by the dispositions recommended. The only other courses open to the enemy would be to stand on the defensive, holding on to what he had got, or to enter on a career of conquest in the East. If he adopted the latter course the offensive operations recommended would quickly compel him to recall his forces, and the Entente would reap the benefits of having obliged him to change his plans. If he chose the former course, which would be contrary to all his principles of war, the Entente must either defeat him on one or other of his main fronts, or would sit down to a trial of endurance.

It will be seen from the above that although British G.H.Q. in France and the Imperial General Staff at the War Office approached the problem from different angles, both arrived at the same solution, and this agreed with the conclusions reached at the allied military conference at Chantilly. Government acceptance of the policy proposed continued, however, to hang fire, and therefore on taking up the duties of C.I.G.S., on December 23, I placed before the War Committee my recommendations as to what should be done. To a great extent they were a résumé of those contained in the War Office memorandum just quoted. I asked that they might be approved, or that the Committee would say what measures they desired to substitute for them. They were to the following effect:—

From the point of view of the British Empire, France and Flanders were to be regarded as the main theatre of operations, and our efforts were to be directed to undertaking offensive operations there in close co-operation with the Allies and in the greatest possible strength.

Egypt was to be allotted eight divisions for its defence. (This I considered to be in excess of actual requirements, but Lord Kitchener thought differently, and as there were abundant troops in the country who could not for the moment be got away the estimate was allowed to stand. It was considerably reduced two or three months later.)

In Mesopotamia the policy was to be defensive (subject of course to the relief of the beleaguered garrison at Kut-el-Amara); and for the present the existing garrison of India was to suffice for the defence of that country.

The operations in East Africa were to be carried out on the general lines already sanctioned, and with the forces already allotted.

The recommendations were discussed and, except for some verbal alterations, were approved on December 28. The principle of aiming at decisive results on the Western Front, which had been laid down in August, 1914, was thus reaffirmed, and for the first time in the war a policy governing all theatres of operations was authoritatively prescribed. This was a great step in advance, and, coupled with a decision of the previous day to withdraw the whole of the troops from the Gallipoli Peninsula, was an encouraging proof of the readiness of Ministers to give to military advice on military matters the attention which it deserved.

Broadly speaking, the policy approved amounted to

the application of maximum strength in the West, subject only to such reductions as might be rendered necessary by defensive considerations in the East. Nominally it held good for about two years, and during that period the General Staff endeavoured, with varying success, to keep it in the foreground as the cardinal basis upon which all action taken in prosecution of the war should primarily rest. Actually, as the narrative will show, it never received complete ministerial approbation and support, even in 1916, whilst throughout the greater part of 1917, with the exception of a few brief intervals, the consistent aim of the Prime Minister, Mr. Lloyd George, was to replace it by a policy of another kind. Eventually, at the end of January, 1918, he achieved his object, the new policy being to undertake a decisive campaign against the Turks in Palestine, in preference to the fullest possible concentration in the West. Within less than two months the British armies in France had to meet an overwhelming attack, and the policy which I had from the first recommended had then to be hurriedly readopted as the only means of staving off defeat.

Some of the early difficulties encountered by the General Staff in maintaining the policy sanctioned on December 28 are shown in the following extracts from letters written by me to Sir Douglas Haig, whom it was necessary to keep informed on the subject :—

5 *January*, 1916.

* * * * *

As you know, the War Committee last week approved of certain conclusions which I sent to you. Mr. Balfour, as a member of the Committee, also approved of them, but rather against his inclinations. Not being able to bring the War Committee round to his point of view, he has now written a long memorandum to the Cabinet arguing quite contrary to the War Committee's conclusions. He has several supporters, as every other member of the Cabinet always has no matter what the question may be. Lord K. asked me to write a rejoinder, but this I have declined to do. I have taken up the position that the General Staff views have already been put forward at sufficient length, and that I have no more to say as regards the strategy to be adopted; that the recommendations of the General Staff have been approved by the War Committee; and until the War Committee tell me that they intend to withdraw their approval, there is no action for me to take. But I do not think they will withdraw, or that anything will come of the Balfour memorandum. It is, however, all very unsettling, and much of my time is taken up in *talking*, and in explaining what these people cannot understand and sometimes do not wish to understand. In course of time there may be an improvement. What we really want is a big success somewhere, and we shall then be in a stronger position. We have not yet been able to get this success, but all being well we will get it in due course.

As regards the date of the offensive that, as you say, must depend upon when the various Allies are ready, and as to Russia I am sending Callwell to Russian G.H.Q. on Monday next to find out as best he can what the state of affairs there really is and when they will be ready. I hope to get some good and useful information from him, which I shall pass on to you. But this will not be until about the end of the month.

The Russian General Staff are rather troublesome. Alexeieff, as you probably know, keeps advocating a big offensive movement through the Balkans, while the Grand Duke in the Caucasus is always urging us to make a big offensive movement in Asiatic Turkey and Persia in co-operation with his offensive in Caucasia and North Persia. Of course we have no intention of doing any of these things. To make matters worse, certain irresponsible people belonging to the Foreign Office, such as temporary-commissioned officers and military attachés in these distant regions, busy themselves with putting before the Russian commanders their ideas as to how we could and should operate in these outlying parts of the world. I am gradually sitting upon these young gentlemen, and getting every one to mind his own business. Lord K. is rather amused with me in the matter, and says I must go carefully. I do not propose to go carefully in so far as concerns irresponsible people dabbling in questions of high military policy. But it will take me a little time to put matters straight. It is hard enough to have to deal with Allies, and when individual officers push their own particular views forward things are of course made much worse. I am afraid I am giving you many accounts of my troubles, but I want you to know what we have to contend against so that you may not think that I am unduly neglecting matters in France. Most of my troubles lie outside the War Office. Everyone inside is playing up well.

* * * * *

13th January, 1916.

* * * * *

There is a fairly strong party in the Cabinet opposed to offensive operations on your front in the spring, or indeed at any time. One wants to go to the Balkans, another to Baghdad, and another to allow the Germans "to attack us." I have used all the arguments which you or any other soldier could use, but not with complete success. In the War Committee decision I sent you a few days ago you will see that we are to make every effort "to prepare" for offensive operations in the spring. In the original draft I put we were to make every effort to "undertake" offensive operations in the spring. By a decision made to-day (which I will send you later) it has now been watered down to the effect that we are "to prepare" for offensive operations in the spring, but without committing ourselves definitely to them. In general there is a great deal of wobbling, and it is bound up with the size of the Army, a matter which is not yet settled. . . .

The terms of the War Committee decision as amended on January 13 were that every effort was to be made to prepare for carrying out an offensive in the spring in the main theatre of operations, and in the greatest possible strength, *but it was not to be assumed that this offensive was as yet fully decided upon*. The military authorities were thus left, not with a specific policy commanding the full support of all State departments which it might concern, but with a formula which, in the endeavour to meet the objections of everybody, settled nothing and was liable to be interpreted in different ways by the different Ministers who were parties to it, and as best fitted in with their individual wishes. Naturally, if circumstances underwent any material change before the policy as proposed by the General Staff was put into execution it would, as in all such cases, have to be suitably altered, or perhaps abandoned altogether, but in the meantime it should have been definitely accepted or definitely rejected, and not qualified by words which threw doubts upon its eventual execution. "If the trumpet give an uncertain sound, who shall prepare himself to the battle?"

On February 21 the enemy commenced the attack designed to effect the capture of Verdun and the destruction of the French armies. He realized, of course, the advantage of dealing with his opponents one at a time, and no doubt hoped that even if his original object were not achieved the attack would at least compel the British armies to counter-attack before proper preparations for it could be made. These results were not attained. The French lines were not breached, the French armies were not destroyed, while the British armies took over the defence of a larger sector of the front so as to allow of French reinforcements being sent to Verdun, and then continued their preparations for the concerted Anglo-French offensive which later became known as the battle of the Somme.

On March 12, when the battle of Verdun had been in progress for about three weeks, the military chiefs again met at Chantilly, and resolved that the general offensive agreed upon by them in December should be started with as little delay as possible. In order that it might not be unduly hurried, the exact date of commencement was in each case to be fixed by the respective Commanders-in-Chief.

On March 27 another conference, composed of Ministers and their professional advisers, was held at Paris, and General Joffre then explained what had been settled at Chantilly. He dwelt upon the importance of Russia, Italy, and Britain concentrating their full strength on the main fronts, and in particular he urged that all British troops not indispensable to other theatres should be sent to France at once. M. Briand, who presided, proposed that Ministers should give their attention during the conference to diplomatic and economic questions, and that military affairs should be left in the hands of the military chiefs. This course was adopted and the operations were not discussed, but Ministers and soldiers combined in laying stress upon the need for close co-operation between the different armies, as well as in the manufacture and distribution of guns, ammunition, and other kinds of war material.

As the non-committal policy formulated by the War Committee on January 13 had not yet been replaced by anything of a more definite character, I asked the Committee on return from the Paris conference to say whether the Chantilly resolution on March 12 had their approval or not, because it was necessary that the British Commander-in-Chief should be informed. I represented that he was well acquainted with the state of our resources, both in men and material, had all the information available about the enemy and the Allies, and that he ought to be trusted to undertake such operations as were appropriate and to select the date when they could most suitably begin. It would also become necessary, if the Committee were unable to approve of the resolution in question, that the Allies should be informed and told what alternative plan was suggested in its place. Realizing that the matter must now be settled one way or another, and that there was in fact no alternative that could be put forward, the Committee at last gave authority for the British armies to co-operate in the manner recommended. Exactly in what terms the authority was given I am unable to say, not having any record of it, but to the best of my recollection it was unanimous, or at any rate was generally accepted.

The decision was, however, not really approved by those Ministers who, from the first, had been opposed to offensive action in the West, and soon afterwards they called upon the General Staff to report whether, in the event of Russia being driven back during the summer towards Petrograd, we could assist her by taking action in some other theatre. To be asked when occupied in making arrangements for a great battle to turn one's attention to an entirely different plan, designed to meet a situation which had not yet arisen, was both vexatious and discouraging. It proved that Ministers were still indifferent to the necessity of adhering to a decision once taken, or did not understand the disadvantages, strategical, tactical, and administrative, that changes of plan always entail. The contingency postulated had not been overlooked when other plans were being examined, and little more could be said about it than that our main object must always be to co-operate with the Allies in the defeat of Germany, and that there was no theatre where we could do that so effectively as in France. This was not merely the view of the British General Staff but had been ratified by the General Staffs of all the Entente Powers, who agreed that in the event of Russia falling into serious difficulties the best way in which we could help her would be to combine with the French in offensive action on the Western Front so as to hold fast such hostile divisions as might be there, and draw in the same direction as many more divisions as possible. This advice prevailed, but it did not satisfy the Ministers who called for it, and apparently nothing would satisfy them short of a passive defence in France, and that was not feasible.

Some Ministers were, moreover, eager to adopt a proposal of M. Briand to use the surplus British divisions then in Egypt for offensive operations in Macedonia, instead of sending them to the Western Front as the General Staff wished to do. Thanks to the support of Mr. Asquith, Sir Edward Grey, and some other members of the War Committee the latter course was followed, but on the other hand none of the 200,000 Anglo-French troops already in Macedonia were taken away, and for this misfortune the French and not the British Government was responsible. In other respects the principle of concentration in the decisive theatre was well observed —for the first time in the war—and the British armies in France increased from a total of 956,000 men in January to 1,400,000 in July.

On June 1 the General Staff commenced to issue a secret weekly summary of events in the various theatres of war, so as to keep Ministers systematically informed of what was taking place, and assist them in appreciating correctly what it meant. The first of these summaries contained a review of the war from August, 1914, to date, and the following extracts from it will be of interest as showing what the views of the General Staff were at the time :—

To understand the plan underlying the German attacks at Verdun, of which the end is not yet in sight, it is necessary to recall the principles which have guided German strategy since the beginning of the war. When war broke out there were only two nations in Europe which were prepared for it in the sense that they were able at short notice to place the whole of their armed strength in the field. Those two nations were Germany and France, and of the two Germany was superior in population, wealth, and military resources of all kinds. She thus secured an enormous advantage at the outset, and the history of all wars shows that to deprive an enemy of advantages once gained, time, patience, and resolution are demanded. No better illustration of this can be found than the South African War, in which a comparatively small force of Boer farmers successfully resisted the efforts of the British Empire for two and a half years. Our state of unpreparedness for that war enabled the enemy to overrun Natal and parts of Cape Colony and to besiege our advanced bases, thus dislocating all our plans and entailing a war both of much longer duration and on a far greater scale than might otherwise have been the case.

Germany had been preparing for the present war for more than forty years, and although she did not conceal either her object in making war or her intention to use any methods however ruthless in bringing it to a speedy conclusion, yet the universal knowledge of her designs did not lead any nation in Europe, with the single exception of France, to take adequate steps to meet the threat. When war broke out England had neither the necessary men nor material, while, although they had great resources in men, the other Powers had not the material or equipment for placing or maintaining their men in the field. The result was that Germany quadrupled her field forces in a very short time, while her enemies could only very slowly and laboriously organize their resources for war.

Certain other factors have combined to render the conduct of the war by the Entente still more difficult, the first of these arising from the grouping of the rival alliances. The intervention of Great Britain was undoubtedly a heavy blow to Germany, but the latter soon found an effective means of discounting this by persuading Turkey to throw in her lot with the Central Powers. The difficulties inherent in securing co-operation and assistance between countries so widely separated as were those of the Entente were thus greatly increased ; and, in addition, we have had to employ for the defence of our Eastern possessions large numbers of troops which would have been invaluable on the Western Front.

A further difficulty has arisen from the fact that the Entente, unlike the Central Powers, have never agreed to submit the conduct of the war to one central directing authority. The periodical conferences of the Entente are in no way comparable as an instrument for the control of military operations with the permanent authority exercised by the German General Head-quarters.[1]

[1] This authority was apparently less powerful than was supposed at the time.

England has invariably given unselfish co-operation, but her allies have been inclined to follow divergent aims having no direct bearing on the defeat of the Central Powers. Russia insists upon gaining Constantinople, and has thereby destroyed all hope of a separate peace with Turkey, and is apparently as intent on beating Turkey as she is on beating Germany. Italy has refrained from declaring war on Germany, and has thus created various difficulties, impairing the sense of mutual confidence which should exist between the members of an alliance. Serbia by her selfish policy rendered an understanding with Bulgaria and with other Balkan Powers impossible. France is responsible for keeping a quarter of a million splendid fighting troops in the Balkans for what appear to be political reasons.

The action of the Entente has accordingly been hampered by the neglect of that fundamental principle of war which can never be neglected without serious detriment, namely, the principle of concentration at the decisive point. Notwithstanding the fact that the Entente were confronted with an enemy far better prepared than they were themselves, they have greatly reduced their main forces by sending detachments to various parts of the world, without, in some cases, sufficient justification.

Germany realized at the outset that it was necessary to concentrate her whole available strength first against France with the object of gaining a decisive victory over the only enemy which, by its state of preparedness, constituted an immediate danger. That accomplished she could deal with Russia at her leisure. She failed to accomplish this object when she was defeated on the Marne, and her subsequent efforts to break the Allied line in Flanders failed to retrieve the situation. She had, however, dealt the Western Allies a blow sufficient to throw them on the defensive for the time being.

Thenceforth she adopted a defensive rôle in France and concentrated all her efforts on overthrowing Russia. The campaign of 1915 in Russia attained a considerable measure of success, but it did not achieve its full purpose. The Russian armies remained intact, their morale was unshaken, and if given time they would recover and be as formidable as ever.

During the autumn and winter of 1915–16 the Central Powers undertook the invasion of Serbia and Montenegro. Their objects were to gain Bulgaria as an ally, to secure direct communication with Turkey, to remove altogether the Serbian danger and thus relieve the pressure on Austria, to discourage Rumania from intervention, to create fresh difficulties for the Entente, and in particular for Great Britain, and to induce them to divert troops to subsidiary theatres of war. In this they succeeded. They may have hoped also that they would be able to use Bulgarian and Turkish troops against Russia or France.

However necessary it may have been to undertake this campaign, it was undoubtedly not an alternative to the two plans of campaign which, as shown above, had failed to achieve their objects. Germany must have expected that her enemies would undertake a combined offensive in the spring of 1916, but no doubt she believed the offensive power of those enemies to vary greatly. The Russians had ample reserves of men, but were deficient in equipment and guns, particularly of heavy guns and ammunition. They had besides been driven back into a country where their communications were far inferior to those of Poland, where the railways ran in diverging directions, and mutual support was thereby rendered very difficult.

Our information is to the effect that Germany, having provided the Eastern Front with heavy artillery and developed the road and rail communications, regarded with equanimity the prospect of a Russian offensive. The British were becoming increasingly formidable, they had still large reserves of men available and had proved themselves stubborn fighters, but their army was an improvised one, containing a large proportion of inexperienced and inadequately trained officers, and its supply of heavy artillery and ammunition was probably insufficient for a prolonged offensive. While an offensive against either of these enemies appeared uninviting, it was probably considered possible to hold them in check with inferior forces for the time being without incurring undue risk.

The French on the other hand are more formidable in attack than in defence, and were provided with the resources in material and equipment required for offensive operations. Moreover, their reserves of men were known to be diminishing, and if a stunning blow could be struck against them, and their reserves be exhausted, it was reasonable to expect that at the least the offensive power of the Entente in the West would be crippled for 1916.

The Italians possessed large reserves of men, but were ill-provided with heavy artillery and ammunition. If they were allowed time to accumulate these they might become a more serious menace to Austria. The disposition of the Italian armies made them peculiarly sensitive to a blow struck through the Trentino, for it would threaten the communications with Italy of the armies on the Isonzo front, and if pressed successfully would force these armies to withdraw and even to abandon Venetia.

The German plan of campaign for 1916 was, therefore, to concentrate all the available reserves of the Central Powers against France and Italy, with the object of dealing each of them so heavy a blow that they would be unable to undertake any serious offensive action in the future. Germany would then be able to concentrate at will against her other enemies. In this she is simply following the old military maxim of " defeating the enemy in detail." The results of her campaign, if successful, will be to place her in an even more favourable situation than that held by her in the autumn of 1915. Two of her enemies will be reduced to impotence, and further successes may then be attained in Russia. Such a situation might well induce the Entente to discuss terms of peace before the winter.

This plan has, however, received a severe check in the failure to take Verdun. The Germans have now continued the attack for fourteen weeks. Their object in continuing it after their first attempt had failed is probably twofold. In the first place, it enables them to retain the initiative, and it prevents the French from concentrating their still available reserves for an offensive. The political and sentimental reasons for holding Verdun compel the French to make its retention their first care. The longer the Germans continue to threaten it, the less danger there is of a French offensive in the future. Verdun may also fall in the end, and this may exercise a great moral and political effect on the situation. In the second place, a continuance of the attack is the only means of avoiding the disastrous consequences on German public opinion of an admission of failure. It would seem, in fact, that the Germans chose the best alternative open to them. To change the front of attack to any other part of the Western Front would have meant great loss of time, and would have offered no better chance of success. It is true that this course entails losses in excess of those incurred by the French, but these will not have been incurred in vain if they succeed in exhausting the remaining French reserves.

The successful defence of Verdun has already affected the whole German plan of campaign, for so much time has been lost in the undertaking that it is doubtful whether Germany will be able to achieve her object in France in time to gain any success in Russia—a project which was probably part of her original plan.

In order to make the attack on Verdun the Germans concentrated in that area, in addition to the units normally there, 8 divisions, of which

2 were taken from the British front, 2 from the area between the Somme and Oise, and 4 from the Central Reserve. Since the commencement of the battle 4 divisions have been brought up from the Central Reserve, 3½ from Champagne, 3 from the Oise front, 3½ from the Woevre, 2 from the British front, 1 from Alsace, and 1, or possibly 2, from Russia, while other parts of the Western Front have received 2 divisions from the Balkans, and 1, or more probably 2, from Russia.

At the same time it must be recognized that the enemy has obtained a considerable measure of success, and that further successes are still within his grasp. He has already reduced the offensive power of the French Army by about one-half, and if the attack is continued on the same scale for another two months and the Entente remain inactive, he may cripple the Entente offensive power in the West, since by that time the French would not be in a position to undertake an offensive at all, and an unsupported British offensive could in that case achieve very little. If, therefore, the Entente undertook no offensive action this summer the enemy would gain his primary object in the West, that of reducing the French Army to comparative impotence.

Summary of the situation in the main theatres of War. France has had to withstand a very heavy attack for more than three months, without direct support from her allies. This attack, if allowed to continue very much longer, will exhaust her remaining resources in men.

Russia considers she is compelled by circumstances to assume the offensive, but owing to her lack of artillery and ammunition, her defective communications, the want of organization, and the corruption of her military and civil administration, it would be unwise to expect great results from any operations she may undertake.

Italy has received a severe blow which has already limited her offensive power and may render her unable to assume the offensive this year. . . . Serbia has suffered a crushing defeat. Her army is composed of fine material and is fully armed and equipped. It is, however, a beaten army, and it is doubtful whether it has yet fully recovered from its defeat. Its training in the use of its new rifles and guns is still incomplete. . . .

England has not yet fully completed the organization and preparation of her resources. Her New Armies suffer from the disadvantages inherent in all improvisations. The officers are, to a great extent, amateurs, the non-commissioned officers are also inexperienced, and discipline is dependent rather on goodwill than on training. The supply of heavy artillery is still below the standard of requirements.

As against these disadvantages, which make it at least doubtful whether the Entente can obtain a favourable decision of the war this year, must be set certain factors which render their prospects for the future distinctly favourable.

The Germans have suffered a check at Verdun which cannot be concealed either from neutrals or from their own people. Their losses have been heavy, and they have already drawn on their younger classes of recruits to a greater extent than France has done.

In Russia they are holding a very long line with forces barely sufficient for the purpose. A Russian offensive will entail a severe strain on the armies of the Central Powers on that front, and should at any rate prevent troops being transferred to the Western and Southern Fronts.

The success of the Austrians has only been achieved by the employment of 8 more divisions than have hitherto been concentrated in that theatre, and as long as Italy can retain on her front the present number of Austrian troops she is rendering more important services to the Entente than she has yet done.

England has up to the present time made only a part of the effort of which she is capable. She has not yet placed in the field a half of the heavy artillery she is manufacturing, her supply of munitions is increasing very rapidly, and she still has troops to place in the field in France. Great improvement is being made in the training of all ranks, and the army as a whole is daily acquiring experience and gaining cohesion.

If the Entente have no immediate prospect of achieving great results, the enemy has still less. Within the last year the Central Powers have increased their heavy artillery more rapidly than have the Entente, but this has been done by utilizing captured Russian and Serbian guns, a source of supply which is at present exhausted. The Entente have far greater resources both in men and material, and their margin of superiority over the enemy will tend to increase. Germany has besides many embarrassments. Turkey has suffered a series of defeats, and is more nearly exhausted than any of the other belligerents ; Bulgaria is reported to be dissatisfied ; Austria's supply of men is gravely depleted.

In such conditions the knowledge that their enemies were assuming the offensive, and that their own armies would be forced to act on the defensive, might have an effect out of all proportion to the actual military results achieved.

Conclusions. The present military situation shows that the armies of the Entente should take such active measures this year as will relieve the pressure upon France and Italy, but they do not possess a superiority either in men or material sufficient to warrant the hope that decisive results will be obtained. In order to obtain these results it is necessary to inflict a crushing defeat on the enemy's main armies.

Great Britain is, as always, by far the most important factor in the Entente, and upon us will rest the chief responsibility for success or failure, but, as stated at the beginning of this paper, in order to develop to the full the resources of the Empire we require time, patience, and resolution. We must have a much greater amount of heavy artillery than we now possess, and be able to turn out an almost unlimited amount of ammunition.

There is no cause for doubt as to the ultimate result, provided the proper measures are taken by the Entente. These are:—

(*a*) Unselfish co-operation and co-ordinated direction.

(*b*) No one Power must remain idle while others are being exhausted.

(*c*) The maximum number of men must be placed on the main fronts and commitments in all other theatres reduced to a minimum, even to the extent of taking considerable risks in those theatres.

There is nothing new in any of these doctrines. They have been consistently advocated by the General Staff for nine months past, and recent events fully prove the truth of them.

In the above review only military considerations have been taken into account. Those of a financial, industrial, political, or economical nature have been omitted. Their importance is recognized to be very great, but the General Staff did not feel themselves qualified to discuss them.[1]

---

[1] It is of interest to notice that the above views with respect to German plans correspond very closely with a memorandum written by General Falkenhayn in December, 1915, and published in his book, "General Head-quarters 1914–1916 and its Critical Decisions," page 209 *et seq.* In the memorandum he says that the main factor in the situation was "the enormous hold that England still has on her allies." After explaining why England could not be struck directly, he goes on: "As I have already insisted, the strain on France has almost reached the breaking-point, though it is certainly borne with the most remarkable devotion. If we succeeded in opening the eyes of her people to the fact that in a military sense they have nothing more to hope for, that breaking-point would be reached and England's best sword knocked out of her hand." He accordingly selected Verdun as the German objective, "for the retention of which the French General Staff would

The question as to the date on which the Anglo-French offensive on the Somme should begin required careful consideration. Sir Douglas Haig naturally wished to postpone it as long as possible, so that his armies might become stronger and his stock of munitions more plentiful. Moreover, a large proportion of his officers and men were not fully trained, and the longer the attack could be delayed the more efficient would they become. On the other hand, the Germans continued to press the French at Verdun, while in May the Austrians gained important successes over the Italians in the Trentino, and it was clear that the strain on France and Italy might become too great to be borne unless early steps were taken to relieve it. In June, Brussiloff's celebrated attack on the Austrians caused Germany to transfer some of her troops from the West to the East, but this did not materially ease the position at Verdun. It was therefore agreed between Generals Haig and Joffre that the combined French and British offensive should not be postponed beyond the end of June, and it accordingly commenced on July 1.

Remembering the dissatisfaction displayed by Ministers at the end of 1915 because the operations of that year had not come up to their expectations, the General Staff took the precaution to make quite clear beforehand the nature of the success which the Somme campaign might yield. In the " Summary " of June 29 it was stated, in reference to Brussiloff's victories over the Austrians and their beneficial effect on the position in Italy, that " the

be compelled to throw in every man they have. If they do so the forces of France will bleed to death—as there can be no question of a voluntary withdrawal—whether we reach our goal or not."

It will further be noticed that particular attention was drawn in the review to the necessity for central control and co-ordinated direction.

necessity of relieving pressure on the French army at Verdun remains, and is more urgent than ever. This is, therefore, the first object to be attained by the combined British and French offensive. The second object is to inflict as heavy losses as possible upon the German armies." Incidentally, of course, a third object was to prevent any further transfer of German troops from the Western Front, and in that way to assist our Allies on the other fronts.

The endeavour to prevent disappointment did not quite succeed, and on July 29 I wrote to Sir Douglas Haig as follows :—

The powers that be are beginning to get a little uneasy in regard to the situation. The casualties are mounting up, and Ministers are wondering whether we are likely to get a proper return for them. I do my best to keep the general situation to the front, and to explain what may be the effect of our efforts, and to ask what alternative could be adopted. I also try to make them think in German of the present situation. But they will persist in asking me whether *I* think a loss of, say, 300,000 men will lead to really great results, because if not we ought to be content with something less than what we are now doing, and they constantly inquire why we are fighting and the French are not. . . . In general, what is bothering them is the probability that we may soon have to face a bill of between 200,000 and 300,000 casualties with no very great gains additional to the present. It is thought that the primary object—the relief of Verdun—has to some extent been achieved.

In order to allay the anxiety that prevailed, I took advantage of a Cabinet meeting on August 1 to review the results recently gained by the Entente, and, to quote from a letter sent to Haig after the meeting :—

I pointed out that six weeks ago the Austrians were nearing the Italian Plains and Italy was calling for assistance ; that Russia was on the same front as that to which she was driven back last year ; that Verdun was on the point of falling and the French public were loudly demanding action from us. I explained that all this had been greatly changed to our advantage, and said that the situation was never so good, in general, for us as at the present time, and that thanks mainly to the Somme offensive, which had prevented a single German from being sent to the Eastern Front, Russia had been left free to pursue her victorious career. Also, that Verdun had been attacked only once this month and not at all for some time now, and that many heavy guns had apparently been taken away from there as well as 3 divisions. Also, that Germany had found it necessary to bring up some 27 divisions to the Somme in order to hold her front, and that, notwithstanding all the importance she attached, *vide* documents we have captured, to regaining the lost ground on the Somme, she had entirely failed to regain any of it. . . . I said that we were now engaged in quite a new kind of warfare and that decisive results could not be expected in twenty-four hours nor in twenty-four days, and that relentless pressure on all fronts was the proper course to pursue and was promising good results by the winter. . . . No one of the War Committee [1] made any comment on anything I said, and as far as they are concerned I should say that they are thoroughly satisfied. The trouble is with a few outsiders. . . . L.G. is all right provided I can say that *I* am satisfied, and to enable me to say this it is necessary you should keep me acquainted with your views. . . . If I have to depend almost entirely upon Press communiqués my opinion is not much more valuable than that of anyone else. . . .

Haig at once sent me a statement of his views and remarked that " any weakening of purpose now would certainly have deplorable effect on our Allies' trust in us, on the general faith in our power to achieve victory, and even on the confidence of our own army."

While certain Ministers thought that Haig was doing too much fighting, the French military authorities complained that he was doing too little. I wrote to him on August 29,

Several hints have reached me that Joffre and Co. think you are going too slowly. I spoke to Mr. Lloyd George [2] about this the

[1] i.e. as distinct from the Cabinet as a whole.

[2] Now War Minister.

other day and he repeated what he has said many times lately, that he thinks you are playing absolutely the right game, and doing your job in absolutely the right way. You can attach any importance you choose to his opinion, but it will be satisfactory to you to know that he at any rate thinks you are doing quite the right thing. All the War Committee think the same. M. Briand told Mr. Asquith last week that he was delighted with what you had done on the Somme. Of course we all know that for many reasons you should get going again on a big scale as soon as you can, but we also know that it is useless going off before you are properly ready. Indeed, it is much more serious than being merely useless.

In spite of the great struggle that was taking place on the Somme, Ministers more than once suggested to me that the Mesopotamia operations should be extended to Baghdad, while the French Government, usually supported by Mr. Lloyd George, continued to advocate the expansion of the campaign in Macedonia. They were particularly insistent upon the dispatch of more troops to the Balkans when, after joining the Entente in August, Rumania entered upon a campaign in Transylvania beyond her power to carry out. The situation was very similar to that of 1915, when Anglo-French divisions were sent to the assistance of Serbia, and the proposal to help Rumania with troops was likely to be no less futile. The War Committee was naturally reluctant to reject the French proposal outright, and a British division from France, with some details from Egypt, aggregating about 40,000 men, were sent. It was an unfortunate measure which brought not the least benefit to Rumania, while it aggravated the dispersion of forces from which the Entente were already suffering. These and other proposals for extending operations in the East led to the waste of much time and energy at head-quarters in London, but by one means or another they were kept in check, and usually the majority of the War

Committee and of the Cabinet well supported the military authorities in trying to make the Somme offensive a real success.

When unfavourable weather brought the operations to an end about the middle of November the three objects we had set out to attain had been achieved and, in the words of Sir Douglas Haig's dispatch :—

Any one of these three results is in itself sufficient to justify the Somme battle. The attainment of all three of them affords ample compensation for the splendid efforts of our troops and for the sacrifices made by ourselves and our Allies. They have brought us a long step forward towards the final victory of the Allied cause. . . . During the period under review a steady deterioration took place in the morale of large numbers of the enemy's troops. Many of them, it is true, fought with the greatest determination, even in the latest encounters, but the resistance of still larger numbers became latterly decidedly feebler than it had been in the earlier stages of the battle. . . . As our advance progressed, four-fifths of the total number of divisions engaged on the Western Front were thrown one after another into the Somme battle, some of them twice, and some three times ; and towards the end of the operations, when the weather unfortunately broke, there can be no doubt that his power of resistance had been very seriously diminished.

As to the future, the Commander-in-Chief said :—

The enemy's power has not yet been broken, nor is it yet possible to form an estimate of the time the war may last before the objects for which the Allies are fighting have been attained. But the Somme battle has placed beyond doubt the ability of the Allies to gain those objects.

With these views the General Staff in London were in general agreement. The position as seen by them, and reported to the War Committee, in the month of October was that the enemy had been dealt a staggering blow [1]

[1] Referring to the position on the Western Front as he saw it in September, General Ludendorff says in his "War Memories," page 266, that "The loss of ground up to date appeared to me of little

from which he would find it very hard to recover, but there was still much to be done before his final overthrow could be accomplished. More than two years had elapsed since the struggle began and we were yet far from putting into it the full efforts of which we were capable. Peace customs and considerations were still too predominant, and there was no sufficient recognition of the fact that we could not expect to win through with anything less than the full services of every man and woman in the country. The people themselves were ready enough to give their services without stint, but some Ministers did not seem to think so, and hesitated to initiate those comprehensive measures which the military position required, and which the nation, if properly informed, would have willingly accepted.

In order that suitable preparations for the future might be undertaken, a fresh review of the situation was laid before the Government on October 26. It showed that the Entente forces in Macedonia, now amounting to some 300,000 men, were holding a certain number of Bulgarian and German troops, but were not in the least likely to achieve anything of real value. In Egypt the operations against the Senussi were drawing to a satisfactory close, while on the eastern side the Suez Canal was now secure and arrangements were well advanced for disposing troops beyond it as a more economical

importance in itself. We could stand that; but the question how this and the progressive falling off of our fighting power of which it was symptomatic, was to be prevented, was of immense importance."

Again, on page 278: "The fighting had made the most extraordinary demands both on commanders and troops. . . . The troops were getting exhausted. Everything was cut as fine as possible. The strain on our nerves in Pless was terrible."

system of defence. In Mesopotamia the communications had been put on a proper footing, and the force would soon be ready to meet any calls likely to be made upon it. In East Africa the ports along the entire coast had been occupied and the enemy everywhere driven into the interior. The ravages made by sickness had necessitated a temporary suspension of operations, but it was hoped that all white troops would be dispensed with by the end of the year. In all four theatres, therefore, a great improvement had been effected as compared with the situation at the end of 1915, except in the Balkan Peninsula, and there it would never be satisfactory.

On the Western Front the enemy was inferior to the Entente in numbers, and also in aircraft, artillery, and probably in the supply of ammunition. His armies had been driven from positions of great strength, and compelled to prepare new lines only to lose them in turn, and in spite of stringent orders to hold them at all costs. The demoralizing effects of these continuous retirements were aggravated by the ever-diminishing support which the hard-pressed infantry received from the aircraft and artillery, and in general the enemy was being made to feel much the same anxieties as those we ourselves had experienced in the autumn and winter of 1914. This did not mean that he was yet on the verge of a collapse, any more than our retreat two years before meant that our resistance had broken down. But his future prospects were worse, for he had no great undeveloped resources as we then had, and his present increase in material bore no relation to our own. In January, 1916, we had in France 1,938 field guns and 785 howitzers and heavy guns. In October we had 3,060 and 1,879 respectively, while the average income of gun ammunition had risen from 30,000 rounds a day to three times that amount. The increase in machine guns, trench mortars, and other appliances of trench warfare had been on a corresponding scale.

The position in Great Britain as to man-power was less good, notwithstanding the measures which had been introduced since the beginning of the year, and the whole of our man-power policy required to be overhauled. As to the belligerents in general the following figures were arrived at :—

	Entente Armies, including troops in home territory, and excluding coloured troops.	Reserves still available.
British	3,516,000	?
French	2,978,000	775,000
Russian	4,767,000	6,500,000
Italian	1,676,000	1,250,000
Rumanian	590,000	380,000
Belgian	128,000	10,000
Serbian	117,000	22,000
Portuguese	65,000	—
Totals	13,837,000	8,937,000
	Enemy Forces.	
German	5,470,000	2,000,000
Austro-Hungarian	2,750,000	800,000
Turkish	500,000	300,000
Bulgarian	400,000	112,000
Totals	9,120,000	3,212,000

The resources of the two groups could not, of course, be evaluated merely by arithmetical calculations. For example, the advantage enjoyed by the enemy of operating on interior lines, augmented by the still greater one of central control, enabled him to make the best possible use of the troops he possessed. The Entente could not do this. It was not practicable for them to reinforce the West by troops from the East, or vice versa, and there was at the time no probability of the superabundant Italian troops being employed to reinforce the French. France and Britain were working in the utmost harmony, but there was no real co-operation between their activities and those of Italy.

There was also the question of armament and quality of personnel to be taken into account. With regard to the former, the Western Powers were still unable to provide Russia with a tithe of the heavy artillery which she needed, the result being that while the Entente field armies exceeded those of the Central Powers by 4,700,000 men, they included nearly 5,000,000 Russians who were only partially equipped. Similarly, of the 9,000,000 Entente reserves 6,500,000 were Russians who could only be used a few at a time. The 2,000,000 German and 800,000 Austrian reservists were a much more liquid asset, and the disparity between the reserves of the two groups was therefore much more apparent than real.

The memorandum containing these statements also dealt with the length of time which the war might be expected to last—a question which, with some display of impatience, constantly cropped up at this period in ministerial circles as well as elsewhere. The answer obviously depended to a great extent upon the staying powers of the belligerents, individually and collectively. As a result of Brussiloff's offensive Austria had at one time seemed to be beaten, but the anticipation had proved to be unfounded. Although she was acutely feeling the strain and her reserves were diminishing, her armies had been so strengthened by German leadership and the admixture of German troops that the prospect of an early debacle seemed remote. The morale of her armies, too, was partially restored by the successes just obtained over Rumania, and the slackening off of the fighting during the winter would afford a further opportunity for rest and refitment.

Turkey and Bulgaria were showing signs of weakness and were without the reserves needed to meet the wastage of a sustained offensive, but they might be expected to offer a stout resistance in defence of their own territories, and had sufficient men to meet all probable needs for some months to come.

Germany had recently increased her effectives by some 300,000 men, and in doing so had drawn deeply on her reserves, but as she still had some 2,000,000 men remaining it was clear that she could continue the war for a period the duration of which could not yet be estimated. Captured documents showed that orders had been issued enforcing the necessity for economy in the expenditure of ammunition, but there was no reason to anticipate any reduction in output. Further, diminution in the intensity of the fighting during the winter season would enable a reserve of ammunition to be accumulated which might permit of more men being combed out of industries if and when the need for them became urgent. More men might also be released by an extension of the employment of Poles and prisoners of war.

On the other hand, the economic position was likely to become serious within the next six months. The harvest had not been good and there was a shortage of potatoes, which would be acutely felt both by the poorer classes and breeders of live stock. Milk, butter, and fats of all kinds were deficient, and there was a great dearth of lubricating oils and rubber. Before she joined the Entente large quantities of grain and oil had been obtained from Rumania, and if this source of supply continued, as at present, to be cut off the conditions of life in Germany might become almost intolerable. But there was no certainty that it would so continue, and in any case the economic stress would have to be very severe before the German Government would consent to unconditional surrender.

The deduction drawn by the General Staff from these considerations was that any attempt to predict what was called the end of the war would be quite valueless. Indeed, it might be very dangerous, since it might create a halting and vacillating attitude in regard to those measures which were essential to the execution of the policy which had caused us to enter the war.

The memorandum concluded with these words:—

> In order to secure complete victory we must continue to develop to the full all our offensive and defensive resources; we must have the strictest blockade of the enemy's coasts; the utmost assistance which the Navy can give to the Army in home defence, so that the greatest possible number of troops may be placed in the field; we must make available for the Army all men fit for military service who can by any expedient be released; and having got the men we must place them where they can best make their weight felt: there must be no mistakes in our grand strategy. Finally, we must expect, and at once prepare for, harder and more protracted fighting and a much greater strain on our resources than any yet experienced before we can wring from the enemy that peace which we have said we mean to have. It remains for the various departments concerned, under the instructions of His Majesty's Government, cordially and resolutely to take immediately the action required to meet these demands.

So far as I am aware, no such action was taken on these important and urgent recommendations—an omission which may be largely ascribed to the unsettled state of political affairs at the time. For some weeks past a feeling had been growing in the country that the war was not being efficiently managed; there was considerable discord within the Cabinet itself; and in these circumstances vigour and precision in the conduct of the war were bound to be lacking. Moreover, in spite of the warning which the General Staff had given, there was distinct disappointment amongst Ministers because the Somme operations had not been productive of more tangible results, and had apparently left the end of the war as far distant as ever. Not only so, but there was a growing fear that the end, when it came, might not be in our favour, and more than a few people in authority were beginning to think that a discussion of possible peace terms could do no harm and might do much good.

One example of this disquieting attitude came to notice in the third week of November, when Mr. Lloyd George asked me to furnish a report saying whether, in the opinion of the General Staff, the Government might rely upon the enemy being eventually dealt such a "knock-out" blow as would enable us to impose upon him the terms of peace that we desired—in other words, whether we could hope to win the war. Unless this were reasonably certain the advisability of continuing the war *à outrance* would call for reconsideration. Without being told exactly what had taken place, I gathered that a question of this nature had just been raised in the Cabinet, and that, in Mr. Lloyd George's view, it needed to be very peremptorily stamped upon. For this he wanted the support of the General Staff, and he suggested that, in framing a reply, I should speak out quite plainly and not "be afraid to let yourself go." I was not.

The question was of course not one for the C.I.G.S.

alone to answer, and, moreover, it had already been dealt with in the memorandum of October 26, since when the situation had not materially changed. I could therefore do little more than refer to the memorandum and add a few observations emphasizing what was necessary in order properly to secure our future position. This was done in a paper dated November 24, the gist of which was as under:—

Before the war we had rejected the system of universal service followed in other countries, and consequently we were now engaged in producing large new armies with inadequate machinery and during the course of the greatest war the world had ever seen. It was inevitable, in these circumstances, that we should have to pay for our omission with losses which might have been far less had our preparations been more complete. Still, it was unthinkable that we should shrink from facing the results of our past mistakes, and before making the full effort of which we are capable.

It was not for me to suggest what terms of peace should or should not be regarded as acceptable, but it was my duty to advise the Government as to the military consequences of such terms as they might be prepared to consider. As to this, the view of the General Staff was that any peace which left the military domination of Prussia intact would entail upon us in the future such a strain as might render our position intolerable, and that to conclude peace before we had made our greatest possible effort would be to estrange the oversea Dominions, to betray our Allies, to sacrifice our own interests, and to dishonour the memory of those who had laid down their lives for the Empire. Unquestionably, it would be a crime to prolong the war for a day longer than was necessary: but it would be a greater crime to flinch from the effort which we might hope would give us a just and lasting peace while it was within our power to make that effort. As so many times suggested already this power depended upon the full development of our resources, and, given this, the General Staff had complete confidence in the result—a confidence that was shared by the armies at the front, notwithstanding the adverse and uncongenial circumstances in which some of them were called upon to operate.

It was also necessary to take into account many other factors, such as the comparative staying power in money and commerce of the opposing sides, possible submarine developments, power of the Navy to safeguard the sea, and the solidarity of the Allies. While not venturing to express any definite opinion on these matters, which lay outside the General Staff's sphere, I observed that there still seemed to be great affluence in the country, and that there were many directions in which waste and extravagance in the national life could be checked. As to the Navy, there was no reason for supposing that the sailors were any less sanguine of the ultimate result of the war than were the soldiers ; while as to the Allies, their stability must necessarily be a constant cause of anxiety, but on the other hand there was not much to complain about. Some of them, especially France, had displayed splendid fortitude, though, on the other hand, there were some who were not too modest in their requests for financial assistance, and had perhaps succeeded in extracting from us far more money than they had expected to get.

With regard to the attitude of our own people, it was admitted that, as in every country, there were a certain number who would be glad to see peace made on any terms, and who were almost ready to argue that we stood to gain more by losing the war than by winning it. These were the same people who, before 1914, had told us that civilization would not tolerate such a war as that which others then saw must inevitably come, and no attention need be paid to them. It was more pleasing to remember that the Empire as a whole

> is ready to face anything in order to win the war, if only the situation is clearly made known to it. Of course we must not ignore our difficulties, but we should equally avoid taking counsel of our fears, and we might with advantage think more frequently about the difficulties of the enemy, and seriously ask ourselves whether we would like to change places with him. It is the essence of a national war that difficulties should arise in every sphere of national activity, and that sacrifices should be required of every member of the community in the common interest. Having entered into the war this fact must be accepted. Up to the present time the people of this country have not been called upon for such sacrifices as I believe them to be capable of bearing and willing to make. If I am correct in my appreciation of the attitude of my fellow-countrymen, it should not be beyond the power of good administration to overcome such difficulties as are arising and will arise. . . . In short, we need to have the same courage in London as have our leaders in the North Sea and in France. The whole art of making war may be summed up in three words—courage, action, determination. In peace-time half-and-half measures may not be very harmful. In war-time they are deadly. We must make up our minds either to fight or to make peace. The most pernicious and paralysing thing that could happen would be to try and make war while in our hearts we are afraid to take punishment.
>
> My answer to the question is: "I am satisfied that the knock-out blow can and will be delivered if only we take the necessary measures to give us success, and take them in time. We shall win if we deserve to win."

After this paper had been circulated to Ministers, one of them wrote me a letter to the effect that the question of our power to win the war had not been raised, as I had supposed, with the intention of suggesting that peace should be made at the first opportunity, but rather for the purpose of taking careful stock of our position—quite a different matter. Had I been aware of this, the paper would have been drafted in more moderate terms.

It was followed on November 28 by a memorandum from the Military Members of the Army Council recommending the introduction of all-round national service. The recommendation was accepted by the War Committee, but before parliamentary sanction for it could be sought Mr. Asquith's Ministry fell to pieces under the weight of its own dissensions, and a new one was formed under the leadership of Mr. Lloyd George. The climax came as a welcome relief, for while the result of the crisis hung in the balance there was much running to and fro in Whitehall by those who were undecided as to which political leader to follow, and the direction of the war was neglected in consequence. When at last it was seen that the Premiership would probably fall to Mr. Lloyd George, three different aspirants for his post of War Minister made their desire known to me, thinking, apparently, that my recommendation would be of assistance to them. I could have told them that in the course of conversation Mr. Lloyd George had already referred to myself as a suitable successor, and that when I demurred on the grounds of parliamentary inexperience he was good enough to say that the difficulty could be overcome by my going to the House of Lords. The post had not the least attraction for me, and on my suggestion the matter was dropped.

It is not for me to appraise the value of Mr. Asquith's services whilst head of the Government during the first, and in many ways the most anxious, half of the war. But having worked in close intimacy with him for a year of that period it is permissible to say that he was always ready, in bad times no less than in good, to support and encourage the Army and its leaders in the execution of the tasks assigned to them. From a military standpoint, the chief defect in the management of the war during his Premiership was the continuance of the traditional system of collective Cabinet responsibility for all Government action taken. Had he amended the system by some more autocratic and efficient organization than the formation of a War Committee, the dispatch of war business would undoubtedly have been expedited. The feasibility of making this change, however, was a matter of which he was the best judge, and there were probably many more obstacles, personal and political, in the way than outsiders might think.

His hesitation to close with the man-power problem at an earlier date was also to be regretted, but here again the majority of his colleagues were equally reluctant, and, after all, it was owing to the measures taken during his tenure of office that the fighting strength of the British armies in France was greater in the summer of 1917 than at any period of the war.

With regard to Ministers in general, it was seldom, with the one or two exceptions referred to in this and other chapters, that any desire was shown to override military opinion on military questions, or to interfere with duties which could more appropriately be left in military hands. There were, of course, occasions when conflicting needs had to be reconciled, and it was not to be expected that military considerations would in every case be given precedence over all others. Delicate questions connected with the length of front to be held by the British and French armies respectively, which sometimes had to come before Ministers for decision, were particularly difficult to settle to the satisfaction of both sides. But on the whole it may be said that, throughout 1916, the General Staff were accorded suitable freedom of action in all matters lying within their sphere, and received from the Government as well as from individual Ministers the guidance and assistance which the proper discharge of their duties required. To this fact, perhaps more than to any other, may be largely attributed the military achievements of the year, which left the position in all theatres of war infinitely more satisfactory and hopeful than it had been twelve months before. Unfortunately, as the narrative will disclose, the same mutually helpful relations were not forthcoming in 1917, and, as was inevitable, the operations suffered to a corresponding degree.

On taking up his new duties of Prime Minister, Mr. Lloyd George asked me to let him have a note of any points connected with the war which particularly required his attention, together with my candid opinion as to our prospects of winning it—a question already twice dealt with by me during the last six weeks. The following extracts from the note supplied will suitably bring this chapter to a close. They are given not because they contain anything original, but because they show some of the questions which the General Staff, as a result of their intercourse with Ministers, felt it desirable to emphasize.

I have no hesitation in saying that we can win if we will only do the right thing. If I thought otherwise I would tell you so. This is the opinion of many other Generals besides myself. In fact I have never yet heard any military officer of standing express any other opinion. But there are many important things to be done, and done quickly.

We must organize our man-power at home.

We must make full use of coloured labour at home, and raise more coloured troops for use in suitable theatres abroad. There is much local opposition to this which must be drastically overridden.

We must insist upon the oversea Dominions sending more men.

We must get the railways right in France, and to do that we must at once get into operation the recent decision of the War Committee regarding railways at home.

We must get a much larger share in the control of the war. The attitude of the British Empire up to the present time has been lamentable. We are contributing far more to the war than any Power, and we exercise less general control than any. We do not control even our own resources, but give way to the Allies on practically every occasion. We shall never do any good if we continue doing this. Our Allies invariably ask for far more than they expect to get, and they say they will do things which they never intend to do. We must be firm with them. At the present time we are practically committing suicide. Even Italy is firmer in her attitude than we are. It will take time to get this control, but it must be got. Germany's successes are largely due to her dominating power. No one else is allowed to count with her. This is due to her Government and diplomatic action rather than to her General Staff, powerful though the latter is.

We must considerably enlarge our ideas as to the magnitude of the war. We do not yet nearly realize the stupendous task confronting us. For months past I have prophesied an increasing strain in every direction. The strain will become greater and greater as time goes on, and we are undoubtedly in for a bad time for the next few months, as we cannot get going until next spring, and the people may become impatient. On the other hand, we may hope to have some little success in Egypt and Mesopotamia during the winter, and the Russians are reinforcing their troops in the Caucasus and seem to mean business. So we may hope to shake up the Turk a little. Still, we must not expect any very great relief before the spring, or expect the war suddenly to come to an end. It is much too big a matter for that. Germany is fighting for her life. She is a powerful opponent. We can only expect *just* to win through and no more, and yet things in England are going on much the same to-day as two years ago. It is upon us more than upon any Power that the final result depends, and I cannot hold out any hope of winning until we have been strained to the utmost. If the nation will not stand that, then the chances are we shall not win. . . .

I honestly think we have done as well in France during the past year as we could expect to do, having regard to our available resources, but in order to obtain better results next year we must have larger forces in the West, and we shall have larger ones I hope. We need to keep our attention on the big things, and not brood and waste brain-power over such petty matters as Rabegh [1] and Persia. It is really pitiable sometimes to see the worried and pessimistic looks of certain people because of some trumpery set-back which matters not at all. I hope you will not mind my saying that some members of the late Government had no proper perspective of the war. They lived from telegram to telegram, and attached as much importance to a few scallywags in Arabia as I imagine they did to the German attack on Ypres two years ago. We are bound to have many set-backs before we finish the war, but so long as we keep determinedly on that path which, after full and careful consideration, we have decided to follow, no great harm can happen and in course of time we shall win. The important thing is to have a definite policy, and to refuse to be diverted from it. In fact we need to make up our minds where we will seek a decision, and not dance attendance upon either the enemy or our Allies.

As regards the enemy, he was in a very bad way last September, and we predicted, what was quite obvious, that he would go for Rumania in order to hearten his country and make a splash in the eyes of the world. For a variety of reasons he has made a great splash, and is making it look as big as he can. But nothing vital has happened. Salonika is the only place in the Balkans which causes me anxiety at the present time, and it is causing me a great deal because of the unsatisfactory way in which the situation is dealt with by the French. . . . Without entering into the wisdom or otherwise of the Balkan operations, it is true to say that the French have never had any real plan, and therefore no good can possibly accrue. M. Briand went there for political reasons ; for the same reasons he does not wish us to come away ; Joffre, to please him, sent troops there, but of indifferent quality and not well supplied with drafts, equipment, and transport. It is necessary that some really definite measures should be taken to put the Salonika affair on a proper footing. If this is done, a hideous nightmare will be removed. One reason for the past muddle is that we ourselves have never had any Eastern policy. . . .

[1] A proposed expedition referred to in a later Chapter.

There is only one way of winning a war, and that is by defeating the chief enemy, and if this principle is kept in view by the War Council a very much smaller expenditure of brain-power will be required to carry on the war. The difficulty that people sometimes find in adhering to the above principle is that they allow themselves to be diverted from important things by those which are not important. I am sure you will readily agree with this and grasp my meaning. There is in this respect no difference between conducting a war and conducting any other business. We must devote ourselves whole-heartedly to essentials. Things of less importance must take care of themselves, no matter how inconvenient and unpleasant they may be for the time being.

The feature which causes me the most anxiety at the present time is the submarine menace. It is not too much to say that the safety of our sea communications is now the dominating factor of the war, and therefore the less we use the sea the better so far as military operations are concerned.

To sum up, I believe that Germany is feeling the strain of the war very much [1]; that her allies are a great burden to her; that we must learn to set our teeth and refuse to be discouraged; and, generally, put into our task more spirit, soul, courage, and determination to win no matter at what cost, and in any event to go down, if we must, with our colours flying. But there will be no question of going down if we are brave and resolute, and stick to a definite plan once it is made.

8th December, 1916.

---

[1] Post-war statements by senior German military authorities more than confirm the accuracy of this view.

CHAPTER VII

MAN-POWER

Difficulty of introducing Conscription on Outbreak of War—Was a Question for the Government, not merely for the War Minister —Munitions Act, July, 1915—Derby Scheme, October, 1915—My Recommendations, January, 1916—Cabinet Inquiry—Resulting Decision—Army Council's Anxiety as to Deficiencies—Renewed Cabinet Inquiry—Further Inadequate Legislative Measures —Formation of Man-Power Distribution Board—Military Members of Army Council recommend All-round National Service —Government approves of it but is replaced by a New Government which Rejects It—Further Representation by Army Council —Lord Rhondda's Committee—Government again urged by Army Council to Provide More Men—Complaints by Commanders-in-Chief—Appointment of Minister of National Service—Final Representation by Army Council—Another Cabinet Committee appointed to Investigate, December, 1917—Its Erroneous Decisions—Infantry Battalions in France reduced by 25 per cent. —War Cabinet and Sir Douglas Haig—More insufficient Legislation Introduced—Unsuccessful Attempt to obtain Assistance from America—Necessary Measures at last Taken.

THE voluntary system of recruiting with which we began the war brought undying honour to those millions of men who, being under no obligation to serve, joined the Army solely from a sense of public duty, but by the autumn of 1915 it was rapidly breaking down and a new system had to be found. The search for it was beset with difficulties on all sides, and many makeshifts were tried before the simple and straightforward policy was adopted of placing all able-bodied men at the disposal of the State, and organizing them for a great effort in whatever direction they could most profitably be used. This policy was many times suggested by the soldiers from the beginning of 1916 onwards, but it was not fully put into practice until forced upon us by the enemy in March, 1918.

It has frequently been said that national service could have been instituted in 1914 had Lord Kitchener chosen to ask for it, and he has been widely criticized for not doing so. But at least one member of the Government did not share this opinion, and there were doubtless others who agreed with him. "Conscription," says Lord Grey, "in the early days of the war was impossible; public opinion was not ready for it; it would have been resisted. Voluntary enlistment gave the country a good start in good-will and enthusiasm; conscription would have given a bad start. There would have been division of opinion, much resentment; the country might even have foundered in political difficulties."[1]

Everybody may not accept these views, but there was one good and sufficient reason for adhering at first to the voluntary system—namely, the registration and legislation needed to start a compulsory system would have taken a long time to complete, and there was not a moment to lose in getting a larger army of some sort together. Moreover, neither equipment nor training facilities were available for larger numbers than those which came forward voluntarily. The case would have been quite different if the machinery for compulsion had been prepared before the war. Men could then have been systematically called up in the quotas required, and put at once into their proper places, but as no preliminary preparations of the kind required had been made, Lord Kitchener had to do the best he could without

[1] "Twenty-five Years," Vol. II, page 70.

them. Why they were not made has already been recalled,[1] and however justified the omission may have been, politically, when war came upon us there was immense waste of valuable material owing to men who should have been trained as officers being put into the ranks, and men who should have remained in the factories leaving them, and in many other ways.

Again, the question was essentially *national* in its scope, not merely *military*, and therefore required to be dealt with by the Government and not merely by the War Minister. Men were wanted for many duties besides service in the Army, all of which had to be taken into account, and with them Lord Kitchener was no more concerned than any other member of the Government. The mistake most to be regretted was not the temporary continuance of voluntary recruiting in the early stages of the war, but the timorous and piecemeal manner in which the bolder policy of all-round national service was dealt with when seen to be the only system which could effectively meet the situation.

One of the first steps taken was the passing of the Munitions Act in July, 1915, a form of compulsion which applied to certain industries only and therefore was certain to break down. National Service all round was a policy that could be understood by everybody, and whatever its defects might be it was at least fair to all alike, whereas there was nothing good to be said of applying compulsory measures to some classes and not to others.

About the same time a National Registration Act was passed, and by it every person in Great Britain (not in Ireland) between the ages of sixteen and sixty-five years was registered. This was a useful preliminary to any

[1] *Vide* Chapter I.

subsequent legislation for national service, but it was no more than that.

In October, 1915, the " Derby Scheme " was started as a final attempt to keep the voluntary system alive, and by it men " attested " their willingness to join the Army when wanted, and then entered a reserve where they remained undisturbed in their civil occupations until called up. It was officially announced that the young unmarried men would be taken before the older, and the single men before the married. A further pledge was given that married men would not be called up unless practically all the unmarried were first accounted for. The result of the canvass was that out of some 2,000,000 single men who were available for attesting some 650,000 did not attest, and therefore there was no other course, if the pledges given were to be respected, but to compel them to come forward. This was done early in January, 1916, by the passing of the first " Military Service Act," which was made applicable to all single men and widowers (having no children dependent upon them) between the ages of eighteen and forty-one years. Opportunity was still given to attest voluntarily under the Derby Scheme, which remained in force, but after a specified date those men who had not so attested were to be deemed to have enlisted for the duration of the war, unless in the meantime they had been exempted.

It so happened that the Bill was still under consideration when I became C.I.G.S., and, thinking that the Government would wish to have before them the views of the General Staff as to our future military needs, one of my first acts was to submit them.[1] Personal experience on the Western Front, conversations there with Army commanders, the man-power position in France,

[1] General Staff memorandum, December 27, 1915.

Russia, and Italy, and information regarding the enemy's intentions, combined to convince me that much greater efforts must be made than anything yet attempted, and that we ought to aim at producing our maximum strength during 1916. I purposely refrained from attempting to give a specific estimate of our total requirements in actual figures. That was impracticable owing to the world-wide character of the war and its possible developments. The only safe basis of calculation was to assume that every man in the country would sooner or later be needed for one kind of national work or another. My advice to the Government was that we should first aim at putting into the field the whole of the 67 divisions whose formation had already been started, if not completed (in addition to the three British divisions then in India and such divisions as might be furnished by the oversea Dominions), and at keeping them at full strength for the period of the war. This meant that we must arrange to provide 130,000 men per month, or about one and a half millions by the end of 1916. How many divisions we might later require and be able to raise were matters for consideration after the 67 had been completed, which they were far from being at that time.

There was quite a strong body in the Cabinet who, apart from the actual provision of men, thought that we could not, having regard to our other liabilities, find the money to pay for as many as seventy divisions, and that the attempt to maintain them might land us in financial ruin. Writing to Sir Douglas Haig on January 4, 1916, I said:—

Not being able to go back on the Prime Minister's pledge to call up the single men before the married, certain Ministers are trying to render compulsion useless by making out that although we may have power to take the men we cannot pay for them, and that they cannot be spared from their trades and at the same time admit of keeping up the necessary exports and so provide the money we need with which to subsidize our Allies. . . . The arguments I advanced were that we need every man we can get, and that it is for the Government to say how many they can pay for and how many they can find. The idea of some of the politicians is to abolish some if not all of the second line Territorial divisions now at home, thirteen in number, which are preparing to go out later. But I do not think this will be done. I have shown many directions in which economy can be effected, and how there would be very little saved if any divisions were disbanded, to say nothing of the money which has been already spent upon them.

A " Cabinet Committee on the Co-ordination of Military and Financial Effort " was appointed to investigate the matter, the Prime Minister himself acting as chairman. The inquiry was exhaustive and lasted for some weeks. The General Staff and other War Office representatives were given a very patient hearing though they were closely cross-examined on, and expected to justify, each and every item of their demands. As these were frequently of a technical character they were not easy to explain to men having no technical knowledge, and more than once the proceedings became tiresome and irritating. There was also a tendency on the part of some members of the Committee to insist that the soldiers ought to be more specific as to the number of men that would ultimately be required, but, as just suggested, the question to be decided was not the smallest number of divisions needed to finish the war, but the largest number that could be found. On the whole, there was little to complain of, the inquiry being conducted with a desire to elicit information, palatable or not, on an important subject which had not yet been systematically examined.

The evidence of the Board of Trade (then the recognized authority on man-power questions) went to show that about 1,275,000 men could be made available for military purposes during 1916, provided their withdrawal from trade was spread carefully over the year. In the first three months 340,000 could be taken " without great disturbance of trade," and as many as 530,000 " without disaster." Upon these data the Committee decided that 358,000 should be taken as a first instalment, and a scheme was to be devised for placing 62 divisions in the field by the end of June with three months' reserves in hand. The remaining 5 divisions were to be brought up to strength, but without reserves, and be retained for Home Defence. The Committee were of opinion that the men required by this scheme could be found " without industrial disaster, though not without grave dislocation of industry, and even some risk." The further supply of personnel was postponed for consideration the following April.

The scheme approximately conformed, so far as it went, to the recommendations made by the General Staff, and in due course it received Cabinet approval. The number of men actually produced, however, fell far short of the number which the Board of Trade had agreed could be found. Of the 358,000 the yield was only 212,000, the chief reason for this being that more than 25 per cent. of the single men called up under the Military Service Act did not put in an appearance. The shortage was felt the more because, as a rule, there was no power to transfer men from one branch of the Army to another where their services might be urgently needed. Hence it frequently happened that while one branch was deficient in men another would have more than it wanted. Again, men belonging to the regular Army were allowed to take their discharge on the expiration of their engagement as in pre-war days. Looking back it seems incredible that as late as the summer of 1916 some 5,000 non-commissioned officers and men should be leaving the Army every month because there was no legal authority by which they could be retained. In numerous ways further legislative action was required to remove the vexatious arrangements by which recruiting and distribution were hampered.

The result was that the end of March found the position but little better than it had been three months before. The infantry battalions abroad were 78,000 below establishment, the Territorial divisions at home required 50,000 men, and the reserves in training were also much below the requisite number. The intake of recruits was, in fact, scarcely more than enough to meet normal wastage in France alone, and it provided no reserves to meet the case of a great battle there or reinforcements of any kind for other theatres of war. Once more, therefore, I had to bring the matter before the Government, and in asking that steps might have to be taken to ensure decisions being properly carried out, I suggested that the country was not yet really at war, that the people did not know how serious the situation was, and that they ought to be told, when they would doubtless be found ready to respond to any call that might be made upon them. The advantage of clearly telling them what they had to do seemed to outweigh the disadvantage of conveying to the enemy certain information from which he might derive some temporary encouragement. The suggestion was not acted upon.

While it was the duty of the General Staff to tender military advice on questions of policy, it was the business of the Army Council to see that the field armies were maintained at such strength as the nature of their missions required. I therefore proposed to Lord Kitchener, and he agreed, that the Council should confirm the representations which the General Staff had made, and this was done in a memorandum laid before the Government during the first week of April. In it the Council expressed " grave anxiety " at the failure of the existing system to produce the requisite men ; said that no remedial measures would be of much value so long as the system of obtaining recruits by a combination of the Derby Scheme (or voluntary enlistment) and the Military Service Act (or compulsory enlistment of single men) remained unchanged ; and concluded with the statement that the circumstances attending the war were such as to render it absolutely necessary that every man of military age who was physically fit and could be spared from naval service or other indispensable employment should be made available to serve in the military forces.

The Cabinet Committee thereupon reassembled, and, as often happens when figures come into a discussion, a difference of opinion arose between the Committee and the Council as to the number demanded and the number available. Eventually the Committee decided that although it might become necessary later on to take legislative powers for securing the service of every man capable of bearing arms, they were not prepared at the moment to enter into that question.

Obviously the Army Council could not allow the matter to rest there. They quite appreciated, as they informed the Government, the considerations which the Cabinet Committee had impressed upon them as to the difficulty of passing fresh legislation for the compulsory enlistment of married men, and they realized the great strain placed on our financial resources by the increasing demands of the Allies, and by the withdrawal of large numbers of men from industries. On the other hand, they were compelled to look ahead, and calculations showed that the supply of recruits would practically cease altogether in the autumn unless immediate action was taken to increase it. All men were entitled to be given fairly long notice before being called up, and at least three months must be allowed for training them. Consequently, the effect of any legislation that might be introduced in April would at the earliest not be felt at the front before September. It was therefore evident that any such postponement of action as that proposed by the Committee would be dangerous.

The Government reluctantly agreed, and the following month the provisions of the Military Service Act were extended to include married men or widowers with dependent children. Ireland was still left out, and in other respects the Act was not as free from hampering conditions as could have been desired, but, within its limits, it provided a more reliable flow of recruits; constituted a further step towards the principle of universal national service; and close upon 1,200,000 men were produced by it during the year.

By the autumn the situation again became acute. France had stood firm against the attacks on Verdun, but at the cost of such heavy losses that she was no longer able to maintain her original fighting strength. Russia, though possessing millions of men, was unlikely ever to add materially to the numbers she then had in the field. Italy, too, seemed unlikely to increase the size of her armies, though she, also, did not suffer from any lack of men. Rumania was being overrun by enemy forces, and instead of bringing assistance to the Entente armies, as had been hoped, she was herself in need of it.

Britain alone could be regarded as a possible source of increased effort, and she, besides the upkeep of her armies and a superior navy, was expected to assist her Allies with money, shipping, and many other necessities which imposed a constant drain upon her man-power reserves. She had, moreover, suffered heavy casualties in the operations on the Somme, and these had to be replaced. Other men were wanted for numerous new units, such as heavy artillery, machine guns, tanks, medical, and transport. Finally, besides the defective system under which she obtained men, there was no guarantee that the best use was being made of those who were taken, for there was no one branch of the War Office charged with their allocation. The men taken into the administrative services were dealt with by the heads of those services, the Adjutant-General and Quarter-master-General, the C.I.G.S., responsible for operative duties, having no voice in either case. Only the direct action of the War Minister could ensure that the non-combatant (administrative) services, which absorbed many hundreds of thousands of men, did not, either at home or abroad, appropriate to themselves personnel which could more usefully be employed in the fighting ranks. I had hoped that Mr. Lloyd George, with his well-known energy, would follow the example of his predecessor, Lord Kitchener, and give special attention to the matter, but it was tedious, irksome work, and failed to interest him. It was also difficult, for some departmental objection or other would invariably be taken to any and every reduction suggested. The only way by which redundant men could be extracted was for the War Minister arbitrarily to issue orders for a fixed quota to be produced, and then leave the branches concerned to produce it in such a manner as they might choose.

A similar evil crying out for remedy was the scramble for men between the different State departments, each trying to satisfy its own wants with little or no regard to the wants of others. Munitions, expansion of the Air Force, enlargement of naval duties, food production, shipbuilding, timber-felling, and many other indispensable services made ever-growing encroachments upon the reserves of men, and there was no appointed authority for adjusting the rival claims which frequently arose. A " Man-Power Distribution Board " was created in August, 1916, but it took no part in recruiting for the Army. Its chief functions were to maintain a supply of labour for essential industries and advise the War Committee on man-power questions, but as the departments concerned were not always prepared to accept its decisions, and as it had no power to enforce them, it was not of much value.

To these defects and demands may be added the fact that the wastage from sickness in the different Eastern campaigns to which we were committed was very high. Figures compiled in November, 1916, showed the rate of admission to hospital per 1,000 men per annum to be :—

France	433
Egypt	656
Salonika . . .	1,036
Mesopotamia. . .	2,135

The figures for France were only slightly in excess of actual sick wastage in peace-time in the United Kingdom.

At the end of October the armies in France were some 80,000 men below their authorized strength, and in bringing this to the notice of the War Committee (General Staff memorandum of October 26) I repeated the opinion expressed on previous occasions that " the decision of this war must come *on land*," and urged " that all demands for men for whatever purpose, and that the policy of His Majesty's Government, whether economical, naval, or military, should be thoroughly reviewed from the standpoint of making our land forces as strong as possible for that decision." Later, as no action of the kind was taken, I suggested to Mr. Lloyd George, War Minister since June, that the Government should be again approached. He agreed, but asked for the case to be put up by the Military Members alone, and not as previously by the Army Council as a whole. He considered that if the representation came direct from the soldiers it would carry more weight than if shared in by the Civil Members of the Council ; that for the same reason he could more effectively support it ; and he desired to avoid all appearance of adding to the Prime Minister's troubles at a time when political affairs were unsettled and might at any moment culminate in a crisis.

I disliked dealing with the question in this way, for it was clearly one that ought to be presented to the Government by the full Council, headed by the President, Mr. Lloyd George. On the other hand, the chief thing was to secure his support, and as he was willing to give it the form of procedure was comparatively unimportant. On November 28 the Military Members accordingly submitted to him for communication to the Government a memorandum in which the previous recommendations of the Army Council were recalled, and it was pointed out that, as fighting of a heavy and perhaps decisive nature was likely to occur in France early in the spring of 1917, the consequences might be serious unless measures were instituted at once to provide more men than could be secured from the arrangements then in force. It was calculated that 940,000 men would be needed during 1917 to keep the armies up to strength, and as there were still in civil life over two and a half million men of military age, exclusive of Ireland, there was no apparent reason why the requisite number should not be produced. The manner of producing them was a question not for the Military Members but for the Government to decide, and therefore they offered no opinion thereon.

Mr. Lloyd George thought, however, that the memorandum was not sufficiently complete without a recommendation on this point, and eventually, in order to meet his wishes, an addition was made suggesting that the military age should be raised from forty-one to fifty-five years, and that all men in the United Kingdom up to that age should be held liable for such national work as the Government deemed essential to the effective prosecution of the war.

The Government having for so long hesitated to introduce a system of this nature, there seemed to be no prospect that they would introduce it now. Several Ministers had always argued that compulsory methods would be of no benefit to the Army, since the additional men yielded would probably be more than counterbalanced by the additional number of troops required to keep the peace in the large industrial centres where, it might be expected, compulsion would be resented. Others, again, though not anticipating actual disorders, agreed that the system would be very unpopular, and they, too, were averse to becoming in any way associated with it. In general, the amount of support which the Prime Minister could rely upon receiving from his Cabinet colleagues, whether Conservative or Liberal, was, so it seemed to me, very much less than the public were sometimes asked to believe. Up to the date here referred to I cannot recall a single instance of national service having been definitely proposed by any Minister, except in so far as Mr. Lloyd George may be said to have proposed it in putting forward the Military Members' memorandum. There may have been instances of which I knew nothing, but there was no indication of them in the many ministerial man-power discussions at which I was present.

To my surprise the memorandum met with practically no opposition when, on November 30, it came before the War Committee for consideration. Mr. Asquith, emphasizing the necessity for keeping the armies up to strength, clearly showed that he was not prepared to oppose it ; the other Ministers present, whatever they may have thought, said scarcely a word against it ; and within a few minutes the policy of national service was approved in principle, a committee was appointed to work out the details, and the War Committee placed on record that they attached great importance to the enactment of the necessary legislation before Christmas, 1916. No better day's work was done in London at any time during the war.

Exactly how to account for this sudden acceptance of a policy held for so long in disfavour is a question that cannot be answered until the political doings of the time are laid bare. As recalled in the preceding chapter, there had for months past been a growing public demand for the display of greater energy in the management of the war ; and the handling of man-power in particular was a constant subject of criticism. Mr. Asquith and his Cabinet adherents may therefore have thought that the adoption of the soldiers' recommendation would be an effective way of countering the attacks which were being made on his Administration, and of averting the overthrow with which it was threatened. If this was the intention it failed, for within a week the Premiership was taken over by Mr. Lloyd George.

For some time previously there had been, so I thought, close agreement between the new Premier and myself as to the needs of the Army, and the policy by which the requisite men could best be supplied. He was now in a position to give practical effect to that policy, as set forth in the Military Members' memorandum to which, as War Minister, he had given his approval. But, as with others before him, a change of office was accompanied by a change in point of view, and he allowed the defective man-power arrangements to drift on month after month without any adequate remedy until, in March, 1918, their amendment was compelled by the imminence of defeat.

The report of the committee appointed on November 30 to draw up the detailed scheme was considered by the newly formed War Cabinet on December 14, but in the absence of the Prime Minister no decision was reached. On December 19 statements on the general military and political situation were simultaneously made by the Government in both Houses of Parliament, and in relation to man-power Mr. Lloyd George announced that:

> The matter was considered by the War Committee of the late Government, and it was unanimously decided by them that the time had come for the adoption of the principle of universal national service. It was one of the first matters taken up by the present Government, and the War Cabinet have unanimously adopted the conclusions come to by the preceding War Committee.[1]

Further explanations went to show, however, that the action he proposed to take was mainly confined to increasing the mobility of labour. The various industries

[1] "Hansard," December 19, 1916.

were to be scheduled according to their national importance, and labour was to become liable to be transferred from one class of work to another, and also to some extent for employment in the Army. Men were to be "*invited* to enrol at once and be registered as war workers on lines analogous to the existing munition volunteers," and if the requisite numbers (whatever that expression meant) were not obtained by voluntary methods the Government would not hesitate to "ask Parliament to release us from pledges given in other circumstances, and to obtain the necessary powers for making our plans fully effective. The nation is fighting for its life, and it is entitled to the best services of all its sons." It was also announced that a Director-General of National Service had been appointed, who would be responsible both for the military and civil side of the scheme. These measures sounded courageous and promising, but in fact they were a poor substitute for universal national service, and made recruitment for the Army no better than it was before. The new National Service Department, from which much was expected, proved to be specially disappointing. Instead of being a unifier of competing interests, it became merely an additional department dipping into the pool of civil labour ; and instead of allaying, it tended to increase the industrial discontent which prevailed.

"Labour," according to what Mr. Lloyd George said to me not long after taking up his new office, would not "stand" any further compulsion—a statement which could hardly be regarded as being in agreement with facts. The majority of "Labour" was quite as determined to see the war through, and to accept the sacrifices which that entailed, as was the majority of any other part of the nation. What "Labour" did not want was a continuance of the system which opened the door to logrolling and corruption as to who should be sent to the front and who should be kept back. Under the existing system young men employed in munition factories, in agriculture, on the railways, remained safely at home, some of them receiving wages of £15 to £20 a week, while older men from the same factory, farm, or station, were sent into the trenches on a mere pittance. Possibly the latter class were released from their work because their employers deemed them to be less efficient, but they were not likely to believe that they were, and so long as the selection was left to the judgment of an individual, however capable and impartial he might be, a sense of unfair discrimination was bound to prevail. The simplest and fairest plan was to make all and sundry alike liable to serve, and then, within the limits of the number allotted, use for the fighting line the youngest first.

Mr. Lloyd George became Prime Minister at a time when the people were ready to give their political leaders full liberty of action, and he enjoyed the further advantage of having the experience of the past two years to guide him as to what was required and what could be done. So far as man-power was concerned, he made poor use of these opportunities, and under his management the situation became not better but worse. The difficulty of providing men for the various kinds of national work to be done naturally increased as the stress of war became more pronounced, but that was the very reason why effect ought to have been given to the policy adopted by Mr. Asquith's Government, and admitted in principle to be necessary by Mr. Lloyd George's.

There were other reasons why delay was to be deprecated. In January, 1917, the War Cabinet agreed to the plan of campaign prepared by the new French Commander-in-Chief, General Nivelle, and in accordance with their special instructions the British armies in France were reinforced by all the divisions which the United Kingdom could supply. This action was quite sound, but of course larger field armies meant the provision of larger drafts for keeping them up to strength, and under the existing recruiting system these were not procurable. Moreover, our share in the plan was to create an opportunity for a decisive blow for the French armies. This meant drawing the enemy's reserves towards our own front, which could only be done as a result of prolonged fighting, that is at the cost of many casualties for whose replacement ample drafts must be made ready.

The shortage of drafts was likely to be the more serious because it was believed at the time that Germany would make her maximum effort in the forthcoming summer. It was known for certain that she would start the season of active operations with 55 more divisions than she had in 1916, and it was probable that she might have as many as 68. These divisions had been partly formed by reducing others from 12 battalions to 9, and then making use of the 3 battalions as a nucleus, but in the main they had been raised by tapping new supplies of men. An Auxiliary Service Law had been passed the previous November, placing at the disposal of the Government the services of all persons between the ages of seventeen and sixty. Belgians had been forcibly deported from their homes to work in Germany, and citizens of Russian Poland had been embodied in the German forces. The net increase made to the strength of the German field armies by these measures was, according to the calculations of my Intelligence Branch, about a million men and a proportionate number of guns.

In February the Army Council informed the War

Cabinet that, as represented by the Military Members three months before, it would not be possible to keep the armies in France up to strength during the heavy fighting about to take place, since it was now too late to make the men ready even if they were provided. In answer to this unpleasant news the Cabinet directed the Council to consider the feasibility of reducing the number of battalions per division from 12 to 9, as Germany and France had done. With such a reduction the provision of drafts had, of course, no connexion, and to it the Council could not agree. Germany had made the change for the purpose of forming additional divisions. There could be no question of our following her example, for we could not find the necessary artillery and other non-infantry units or the trained staffs which additional divisions would require. As to France, she had reduced the number of battalions because she could no longer maintain the original number at their proper strength. We might be compelled to do the same, but until then there was no point in the reduction proposed.

In order that the various Commanders-in-Chief might be informed of the drafts they would receive and so be enabled to prepare their plans, the Council next asked the War Cabinet to say whether measures would or would not be taken to provide more men than were at present in sight. A definite answer to this plain question was necessary because if more men could not be provided—and it was for the War Cabinet to say—and the armies could not be kept up to strength, plans of operations and administrative arrangements for the maintenance of the various forces would have to be revised. It would have been unpardonable for the Council to have allowed Commanders-in-Chief to embark on operations on the assumption that drafts to keep their armies up to strength would be forthcoming, and leave them to discover at the critical moment that they were not. Such an error would be tantamount to a breach of faith both to them and to the Allies with whom they might be co-operating. No answer being given by the War Cabinet, the question was renewed early in March. Again no answer was returned, and Commanders-in-Chief were thus left to do the best they could.

On numerous occasions during 1917 the War Minister (Lord Derby) and the Adjutant-General pointed out to the Government that the shortage of recruits was not so much due to the lack of men of military age as to the want of a proper system for making use of them; that the powers of exemption conferred on Tribunals and Government departments were excessive; and that the whole arrangements were unsatisfactory to everybody and would never be anything else. The General Staff as frequently, and as unsuccessfully, repeated that risks were being incurred which could not be justified. Certain improvements were introduced, but they were mostly of a minor nature and left the root of the trouble untouched. Some of them, though quite good in themselves, were rendered abortive by the way in which they were carried out, or by the chaotic state of affairs into which the Government had allowed the matter to drift. As an example of this it may be mentioned that one of the first proposals made by the Director-General of National Service for supplying the Army with men was considered by the War Cabinet on January 19, 1917. It was decided that 30,000 men engaged in agriculture, 20,000 miners, and 50,000 semi-skilled and unskilled munition workers should be released by the end of the month. As late as the end of May the first figure had not been attained, of the second less than one-half had been received, while of the third the number received was less than quarter.

In March another committee, under Lord Rhondda, was appointed to consider the question of the supply of men, the policy as to future legislation, and the modification of existing methods of exemption. It, also, reported that compulsory national service was necessary, but when, on March 23, the report came up for approval the War Cabinet announced that compulsory methods could not be entertained.

The recommendations of this committee regarding the release of men from certain protected industries were left to be disposed of by two members of the War Cabinet, Lord Milner and Mr. Henderson, and it was eventually settled by them that during the four months April to July a total of 215,000 men should be set free. The War Cabinet instructed the departments concerned (Board of Trade, Ministry of Munitions, Home Office, and others) to make the men available, but up to May 25, two months after the order was given, the Army had received of the allotted number one man! Effective prosecution of the war was impossible under such conditions as these, and I may add that the number of category A men who were received into the Army during the first five months of the year was little more than one-half the number asked for by the Military Members in the previous November.

In a memorandum[1] bringing these facts to notice, the Adjutant-General stated that a most dangerous situation would arise unless the War Cabinet compelled the departments to carry out the instructions that had been given, and that the belief prevailed in the country that men were not really needed for military purposes but for purposes of industrial compulsion. This belief was

[1] Dated May 31, 1917.

being fostered by Government departments writing to Tribunals saying that the need for men in some civil occupation or other was paramount, and in the opinion of the Government was more important than securing men for military service. Tribunals, faced with the uncongenial duty of sending men to the front, made use of these letters to retain them in civil life. They saw Government departments protecting large numbers of young men in different occupations, and naturally they were apt to conclude that the needs of the Army were not pressing. Moreover, opposition was stirred up by certain Members of Parliament against recent revisions of the Military Service Act, and by other people against the Medical Boards. In short, the position was, as the Adjutant-General said, " impossible," and he submitted, as had been done several times already, that there was only one way of obtaining the men required, and that was to inform the country clearly and plainly that they must be provided. He repeated the request made by the Military Members for raising the military age, and he again asked for new legislation with respect to the constitution and functions of the Tribunals.

In forwarding this important document to the War Cabinet the Army Council remarked that, according to it, the Army was, for all practical purposes, being supplied with men only after all other national needs had been satisfied. They admitted that in the distribution of man-power many other factors had to be taken into account besides those of a military character, but they reminded Ministers that the war could not be won unless our achievements included the defeat of the enemy's military forces, and that this could not be accomplished unless our own forces were kept up to strength. They urged the War Cabinet to sanction the measures which the Adjutant-General had recommended, and again expressed the belief that no satisfactory solution of the man-power problem would ever be found short of general liability to national service, as suggested by the Military Members several months before. Once more no sufficient action was taken, and consequently the fighting strength of the armies in France, brought by the measures of 1916 to its highest point in the summer of 1917, began seriously to decline.

The view taken of the position at this period by the Prime Minister is referred to in the following extract from a letter which I wrote to Sir Douglas Haig[1] :—

> It is necessary that you and I should have a talk over your proposed plans, in order that there may be no misunderstanding as to what they involve. I say this from the point of view of man-power, regarding which the outlook is not good by any means.
>
> Lord Derby and I had a long talk on the subject with the Prime Minister last night, and as an indication of what the position is I may say that the Prime Minister told us that he was afraid the time had now arrived when we must face the fact that we could not expect to get any large number of men in the future, but only "scraps." He said this was so because of the large demands for men for shipbuilding and food production, and owing to labour unrest. I am afraid there is no getting away from the fact that there is some unrest in the country now as a result, partly, of the Russian revolution. There have been some bad strikes recently, and there is still much discontent.

As time went on, prospects grew steadily worse, and in July the War Office Director of Recruiting recorded his "firm conviction that the present method of recruiting is thoroughly bad." The injustices which were being perpetrated daily under the Military Service Acts were, in his opinion, undermining the morale of the nation and fanning the embers of pacifism. The

[1] Dated May 26, 1917.

Adjutant-General agreed, and added that in order to augment the flow of drafts he had been obliged summarily to send to France all available men in reserve and at convalescent hospitals who had returned from the front —a most objectionable expedient, but the only one that remained. He stated that the reports received regarding unrest in certain circles all bore witness to the dissatisfaction that prevailed, and that men were resorting to every possible device to seek exemption. In Wales eleven Tribunals had recently refused to continue their duties on the ground that elderly married men were being taken while young men were left in civil life.

The following month the Director of Recruiting was replaced by a Minister of National Service, who was given, subject to the general direction of the War Cabinet, complete control over all man-power resources, and the provision of men for all national purposes thus came for the first time into the hands of one agency. This greatly overdue reform was excellent in itself, but it did nothing to increase the number of Army recruits. More calculations, more recommendations, were subsequently put forward by the Army Council and the War Minister, but as they were as barren of results as all the others had been it is not necessary to describe them. The War Cabinet continued to regard all-round national service as an impracticable or unnecessary policy, and the supply of recruits continued to decrease in consequence.

In view of the great reverses suffered on the Western Front in the following spring, it is necessary to mention that on November 24, 1917, the Commander-in-Chief brought formally to the notice of the Army Council that, according to the figures supplied to him, there would apparently be a deficit of nearly 250,000 men in his infantry by the end of March, 1918, and that, under these conditions, not only would the offensive power of the armies be paralysed but their defensive capabilities would be seriously curtailed. Referring to a renewal of the suggestion that the shortage of men should be met by reducing the number of battalions per division, he maintained very strongly that if reductions of infantry must be made the divisions should be reduced in number and not in size. He asked to be informed whether it was or was not the intention to provide sufficient men to keep the existing divisions up to strength, because if that could not be done he would wish to proceed at once with the disbandment of such as was necessary. There was no time to be lost, since his plans and training arrangements depended upon the number of divisions which he could count upon having at his disposal.

This letter was but one of many similar communications received during 1917 from the same source as well as from other theatres of war. The ever-recurring requests made to the Government to provide the Army with more men did not, as some people have thought, always have their origin in the War Office. In one form or another they were constantly being received from Commanders-in-Chief, particularly from Sir Douglas Haig, and when of special importance there was no choice but to lay them before the War Cabinet. It was the duty of the War Office to keep the Government systematically informed on such matters, as otherwise intelligent direction of the war would be impossible. In the course of a conversation I had with the Prime Minister in regard to the letter here in question, he suggested that the Army Council should themselves submit a scheme showing how more men could be obtained than were already being provided.

I communicated his request to the Council and they discussed it on December 3. Their view was that as the machinery which had formerly existed at the War Office for dealing with man-power and advising the War Cabinet thereon had been handed over to a Minister of National Service, any proposals which they might submit would be based on insufficient knowledge of our national needs as a whole. Moreover, the Minister himself had quite recently dealt with the position in a memorandum which contained a full summary of the available man-power resources, and the quotas which could be taken without disturbing the industrial policy of the Government. With the memorandum the Council had expressed their agreement, save on a few points of detail, and therefore without intruding into the sphere of politics—which they did not wish to do—there was nothing more that they could usefully say.

They drew attention, however, to the various memoranda which they had laid before the War Cabinet during the past twelve months. In these were several proposals as to the manner in which more men could be obtained, but instead of steps being taken to produce them every succeeding month had seen the recruiting field narrowed, while tens of thousands of men had been withdrawn from the Army for civil employment on the demand of other departments of State. The Council again repeated that they quite realized that the Army could not be given absolute priority in the supply of men regardless of all other considerations, but at the same time they warned the War Cabinet that as large enemy forces would soon be released from the Eastern Front the war might well be lost unless, while awaiting American assistance, the armies in France were maintained at a proper strength.

The War Cabinet now decided, much in the same way as was done two years before, to refer the whole matter to a "Cabinet Committee on Man-Power," the Prime Minister being chairman. To the best of my recollection the General Staff were not called upon to give evidence, nor were the Army Council asked for their opinion in regard to the conclusions to which the Committee ultimately came. When, however, Lord Derby, in his capacity as a member of the Government, received a copy of the Committee's draft report he showed it to the Military Members of the Council so that they might express their views upon it. These met with his approval, and on January 7 he communicated them to the War Cabinet. The Committee's report contained, as future events were to prove, fatally erroneous calculations as to the number of drafts required, and displayed the most amazing misconception of the nature of war.

The Navy, Air Force, shipbuilding, food production, timber-felling, and the provision of cold-storage accommodation were all given priority over the needs of the Army—a formidable list, having regard to the defection of Russia and the military situation in general—and it was recommended that, exclusive of 120,000 boys who could not be sent to the front before 1919 on account of being under age, only 100,000 category A[1] men should be allocated to the Army during 1918 as against the 615,000 requisitioned by the War Office. The Committee considered that the lesser number would suffice because a defensive policy was to be pursued on the Western Front, and, in their opinion, that would automatically entail fewer losses than the offensive policy of the past. This argument was so utterly fallacious as to be almost incredible, for the losses sustained would

[1] i.e. men physically fit in every way for the fighting units.

depend, as always, upon the intensity of the fighting, and, as was pointed out, this in its turn would depend not so much upon the policy of the Entente as upon that of the enemy. " We have had," said the Military Members, " to assume a defensive rôle for the time being not from choice but from necessity, and the initiative has, therefore, passed temporarily to the enemy. If he forces the fighting—as he is almost certain to do—the Entente must also fight, and there are no grounds whatever for supposing that, in that event, our rate of wastage this year will be less than in the past three years."

In order further to justify the provision of a smaller number of men than that asked for, the Committee took as the basis of their calculations the French, not the British, wastage rate, the former being lower than the latter. It was arrived at in consultation with an officer of the French Army whom the Committee had asked the French Government to send to London to explain the French system to them. (" Wastage," it may be observed, can be calculated in different ways according to the manner in which incapacitated men are returned to the different kinds of duty.)

With the French estimate the Military Members quite properly declined to have anything to do, since they had not the necessary data upon which to form an opinion as to its accuracy. They contented themselves with saying that any comparison between British and French figures would probably be misleading, and that they were unable to agree to any lower basis than that taken by the Adjutant-General. The experience of the past three years had shown it to be reliable, and there was no reason why it should be rejected in favour of one which they did not understand.

The Committee also reverted to the old proposal

to reduce the divisions in France from 12 to 9 battalions each, and with the infantry thus withdrawn additional divisions were to be formed so as to create a larger mobile reserve. But even the Committee, though composed for the most part of civilian Ministers, should have remembered that about half the personnel of a division consisted of artillery and other non-infantry units, and that shortage of men in those units was fast becoming as great as it was in the infantry. Further, the deficit in the infantry was already 130,000 men, and a very simple calculation would have shown that the reduction of divisions to a nine-battalion basis would not only not enable additional divisions to be formed, but would not provide sufficient men to keep up to strength the divisions already existing, even on the reduced basis. In other words, if no more men were provided during 1918 than the Committee proposed, ten divisions would have to be broken up in order to find drafts for the remainder.

In these circumstances the Military Members stated that they could not help thinking that the Committee had completely failed to realize the perilous situation in which we stood, and that they

> must warn the War Cabinet again of the results that may ensue from the inevitable diminution of the fighting forces at the front which must occur unless a far greater number of men are made available than that foreshadowed in the draft report. There is every prospect of heavy fighting on the Western Front from February onwards ; and the result may well be that, even if the divisions successfully withstand the shock of the earlier attacks, they may become so exhausted and attenuated as to be incapable of continuing the struggle until the Americans can effectively intervene. In short, the Council would regard the acceptance of the recommendations in the draft report without further effort to provide the men they consider necessary for the maintenance of the forces in the field during 1918 as taking an unnecessarily grave risk of losing the war, and sacrificing to no purpose the British Army on the Western Front.

I well remember that these grave and prophetic words were deliberately chosen in the hope that the War Cabinet might yet realize the appalling short-sightedness of the policy which they were bent upon pursuing, but the warning fell upon deaf ears and unnecessary sacrifice of life was the result.

Meanwhile the General Staff had also twice drawn attention to the position,[1] and on January 7, while the Committee's report was still in its draft stage, the question was brought up at a meeting of the War Cabinet in connexion with the extension of the British front, about which there was some disagreement with the French. In the course of the discussion a Minister asked Sir Douglas Haig, who was present, whether, if he were the German Commander-in-Chief, he would think that there was a sufficiently good chance of breaking through the Entente defences as to justify accepting the losses which would thereby be incurred. Sir Douglas replied to the effect that, if the Germans were wise, they would think twice before making the attempt, because if they failed their position would be critical. What his exact words were I do not remember, but they were at once seized upon and developed by certain members of the War Cabinet because of their intimate bearing on the man-power question.

The situation at the moment was not an easy one for any soldier to discuss with Ministers without the danger of being misunderstood, especially if he was not acquainted with the way in which they are apt to look, and to some extent are compelled to look, at the problems with which they are called upon to deal. The recent operations in Flanders, commonly spoken of as Passchendaele,

[1] Memoranda dated December 29 and January 3 respectively.

had been severely criticized as furnishing no adequate return for the heavy losses suffered, and Sir Douglas Haig probably had this in mind when he dwelt, as he did, upon the losses sustained by the enemy, not only in men but more particularly in morale. At the same time he was in need of large drafts himself, and therefore, while claiming such success over the enemy as he might, the line had to be so drawn that the success would not appear to render the provision of the drafts any less necessary than in reality it was.

The War Cabinet were also in a dilemma. They were being constantly pressed to produce more men, and statements by the Army Council and General Staff were on record pointing out that unless more were produced the war might be lost. On the other hand, the political and man-power situation was, in their opinion, such as to necessitate cutting down the demand for men by no less than five-sixths. Consequently nothing could be more welcome to them than an assurance (no matter how qualified it might be) that the enemy had been so severely handled during 1916–17 as to be incapable of breaking through our defences, or unlikely to attempt to break through, before the American armies had time to arrive.

Given these circumstances, it was not surprising that by the time the meeting terminated Ministers should have extracted from the Field-Marshal such a favourable account of the situation as brought to them the relief of which they were in search. The General Staff had for some weeks past persistently asserted that the enemy would make a determined attack on the Western Front early in the spring, with the object of gaining a decision before strong American help could arrive. Now, the Field-Marshal, who commanded on the Western Front, and who could be regarded as a better judge of the situation there than the General Staff at the War Office, was understood to throw doubts upon the enemy attempting to make this attack. The War Cabinet were thus left in the position of having two different military opinions from which to choose. Not unnaturally they embraced the one which rendered their task easier and not harder.

This, at any rate, was the impression which the proceedings left upon me, and when coming away from the meeting I remarked to the Field-Marshal that it would now be quite impossible for the War Office to secure for him the drafts which he required, since the War Cabinet would conclude from what he had told them that no serious attack need be apprehended, and consequently there was no urgency with respect to drafts. He denied having said anything that would bear that interpretation, and I could only reply that I was afraid the War Cabinet would think differently. Lord Derby, who was present, took the same view as myself, and we mutually hoped that the written statement which the Field-Marshal had been asked to send to the War Cabinet on the following day would help to restore matters to their true perspective. The better to ensure this, Lord Derby afterwards requested me to write to Sir Douglas Haig, who was remaining in England for a few days, and the letter reproduced below was dispatched the same (Monday) afternoon. The Blue Paper mentioned in it was a copy of the Cabinet Committee's draft report referring to the provision of men.

War Office,
7th January, 1918.

My dear Haig,—

I understand you are to see the Prime Minister on Wednesday. Before then you should carefully read the paper enclosed. For months past, as you know, we have been trying to get more men for the Army.

The Cabinet on the other hand find great difficulty in providing more men, and therefore make every excuse for not providing them. The paper shows their arguments for allotting fewer drafts than we have demanded. Amongst the arguments are that as we are now on the defensive we shall have fewer losses, and great importance is attached to numerical factors while moral and other factors are ignored. For a long time past they have been trying to induce me to say that the Germans may not attack us this year. Unfortunately you gave as your opinion this morning that they would not do so, and I noticed, as Lord Derby also did, that the Cabinet jumped at this statement. Of course you did not mean that for certain the Germans would not attack, but I think you will find in the "Cabinet Proceedings" the opinion recorded that you anticipate no attack. The "Cabinet Proceedings" will I presume be sent to you to see, and perhaps you will have an opportunity of making clear what you intended to say.

The long and short of it is that the Cabinet think that by giving us 100,000 men this year in place of the 600,000 we asked for you will be able to hold your own. Personally, I think that is doubtful. My belief is that the Germans will make the heaviest attack possible. They have a better chance of winning this year than they will have later, and we may suppose that they are bent on winning as much as we ourselves are. I suggest therefore that when you see the Prime Minister you make it quite clear to him that what you can do, and to what extent you can oppose the enemy, depend entirely upon your divisions being kept up to strength. You will see in the paper that we are asked to form 9-battalion divisions, and an order to this effect is going out to you in the course of a day or two. So long as the Cabinet are of opinion that you can hold your front this year with 9-battalion divisions (and even these will not be up to strength) I am afraid we cannot get any more men than those now promised, namely, 100,000 as against the 600,000 we consider we require.

I am going to France early in the morning, but if you would care to obtain further details as to the draft situation I suggest you see Whigham [1] to-morrow. He knows the case fully. I will send you first thing in the morning a copy of an Army Council paper on the subject of drafts which we sent to the War Cabinet on the 3rd of last month, and also a copy of the one we are sending them to-morrow.

I am quite sure that the idea the Cabinet have now got is that you

[1] Deputy-Chief of the Imperial General Staff.

are perfectly all right, and that they need not trouble to give any more men than those they have arranged to give, *vide* the Blue Paper.

I did not think it necessary to say anything to you before the meeting on the subject of men as I felt you would not fail to rub that in. Curzon's questions were intended to give you that opportunity. Of course you do not quite understand these people as well as I do.

Derby is very anxious, and so am I, that you should write the paper they referred to. It may be short. You do not know all the factors. But you know you must be kept up to strength, and you will not be unless we get far more men.

Yours very truly,

W. R. Robertson.

In the written statement which he submitted Sir Douglas Haig urged no less strongly than the Army Council had done the necessity for bringing and keeping his divisions up to strength, but his advice, like theirs, was of no avail. When the statement came before the War Cabinet the Prime Minister tossed it aside with the remark that it was entirely inconsistent with what Sir Douglas had said verbally, and the final decision was that no more men should be allotted than the Committee had recommended.

This decision was, to the best of my belief, accepted by the Army Council without further objection, though, being frequently called away to Paris during the next few weeks on important matters relating to other theatres of war, I do not know all that passed at the War Office with respect to it. The Council had repeatedly pointed out, in the plainest language, the risks incurred by allowing the Army to decrease in strength at a time when threatened with the greatest attack that the enemy could possibly build up. They had suggested various measures by which the decrease could be partly if not wholly avoided. The War Cabinet had now definitely decided that the risks must be accepted, and therefore with them would rest responsibility for the consequences. This, as I understood it, was the view which the majority of the Army Councillors took of the position. Whether they were justified in taking it, seeing that, in their judgment, the safety of the Army entrusted to their care was being jeopardized in a way for which there was no sufficient excuse; or whether they ought to have taken the alternative course of asking to be relieved of their offices, on the ground that they could no longer retain them with satisfaction to their conscience, is a question on which opinions may differ, and it was certainly a hard one to answer at the time. In the crisis through which the country was then passing it was necessary that everybody should endeavour to work cordially together, to help and not to hinder, and therefore whilst some members of the Council thought the alternative course to be the right one, others were content to abide by the Cabinet decision and hope for the best.

On January 14, following the adoption of the Committee's report, the Minister of National Service introduced a Bill for empowering the Government to call up from civil employment a number of young men who had previously been exempt, but the Bill proved to be inadequate and illusory as in the circumstances it was bound to do. The Minister announced that it was not intended either to raise the military age above forty-one years or to apply compulsion to Ireland, nor would the military age for service oversea be lowered. He further stated that " the secession of Russia from the Allies has added to the potential enemy's strength on the Western Front, including Italy, possibly as many as 1,600,000 men, without taking into consideration the reserves which would otherwise have been required for service on the Russian front." This statement was presumably meant to render easy the passage of the Bill, but how the Government reconciled with it the trivial measures which they were proposing is difficult to understand. It may also be observed that the credit for not reducing the age for service at the front below nineteen years was due to the Army Council and not to the Government. The Minister of National Service had suggested lowering it to eighteen and a half years, but the Council objected to the change as being unfair to the youths concerned.

During the course of these events an endeavour was made, on a suggestion I put before the Prime Minister at the end of November, to alleviate the position by seeking the aid of America. Like ourselves three years before, she was engaged in creating large new armies, which could neither be made ready, as such, nor brought to France for several months to come. The provision of shipping for conveying them across the Atlantic was the chief difficulty in the way, and calculations showed that as much tonnage was required for three divisions (having in them 36 battalions) with the necessary equipment, transport, etc., as would be needed for the conveyance of 150 individual battalions, if unaccompanied by transport. Infantry being the arm of which we were the most deficient, 150 battalions would clearly constitute a more helpful reinforcement than three divisions, and my suggestion was that the American Government should be asked whether, as a purely temporary measure, they could possibly consent to a portion of their infantry being embodied in British divisions, their transport—a comparatively small amount—being found from British sources. The employment of American troops in this manner, temporary though it might be, would make a great demand on American goodwill and self-esteem, but the situation was becoming so critical as to justify the question being asked.

The Prime Minister agreed, and on December 2 Lord Reading, acting on his behalf, personally handed a General Staff memorandum on the subject to Colonel House, who was then in France and was understood to be empowered to report unofficially to the President on matters which specially required attention. Colonel House referred the request to Washington, and showed the memorandum to the American Commander-in-Chief, General Pershing. The Washington authorities treated the request with sympathetic consideration, and accorded General Pershing full authority to use his troops in whatever way he might deem best. He was reminded, however, that it was undesirable that the troops should lose their identity. This instruction placed him in a difficult position, for the employment of American troops under a foreign flag was certain to be unpopular with the American people, and the responsibility for permitting or refusing it should, one would think, have been definitely assumed by the American Government. The General himself was apparently of the same opinion, for the proposal was not seriously considered by him until I went to Paris, by request of the War Cabinet, to discuss it with him in the second week of January, five weeks later.

At the time the American programme contemplated the raising of 45 divisions, of which four and a part of the fifth had arrived in France. When the remainder would be ready " no one in the world could even guess," said the General to me, because so much depended upon the rate at which the necessary equipment could be produced and the amount of available shipping, of which America herself had far less than might be supposed.

The General declined to make any forecast beyond saying that he hoped to have ten more divisions (or fifteen in all) in the country by the end of June, while a maximum of fifteen others might perhaps be ready by the end of 1918, thus leaving a balance of fifteen in America.

I suggested that it would be a pity if the last-mentioned fifteen were not brought into the field before 1919, as the war might be over before then, and the rate of arrival of the other divisions also seemed dangerously slow, having regard to the fact that Germany would without doubt strive her utmost, if not to win outright, at least to place herself in a winning position before the end of the summer. There were already twenty-eight more German divisions on the Western Front than a year ago, and forty more could easily be brought there from the Russian front by the month of May, as well as a large amount of artillery. As compared with this increase, eleven British and French divisions had just gone to Italy, while in future all British divisions in France were to be reduced from four battalions per brigade to three—that is, to contain 25 per cent. less infantry than before.

This situation was, I represented to the General, causing the British and French authorities very great anxiety, for even if the impending German attack was successfully withstood, as we hoped it would be, the British divisions might still suffer such heavy losses as to be fit for little employment afterwards. It was therefore a matter of vital importance that arrangements should be made, if possible, for supplying infantry reinforcements at once. If the General could see his way to provide, say, 150,000 men (or 150 battalions) from the divisions not expected to reach France until 1919, the British Government on its part would be prepared to run very considerable risks in the reduction of stocks of food and war material so as to provide the shipping required to bring the men over. There would thus be no interference with the sea-transport for the American divisions as already arranged, and it was estimated by the Shipping Controller, who had been deputed to accompany me, that all the 150,000 men could arrive in France within about three months. Exactly how the battalions could best be fitted into British divisions, the time when they should be recalled to join their own divisions, and similar details, could be settled later in accordance with the General's wishes. I repeated that the British Government fully appreciated the natural desire to retain national identity, and felt that if America could accept the proposal she would thereby display the greatest possible magnanimity and sacrifice.

The discussions continued for the best part of two days, and sometimes an agreement seemed to be near, but it was never actually reached. For some reason I could not convince the General of the seriousness of the position. He seemed to think that I was exaggerating the imminence and possible consequences of the attack which threatened, and he shrewdly observed that it was difficult to reconcile my request for assistance in defence of the Western Front with Mr. Lloyd George's desire to act offensively in Palestine. There was, unfortunately, no answer to that argument, except that, so far as I was personally concerned, not a man or gun more would be sent to Palestine from anywhere. The General feared, moreover, in spite of what I had said, that the arrival of his complete divisions would be delayed by the transporting of the 150 battalions, and of course he disliked putting the latter under the command of officers of another country. Instead of placing them in

British brigades, he suggested withdrawing all British battalions from a certain number of divisions, their places being taken by his battalions. The infantry of these divisions would then be entirely American, while the remaining units would be entirely British.

I replied that as the change would have to be made in the spring or early summer, it might not be feasible, since by then we would probably be engaged in repelling attack; that the change, whenever made, would mean putting the newly constructed divisions out of action for some weeks while they were settling down; and that the divisions would still be partly American and partly British. He agreed, but said that he had to bear in mind that there was a strong desire on the part of his people to keep their troops together, and to have a large army of their own. Except for this he might fall in with the proposal, but circumstances being what they were he could do no more than refer the question back to Washington. This he did about the middle of January, and recommended that serious attention should be given to it, subject to certain conditions being fulfilled as to the nature and duration of the proposed attachment, and to the British Government exerting "every energy to keep its own forces as strong in man-power as possible." In return he asked to be furnished with a full statement "as to British resources in this regard, including those at present available and to become available during this year." He required the information in order that his Government might have all the facts before them in coming to a decision.

Exactly what reply was received from Washington I do not know, but the proposal never materialized in its original form, and one could hardly expect that it would. At a meeting of the Supreme War Council held at the end of January, General Pershing suggested that the British Government should use all its available shipping for bringing over the personnel of complete American divisions, the infantry portion to be trained with British divisions and then rejoin their own. Some such system as this was eventually adopted, the result being, of course, that the arrival of reinforcements in the shape of infantry was very much slower than would have been the case had the British proposal met with approval.[1]

About a fortnight later I ceased to be C.I.G.S. and my dealings with man-power thereupon came to an end. The views of the General Staff did not, I believe, materially change with the change of Chief, for about the middle of March my successor asked for 46,000 men, in addition to those already allocated, with which to man the large numbers of *tanks* he proposed should be provided in substitution for infantry. He reported that already he could not see his way to manning the *guns* which would be turned out during 1918, and that the possibility of keeping the *infantry* up to strength, while the tanks were being produced, depended entirely upon whether heavy casualties could be avoided.

There was never the least chance that the enemy would allow them to be avoided, and a few days afterwards, when the long-threatened attack against the British front was launched, the erroneous views and opportunist

[1] About seven weeks after the discussions with General Pershing, when the great German attack began, the War Office authorities said to the American military attaché in London, " For God's sake, get your men over ! " At the same time the American Ambassador wrote to President Wilson urging him to send troops over at once. " I pray God that you will not be too late."—" The Life and Letters of Walter H. Page," Vol. II, pages 363–4.

methods of the previous fifteen months stood exposed. Drafts amounting to 140,000 men were then hurriedly scraped together and sent out, the number including, contrary to the undertaking given in Parliament on January 14, many youths under nineteen years of age; about 100,000 men were withdrawn for military service from munition works; a similar number was taken from the coal industry; railways and other transport services were ordered to release the greatest possible number of category A men, and further calls were made on the Civil Service. Orders were also issued under the Act passed in January cancelling exemptions in selected industries, and the length of the calling-up notices was shortened from fourteen to seven days. So urgent was the need for men now seen to be that on the opening day of the session, April 9, the Prime Minister moved the first reading of a new Man-Power Bill, and all other Government business was set aside until the Bill was finally passed. By it the military age was raised to fifty and in some cases to fifty-five years; in the event of a national emergency being declared certificates of exemption would cease to have effect, and men could be taken or left on medical grounds only; Tribunals were to be reconstituted, and rights of appeal were to be limited; the Military Service Acts were to extend to Ireland under the same conditions as in Great Britain, being put into force by an Order in Council when the necessary arrangements had been made. The Bill passed through all its stages and became law within ten days of its introduction, and with no alterations in its essential provisions. These measures were estimated by the Minister of National Service to produce 350,000 category A men and 170,000 of lower categories within the next three months—a very different estimate from that made by the Cabinet Committee a few weeks before, when it was said that not more than 100,000 category A men could be provided during the whole of the year.

To what extent the grave losses incurred at this period of the war would have been prevented had the above measures been taken when first recommended by the military authorities in 1916 must always remain a matter of speculation. It is, however, safe to say that the losses would have been much fewer and therefore the ultimate drain on our man-power would have been less, while the necessity for putting into the trenches youths under nineteen years of age would have been minimized if not entirely obviated.

Butler & Tanner Ltd.
Frome and London
F50-926